BUSINESS TO BUSINESS MARKETING

AF652586

BUSINESS TO BUSINESS MARKETING

R. K. SUGANDHI
Deputy Manager
Bharat Heavy Electricals Ltd.
New Delhi

NEW AGE MANAGEMENT

An Imprint of

NEW AGE INTERNATIONAL (P) LIMITED, PUBLISHERS

New Delhi • Bangalore • Chennai • Cochin • Guwahati • Hyderabad
Jalandhar • Kolkata • Lucknow • Mumbai • Ranchi

Visit us at **www.newagepublishers.com**

Copyright © 2009, 2002, New Age International (P) Ltd., Publishers
Published by New Age International (P) Ltd., Publishers
First Edition: 2002 (HB)
First Edition: 2009 (PB)

All rights reserved.

No part of this book may be reproduced in any form, by photostat, microfilm, xerography, or any other means, or incorporated into any information retrieval system, electronic or mechanical, without the written permission of the copyright owner.

Branches:

- 36, Malikarjuna Temple Street, Opp. ICWA, Basavanagudi, **Bangalore**. © (080) 26677815
- 26, Damodaran Street, T. Nagar, **Chennai**. © (044) 24353401
- Hemsen Complex, Mohd. Shah Road, Paltan Bazar, Near Starline Hotel, **Guwahati**. © (0361) 2543669
- No. 105, 1st Floor, Madhiray Kaveri Tower, 3-2-19, Azam Jahi Road, Nimboliadda, **Hyderabad**. © (040) 24652456
- RDB Chambers (Formerly Lotus Cinema) 106A, 1st Floor, S.N. Banerjee Road, **Kolkata**. © (033) 22275247
- 16-A, Jopling Road, **Lucknow**. © (0522) 2209578
- 142C, Victor House, Ground Floor, N.M. Joshi Marg, Lower Parel, **Mumbai**. © (022) 24927869
- 22, Golden House, Daryaganj, **New Delhi**. © (011) 23262370, 23262368

ISBN: 978-81-224-2720-2

Rs. 290.00

C-09-03-3553

Printed in India at Saras Graphics, Rai, Haryana.

PUBLISHING FOR ONE WORLD
NEW AGE INTERNATIONAL (P) LIMITED, PUBLISHERS
4835/24, Ansari Road, Daryaganj, New Delhi-110002
Visit us at **www.newagepublishers.com**

This book is dedicated to my wife Pushpa,
for her constant support and encouragement and to my daughters,
Dr Pallavi and Dr Nidhi for their valuable suggestions and
help without which this would not have been completed

Preface

With increasing competition and globalisation, the business environment has changed dramatically from Supplier's market to Buyer's market. Today every vendor has realized that his business growth and profitability are dependent on the Customer. Hence the last two decades have seen the emergence of marketing and thrust on activities like demand forecast and business trends. In order to get competitive advantage, suppliers are reassessing the needs and requirements of customer; factors that can provide them lead over their competitors. Every supplier is looking forward to create differentiation in the mind of the customers and impress upon them the uniqueness that he can provide. Satisfying the customer and providing quality and timely service has become an integral part of any corporate strategy for growth and success.

Marketing efforts are today oriented towards assessing customer needs and ensuring that the products and services provided by the supplier not only meets his requirement but exceeds it. Marketing has suddenly become a challenging and interesting field. Naturally a large number of young people are choosing it as a career by opting for marketing courses in management institutions, which are doing immense service by acting as a supply chain for professional human resources for industries. However most of the marketing courses are tailored to suit only the Consumer sector. Our educational institutions and other organisations have left the Core sector to fend for itself as far as marketing is concerned. The Business to Business sector, i.e. Core sector is probably as big as Business to Consumer sector but unfortunately it is yet to get the privilege of getting professional marketing executives, educated and trained to cater to this segment. Our management schools may like to reassess and modify their educational syllabus to cater to this unattended segment, which may be around 45 per cent of the total marketing segment. The marketing requirements in these two segments are very different and the concepts and theories applicable to one segment may not essentially be applicable to the other.

In the absence of suitably qualified candidates, most of the companies operating in the core sector have to create their own marketing executives. Unfortunately there is no structured literature or courses available and most of these marketing executives receive their baptism and training by learning on the job. This book is essentially aimed to help them and cater to this segment and to serve as reference or textbook as and when educational institutions introduce the subject of industrial marketing. The book discusses in detail the factors that shape demand and customer needs and identifies tools for assessing and addressing them. The market is a dynamic place with ever changing customer needs and competition. The marketing strategies are discussed considering this market dynamism alongwith the methods for proper utilization and leveraging of this dynamism.

Customer satisfaction and loyalty are vitally important aspects of today's business. In reality the business in core sector is essentially a business through relationships. No business or marketing is complete without CRM (Customer Relationship Management). The concept of CRM is still evolving and there is need for focused and properly structured course material on the subject. The book has therefore devoted one full chapter on CRM considering its importance.

For a business to succeed, one must have proper human resources for the task. It is now being increasingly realized that specialized people are required to man specialized fields in order to get optimum results. Supplier's human resources, their attitude, orientation and negotiating skill assume paramount importance for marketing. These issues are discussed with practical cases alongwith suggestions. Probably this is one area in which core sector marketing needs tremendous professionalism.

The book also discusses in detail business through the Internet as this medium is shortly going to change the way business is done. Reverse Auction has very high unrealized potential to optimize the price and other parameters.

This book has been written from a practical point of view with factual case studies to vividly illustrate the concepts. It is felt that such an approach would help the reader to have quick and complete grasp of the subject.

In the preparation of the book, I have received valuable suggestion from the publisher and especially from Mr Rajiv Banerji and I am thankful to him. I am also grateful to my wife and daughters who have helped me in unraveling human aspect of relationships, which is one of the critical factors for business success and which has helped in giving uniqueness to the book. I am also thankful to my colleagues in BHEL and my customer friends for their help.

I hope the book will be able to bridge the knowledge and skill gap that presently exists in this area. I would be grateful for any suggestions for improvement.

R K SUGANDHI

Contents

1

Marketing and its Role in Business

What is Marketing
Need for Marketing
Difference between Selling and Marketing
Marketing—The Process
Marketing Phases
Advantages of Marketing
Marketing Purpose
Disadvantages of Excessive Marketing

1

WHAT IS MARKETING

Marketing is a simple word with a complex meaning. What is Marketing? Is it selling what you produce or producing what the customer wants? Some writers have even gone beyond that. They consider efforts towards cost reduction, endeavour for better technology, more customer comforts as part of marketing. The definition can be further enlarged to cover product substitution or creating demand. There is no end to it. Marketing can be considered as a tool where the customer is the centre of corporate strategy and all efforts are made to see that he gets more value for the money he spends and not only gets the benefits from the product he wants but that they also exceed his expectations. It is a methodology to ensure that the customer is not simply satisfied but is also delighted.

NEED FOR MARKETING

In business where demand outstrips supply, there is no need for marketing. There was a time in India when the marketing department was either non-existent or was otherwise called the 'Sales Department'. During 1960s, many well-known Indian corporates were having designations such as "Commercial Manager" or "Sales Manager". The company was inward looking. There was no dearth of orders or business and the only corporate function was production. Cost-cutting or engineering improvement were merely decorative words. Meeting customers or enquiring about their opinion were the last priority on the list of a CEO. Customer meets were a waste of time and money. The company basically existed to serve itself and its employees.

The customer was only a captive commodity to achieve this objective. His requirement and needs were of secondary consideration. The concept was simple. If a company is producing, let it produce more, because there is a ready market and the function of the sales department is to sell. Selling was not considered difficult and the only function that used to receive priority in corporate eyes was manufacturing. There was no need to understand the customer and ascertain his satisfaction level or even his requirements or his wants. There was no concept of conducting market research to find out whether the products already being sold needed any improvement or required substitution; or whether the supplier should concentrate on making the products more customer-friendly; or whether to provide customer more value for the money he spends.

DIFFERENCE BETWEEN SELLING AND MARKETING

Table 1.1 basically provides at a glance the difference between selling and marketing. The fundamental difference between them is highlighted.

Table 1.1 *Difference between Selling and Marketing*

Selling	*Marketing*
• Introvert	• Extrovert
• Demand > Supply	• Supply > Demand
• Focus on Production	• Focus on Customer
• Seller's Market	• Buyer's Market
• Supplier has the options	• Customer has the options
• Supplier Satisfaction is the objective	• Customer Satisfaction is the objective
• Supplier is the driver	• Customer is the driver
• Competition non-existent	• Severe competition
• No thrust on Product Improvement, Cost Reduction or Product Substitution	• Major thrust on Product Improvement and Cost Reduction
• No priority for Technological Improvement	• Technological Improvement is the priority area
• Concept of Market Share	• Concept of Opportunity Share

Two examples given below highlight the selling behaviour prevailing in the 1960s in India.

Illustration

A customer of major capital equipment was interested in buying major equipment from a well-known firm. However, he wanted a shorter product delivery period so that he could commission the plant earlier, and approached the Sales Department with his request for early completion. The sales officer contacted his superior to enquire whether they could oblige their customer and got the reply that if he wanted to buy their firm's equipment and wanted to commission his plants by the date he had in mind, then he should have planned better and placed an order on them earlier. The message being communicated was loud and clear that there was no question of even thinking at their end of any improvement. If any compromise had to be made, it had to be made by the customer. They would not change; they would produce and supply what they wanted. If the customer wanted to purchase, he had to adjust according to the seller's dictates. This is a typical attitude of selling. Seller's satisfaction is the prime objective. Nobody is willing to look beyond the boundary walls of the manufacturing plant.

The second incident is a bit comical and was narrated to me by one of my college classmates, who joined an electric motor manufacturing company as a sales engineer. The company received an order from one of the renowned tyre manufacturers of the country for supply of electric motors. As per the contract, the customer was to inspect and witness test on the motors before giving dispatch clearance. The motor was ready and accordingly the sales engineer sent the inspection call. His boss, who was aware of the status, enquired whether the sales engineer had communicated the 'other requirements'. On noticing that my friend could not understand him, his boss took pity on him and told him that scooter tyres were not freely available in the market and that distributors were selling them at very high prices in the black market. The tyre company, in order to expedite the supply of motors which was in any case late, had promised that they would supply scooter tyres to concerned people at the control/regular rate. Since the motor was ready, they wanted to have tyres at fair price. My friend was advised to go to the production shop and collect names of important officials from manufacturing and testing department, who wanted tyres and collect the cash and inform the customer. He did so and the customer brought the consignment and handed it over to the sales department and collected the price of

Contd

tyres. When the customer went to the shop floor, the test engineer enquired from the sales department about the tyres and, receiving a positive reply, gave priority to the testing of the motor of the concerned customer.

MARKETING—THE PROCESS

There was a time when the supplier was the king and the customer was required to stand in a queue for his turn to be served. The world has since swung to the other extreme. Supply has now overtaken demand and suppliers are forced to adopt new and proactive methods. In USA the great depression of the 1930s changed the scenario. Added to this was the change introduced by liberalisation of policies. The vendors could no longer take the customers for granted. They were not sure that whatever they produced would be sold. In the core sector customers were no longer visiting the suppliers to purchase their requirements. Rather, the reverse was happening, Suppliers were visiting the customers to persuade them to buy. They also, in the process, learnt a new term called 'Competition'. They realised the need to make efforts to ensure that their shop floors were booked. Production was only possible if there were customers and orders. A new term was born—Marketing. The emphasis shifted from Production to Business Realisation and this led to a shift of focus to the customer. The transition to Buyer's market was complete. The customer is now having the option to purchase what he thinks is best. It is now the turn of vendors to prove to the customer that their products give him the best value and meet his requirements. Suppliers are also competing with each other to explain long-term services they can offer and customer/user-friendly nature of their products. Customer satisfaction has become the key to success. Figure 1.1 shows this concept in schematic form. The diagram shows that marketing is a closed-loop cycle. It comprises the following activities:

- Assess customer needs
- Compare needs with what supplier is offering
- Identify improvement area
- Re-engineer the product and process to meet the customer needs

- Collect market feedback to ascertain how the product is meeting the market needs and take corrective action
- Business growth and increased profits through customer satisfaction.

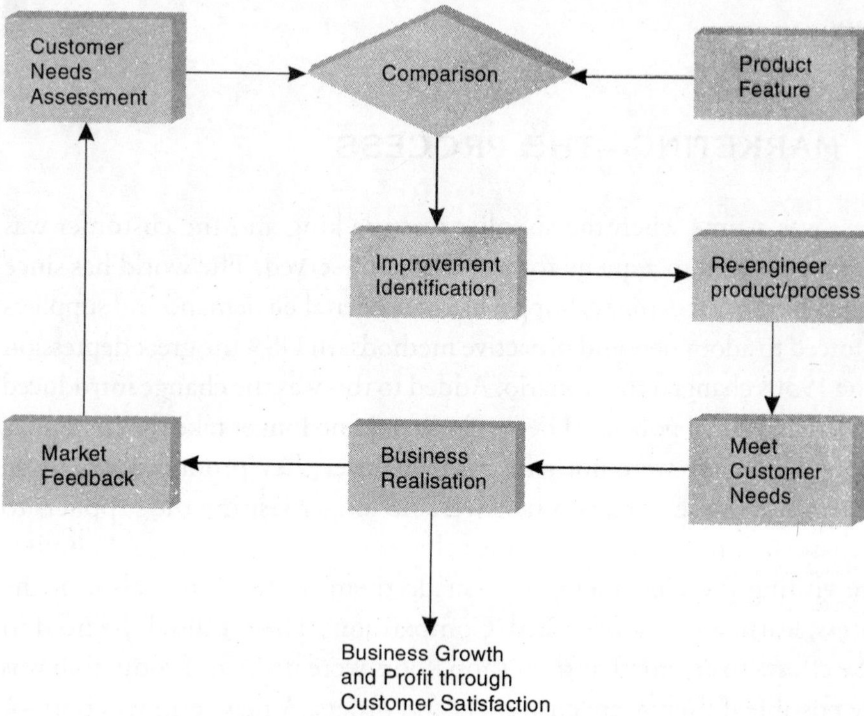

Fig. 1.1 *Marketing—The Process Flow Chart*

This concept led to a whole new philosophy. The marketing man has not only to understand the needs of the customer, but also has to look back and sideways to see how his competitors are doing. He is required to keep track of not only their existing work, but also their future plans and compare them with the status of his own orgnisation's existing work and progress and take appropriate measures to stay ahead. It is like a marathon race in which each player not only looks forward to reach the target, but also looks sideways or back to find out the relative position of his co-runners and assesses how they are doing or what strategy they are adopting to overtake him. No sooner he realizes that they are changing their tactics and his position and leadership is in danger, he immediately reassesses himself and adopts new tactics to meet the challenge and remains ahead. This is like constantly monitoring the market share of self and other competitors, which acts as a parameter or measurable indicator to reflect the relative success of each of the participants.

Some people also assess the percentage capacity utilization of each of the competitors apart from the market share. Low capacity utilization indicates the pressure to do something quickly to correct the situation. The competitors will put this company under a 'watch list' as they expect that either this company will have to change its strategy to remain in business or will slowly fade away. Thus, marketing basically becomes a survival strategy. '*Market yourselves to remain in business*' became the guiding principle. Faced with reduced business and falling market share, the companies start falling back on the marketing techniques to survive in the business. It becomes a business philosophy that places the customer as the driving force and the road map for business growth and profitability is through "meeting the customer's needs and ensuring his satisfaction" and making the supplier market-oriented. According to this philosophy, the most effective way to create a customer is to market the products directly aimed at his needs.

MARKETING PHASES

Figure 1.2 indicates the chronological development of Marketing. Phase–1 of marketing concentrates on the present business and improvement in the market share. The companies start looking into the ways and means of understanding customer requirements, the strategy adopted by the competitors and ways to leave them behind. The activities are:

- Understanding customer needs
- Understanding self and comparing one's readiness to meet the customer needs
- Understanding competitors

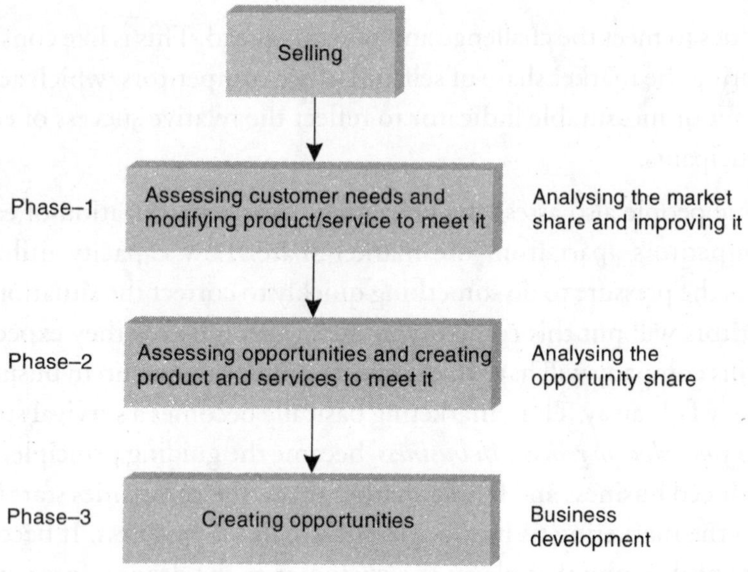

Fig. 1.2 *Marketing—Chronological Development*

The basic framework of marketing for improving the market share is detailed in Fig. 1.3.

However, as the competition became more intense, the customer became more demanding and the suppliers felt the need to increase their business sphere to create more business for themselves. This led to the beginning of Phase–2 of marketing. The supplier started looking beyond existing products and services and projects at those areas where they could logically enter and which suited their core competencies. Thus began the concept of horizontal and vertical integration. The concept of 'Market Share' gave way to the new concept of 'Opportunity Share' and entered the fourth parameter in the existing three parameters of the marketing, i.e. 'Understanding the Environment' and completing the FOUR U THEORY of marketing. This fourth parameter indicates the factors around which the needs can be created and new business opportunities can be developed. The supplier started looking into these new opportunities as they could provide increased captive demand for existing business (Reliance Industry integration plan), or new technological inputs or even lead to cost effectiveness for the existing products. Many suppliers also looked at the new environment from the 'disintegration' viewpoint. They re-visited their business profile and again assessed whether they should continue to operate the business in all segments or become more competitive by stopping operation of some segments. Many companies decided to sell some of their business to other corporates to increase their business focus and bottom line. Reliance decided to come out of L&T and L&T itself is thinking of coming out of the cement business. Tatas decided to sell their holding in ACC and concentrate on business suitable to their core area. The necessity of protecting their business interest inspired the Aditya Birla group to buy a significant stake in L&T. Business suddenly came alive. There was more churning of business now than at any time in the past. These are motivated to sustain a competitive edge and to minimize competition. Sometimes, they are also done to reduce the cost or achieve critical mass to influence the market.

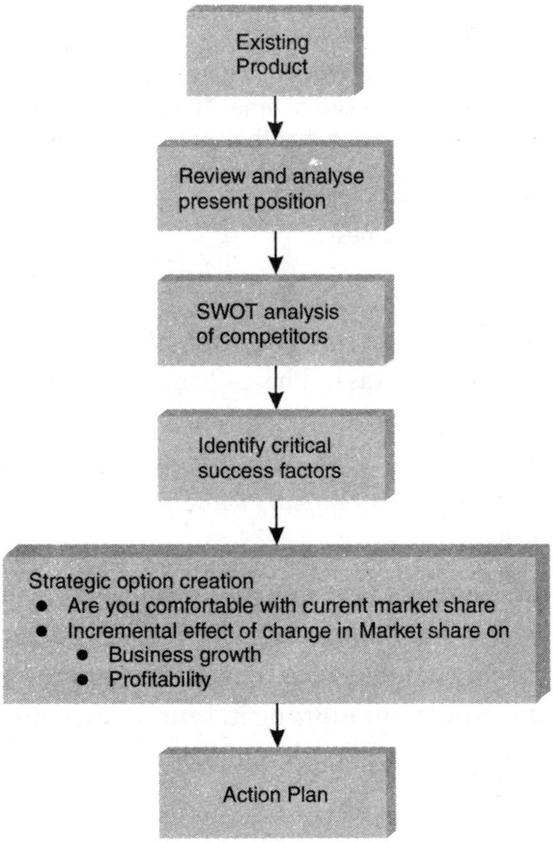

Fig. 1.3 *Marketing for Improving Market Share*

The essence and efficiency of an organisation lies in ascertaining how many of these opportunities were captured by the organisation.

Illustration

Many marketing groups tell the story of a widow who suddenly got a one million dollar bonanza and wanted to spend it. Two businessmen followed her to see how and what she purchased and whether that included products they manufactured. Incidentally, both were in the same line of business and were competitors. They felt that this was the opportunity to judge whose product had better acceptance in the market. The lady saw their products but decided against buying products from either of them or, to be more correct, product of that type. They were greatly disappointed. One of them decided that since he was not getting the business, it was time to go back and do some other useful work, but he found that the other person was still interested in following the lady. He suggested to that friend that the lady had not purchased anything that they were producing, so following her further would be a waste of time. The other man replied that she had not purchased anything that they made, but he wanted to follow her to find out how she spent her money. If possible he would start producing them, so that in future somebody else would not go away without giving him business.

This example clearly indicates that while the first person was still in Phase–1, the second person was in Phase–2 and searching the opportunity and was willing to modify the existing product or create a new product to remain in business. This again reiterates that Marketing is the strategy for both survival and growth. *If a company wants to be lucky, then the best way is to create that luck.*

The basic framework of marketing for utilizing existing opportunity is shown in Fig. 1.4. It shows various stages for getting the business from the existing opportunity. The supplier has to map the opportunity and identify the needs and requirements for utilizing it. Immediately after the opportunity has been sighted, the supplier should identify the following information:

- Total value of opportunity on a short-term, medium-term and long-term basis.

- Resources required for it and comparison with existing resources available with the supplier.
- Additional investment needed.
- Existing competition in the proposed new area and SWOT analysis of existing competitors.
- Identification of critical success factors in the new area and supplier's strength in meeting them.
- Will entry into the new area lead to some benefits in the existing area like reduction in cost due to backward integration, or increase in assured demand due to forward integration, or overall cost reduction due to better utilization of existing resources?
- Will entry into the new area lead to some overall competitive advantage on a long-term basis?
- If, on the basis of positive evaluation of the above factors, the company wants to go in for capturing a new opportunity, then it should work out an implementation plan.

One of the major issues that must be considered before utilizing a new opportunity is that it must be in the core competency area of the supplier. For this purpose, the supplier must identify a functional area in which it is strong. Normally, companies try to enter into areas in which they can have synergy with the existing business profile, but there are cases in which companies have gone into totally unrelated fields. Sterlite Industries has entered into the aluminium sector through acquisition of BALCO, though it has no experience in aluminium. But if the corporate plan of Sterlite is to make its presence felt in basic metal industry, then this is a logical extension of their business. Entry of OSWAL into fertilizers was totally unsynergised opportunity utilization. Tata entered into the passenger car segment as a logical step towards opportunity tapping.

During the last five years many companies have sought to capture new business opportunities. With the increasing competition in the banking industry and continued slow down, the banks are flush with funds. Most of them till now have been mainly lending to industrial houses but with recession in the market, the demand for industrial borrowing has come down. At the same time, due to non-payment, non-performing assets have gone up. This has seriously affected business and profitability of financial institutions. In order to survive and add new business segments, a large number of banks have entered into the household segment by giving loans for purchase of car/vehicle and other consumer items. With the opening up of insurance sector, some of these banks are making efforts in this lucrative area. This is in addition to the entry into mutual fund segment, which many banks have done with the new culture of investment through mutual funds.

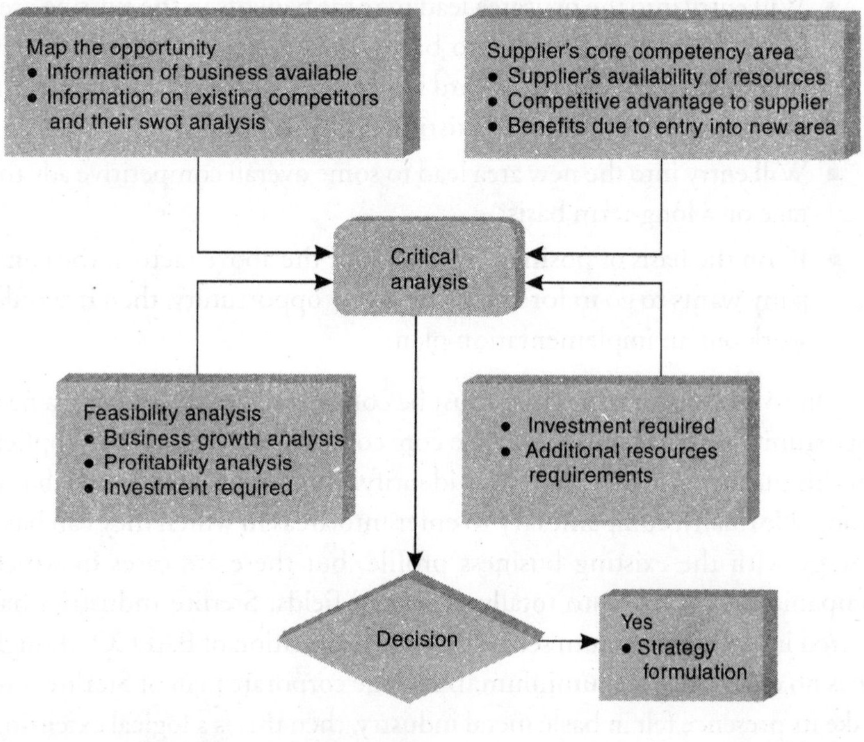

Fig. 1.4 *Marketing for Existing Opportunity*

KRIBHCO, a fertilizer company of repute, is trying to leverage its experience of setting and running Captive Power Plant into setting large power projects and entering into power generation area. These are some of the successful cases of utilizing the opportunity. Success depends on the ability of an organisation to meet the market requirements.

Jaiprakash Industries is another company that has expanded its business profile by capturing existing opportunities. It began as a construction company. One of the biggest requirements of a construction company is cement. It explored and analysed the possibility of entering into cement manufacturing business and decided on it. Thus, from a construction company, it graduated into the manufacturing business. Sometime during this period, it decided to utilise its experience in construction to construct a hotel. Thus began its entry into the Hotel Industry.

The third phase of Marketing, i.e. 'Creating Opportunity' is a most interesting one and the most challenging of the lot. There have been many articles on this subject, which basically convey that marketing means creating demand.

It is often said that '*necessity is the mother of invention*'. What can probably be added to this is that the job of the marketing man is to create that Necessity. One of the best ways of creating opportunity is to identify needs, create needs and publicise them so that they get converted into opportunity. Some of the examples of opportunity creation that immediately come to mind are discussed hereunder.

Illustration

In major cities, accidents at road crossings are going up. One of the major reasons is the changing lifestyle putting time pressure on individuals and growing impatience. It is often seen that when the traffic signal glows green, in order to avoid waiting at the signal, the motorist increases his speed so that he can pass through during this signal itself. When he reaches near the crossing, many times he finds the signal suddenly turning red. By that time the motorist has picked up so much speed that it become difficult for him to stop. He tries to jump the signal and many times collides with the vehicle which are now trying to cross as a result of the green signal. The second possibility of an accident happening is when he decides not to cross and suddenly applies brakes on seeing the signal turning to red. He is banged from behind by the traffic coming at equally high speed. In order to ensure that the motorist clearly knows how much time is remaining for green signal to continue, most of the traffic signal lights now have a stopwatch which indicates how many seconds are remaining before the signal will turn red. Based on this information, the motorist depending upon his position quickly calculates whether he has a chance to cross the road or not. Unnecessary speeding is thus avoided and the vehicle

Contd

proceeds at a reasonable speed and is sure of reaching the destination safely. The motorist can adjust his speed accordingly. This has not only led to considerable reduction in accidents but also increased compliance with traffic rules. The other benefits are reduced pollution and better fuel economy as the motorist can switch off his engine if the time interval expected at junction is high as the time period remaining for red signal to turn green is also displayed.

The essence of this example is that the 'Need' was existing for such stopwatches at traffic lights for long, but it is only now that this opportunity has been seized and utilized for business growth.

Illustrations

Another case of opportunity creation can be utilization of toll tax booth on Highways to be used as Supermarkets for purchase and as restaurant. Nowadays, roads are being built on Build, Operate, Own and Transfer basis, in which the builder is to get his financing charges by collecting toll tax. On such roads at suitable points toll tax booths are created where motorcyclists/vehicle owners have to stop to pay toll tax. This place can be converted as a resting place with facility for purchasing and eating, as any person driving on a long stretch will look forward to a cup of tea and will not mind extending his break. Similarly, in Delhi, city bus stops are shortly expected to have tea/coffee vending machine, STD/Telephone booths. The need for such facilities were there, but they are being recognized only now for utilization.

In the utility sector, since independence, thanks to substantial investment a large number of power plants has come up. Many of them are more than twenty years old. They require major overhaul and repair. If renovation is now carried out then they can be made ready to serve with efficiency for another 10 to 20 years. Major power equipment companies have converted this need into an opportunity by setting up special groups to cater to this type of business. Renovation and Modernisation has become a major business segment for them.

Another example of opportunity creation can be seen at petrol pumps. People, who go to have their vehicle tanks filled up, often find there boys suggesting that if they put this ingredient in the tank, their engine will perform much better and give a higher fuel efficiency

Contd

with minimum wear and tear. The vendors are creating business opportunity from the need for higher fuel economy and reduced engine maintenance.

All the above examples indicate that there are two ways of creating an opportunity. The first way is to identify the needs that are unsatisfied or dormant and make people aware of it, thereby creating a business opportunity. The second way is to create the need itself. Figure 1.5 indicates the flow chart for marketing by creating the opportunity. After creating an opportunity, the organisation must evaluate/find out that what are the ways to use this opportunity, and whether the organisation has the core strength to meet the requirement and make the business profitable. The supplier has to evaluate the quantum of business, investment required, skill and training required along with status of human resources to decide about taking a plunge in converting this opportunity into a business proposition.

Water Harvesting methods and the thrust on them is another example of opportunity creation. The water shortage is increasing every day due to increasing population, continuously increasing standard of living and ever increasing need of irrigation. During the 1960s, the underground water resources were channelised to meet this need, but their mindless exploitation has led to depletion in their level to dangerous levels. Thus a need was created to salvage this situation. Water Harvesting methods converted this need into an opportunity. Today, throughout the country, they have assumed importance.

Another similar example in water management and increasing its availability is conversion of saline sea water into domestically useful water. The sea provides an unending supply of water, but it is not useful for consumption. During the last thirty years, various technologies have been tried to make sea water useful. The market potential is enormous if we also take into consideration the oil-rich gulf countries that are oil-rich and can afford water at any price. This has led to the development of Desalination plants, which are now also becoming an attractive proposition in a country like India.

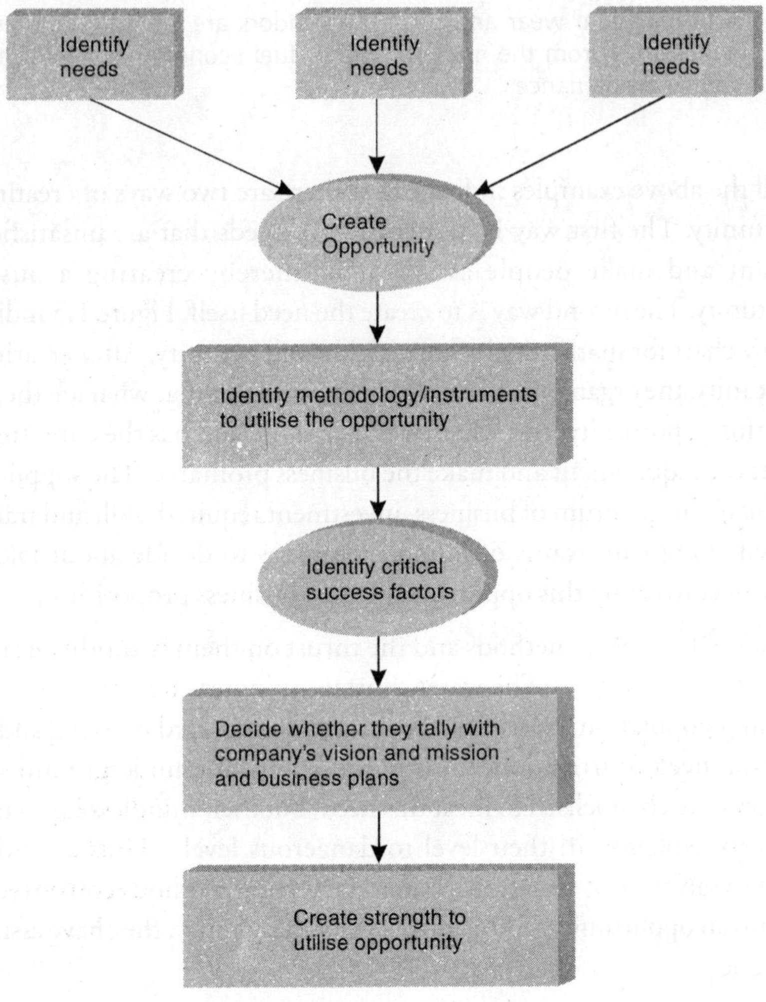

Fig. 1.5 *Marketing with Opportunity Creation*

The development in communication system is another example of opportunity creation. The need to contact and communicate with people was felt for quite some time. This need was on account of business where people need to consult fast, communicate fast and decide fast as time is of the essence. The ability of an organisation to keep itself fully informed is a competitive advantage. Thus, cellular telephone operators realized this need and converted it into a business opportunity. This also helped people to keep in touch with their families, particularly daughters and family members, who are mobile due to their job requirement. Cellular phones have thus become very popular, and with the enormous potential, have the ability to become as essential as the wristwatch. This is a classical example of converting a need into enormous opportunity and then demand.

The other example of converting a need into opportunity is the 'Internet'. The necessity for a fast and reliable mode of communication is ever increasing. People no longer want to transfer only messages. They are looking for means to transfer drawings, sketches, pictures and, if possible, the complete story running into pages. From a letter through ordinary post and crisp telegrams, the development led to courier service and telex. The 'eighties saw arrival of fax that, for the first time, facilitated transfer of drawings and sketches. Now e-mail has revolutionised the world. You can transfer anything right from messages to drawing and photographs. One can zip the file and compress the information, enabling it to be transmitted over any distance. What is remarkable about this form of transformation is that the quality of information remains unchanged and distortion is avoided.

ADVANTAGES OF MARKETING

Value Addition

It is common knowledge that products and services have no value until they are delivered to the right people at the right place and right time. Thus, marketing adds value to the system by making customers aware of their needs and explaining to them how the product being marketed can meet them. A water filter can remain a dignified product on the shelf until somebody is made aware of the need for it and then explains how the product meets it. Thus, marketing of a water filter concentrates on the following:

- It makes the customer aware of the need of filtering by concentrating on its requirement.
- It explains to the customer how the water filter can meet its requirement and satisfy his needs.

In the process, marketing has added *value* to the product. Marketing is thus a bridge between the needs of the customer and 'the way of meeting them' by the supplier. However, marketing can only enhance the value of the product. By itself, it cannot create 'Value'. The product must have its own intrinsic value and be superior. No marketing tool can overcome this deficiency in the long run.

Demand Management

One of the major objectives of marketing is to create demand and manage it. Figure 1.6 shows the mechanism of demand management through marketing. As can be seen from this figure, there are a number of interesting possibilities. If there is no existing demand for the product, then the marketing executive has to identify 'needs' and convert it into opportunities for generating demand and adding value to the product. This is an opportunity creation case.

If there is latent demand, then it is a case of existing opportunity wanting to be utilized/exploited. The marketing executive must develop a suitable product or service to meet this latent demand, and further convert this latent demand into actual demand. Examples of latent demand commonly found in the core sector are increasing stress on meeting the pollution norms by various industries. Whether it is a chemical industry, cement industry or power generation company, there are strict environmental norms to be complied with. Companies, which are in the business of supplying environmental compliance equipments, can study these requirements and see how best they can meet this market. After coming out with a product to meet this requirement, they can make a presentation to the customer demonstrating how the product offered by them can meet his requirements. Hence, marketing not only helps in developing the demand, but in creating products and services to meet it.

The third and fourth cases of demand management fall under the category where demand exists. In one case we re-examine the market needs and the present products and services to create ways and means of adding more value to the products and services by offering more than the customer needs, thereby revitalizing the demand to higher levels. In the core sector, this area of demand management and creation offers tremendous business prospects. A project consists of a large number of smaller products and services, and their specifications are interdependent. If a supplier goes on

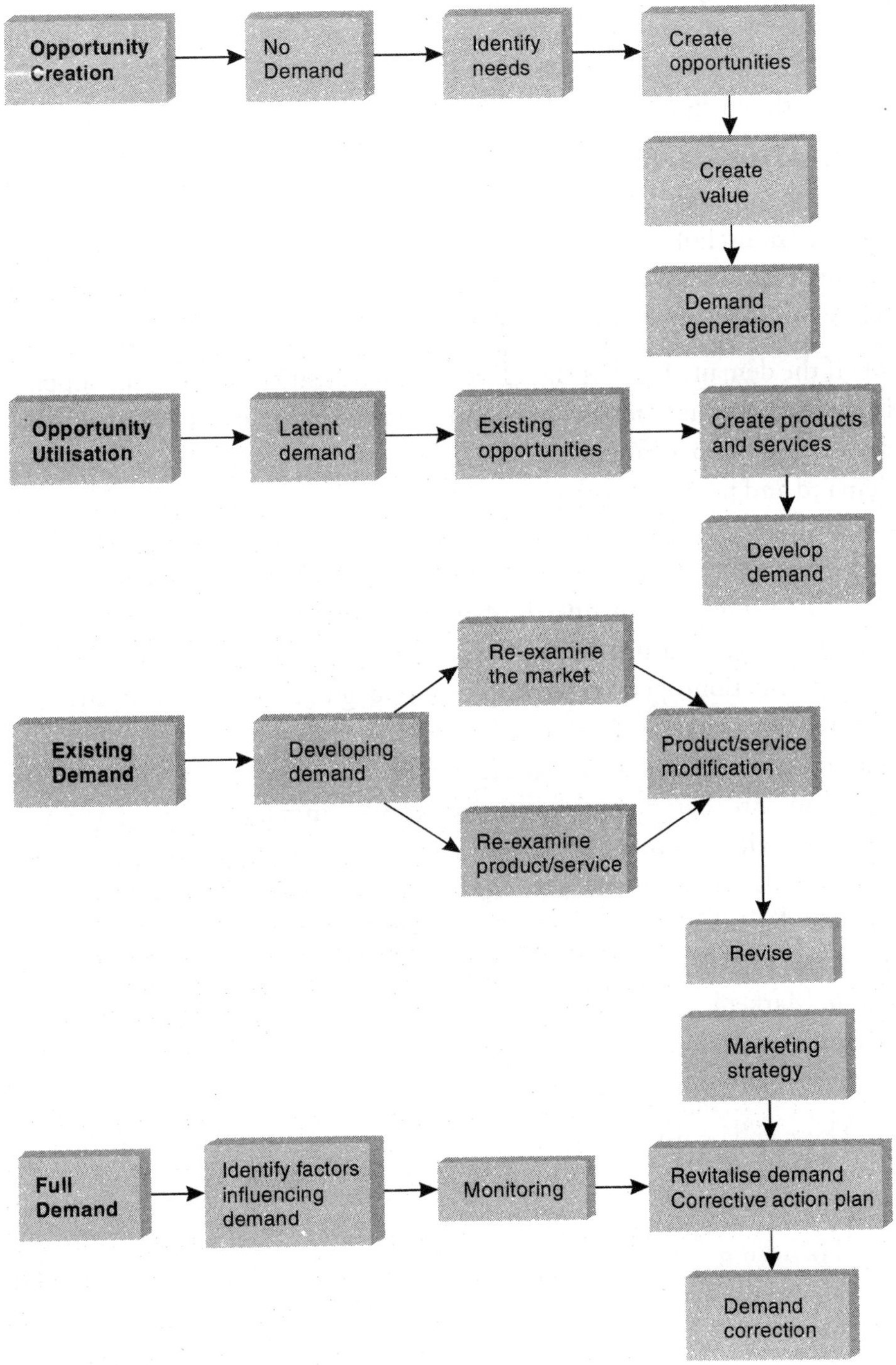

Fig. 1.6 *Demand Management*

accepting more systems in his area of activity, on the one hand he is reducing the difficulties of the customer, and on the other hand, he is giving more value to the customer. In the process, he is also getting more business himself.

If a supplier is offering a desalination plant to convert sea water to drinking water, he might as well take a project to lay pipelines for supplying this water to households. As a logical extension, he can take a total water management contract on a long-term lease, including operation and maintenance of the main desalination plant himself.

If the demand is at the right level and, for business reasons, the supplier is not interested in boosting it, he must monitor the demand to ensure that the demand is not changing suddenly. He must identify the factors affecting demand and take necessary corrective action. For this he must monitor the environment, note the changes in customer needs and keep track of investment climate and macro-economic factors. If declining demand is due to changing customer needs, then the marketing man must identify the quantum, direction and quality of such change and give suitable guidelines to his production/operational people for re-engineering/modification in the product and change the services to meet the new requirements. The marketing man acts as an interconnecting agency between changing environment, changing customer needs and company's in-house agencies entrusted with engineering and production. The supplier must protect his business share and the marketing man must aim in further improving it. One of the basic purposes of the marketing job is to predict demand behaviour sufficiently in advance to enable other agencies to take corrective action. Market intelligence is an integral part of marketing. If the demand is increasing or reducing, the supplier must know in advance and have a workable plan to meet it.

There will be situations, more so in the core sector, where demand will be much less than the supply. Many companies, based on the market forecast of the demand, plan their capital investment to serve the market. Since the actual planning, investment and readiness for commercial operation takes at least two to three years, there is no way of knowing the actual demand at the planning and investment stage. Thus, the planning and investment always take place on predicted demand. In case the predicted demand does not materialise, there is a problem of surplus capacity and price realization becomes less. Many a time it becomes difficult to service the loan and investment and, sometimes the investment may become dead. Marketing has to find ways and means to boost the demand or create alternative demand. It is one of the toughest and most thankless of jobs, but in today's competitive environment, it is required more often. A small change in domestic government taxation policy or changes proposed by other government may have serious effect on demand. The case of steel industry is the best example. Even now, due to high duty imposed by USA, the demand has suddenly fallen.

Thus creating or predicting market behaviour and managing demand is one of the main functions of marketing

Creating Options for Customer

One of the major aims of marketing is to create options for the customer. In the core sector, standardisation is rare due to different and specific requirements of each customer. Under the circumstances, one of the major responsibilities of the marketing person is to make the customer aware of various possibilities. These may be pertaining to better performance or possibility of cost reduction through change in scope of work. The vendor may also suggest a different layout or other alternatives to various tender packages being conceived by the customer. In the process, he is creating different options for the customer with different costs and providing him different values. The customer thus gets the opportunity of knowing and evaluating various possibilities and choosing the best option.

Customer Satisfaction

The word 'Marketing' has its origins from the customer. *The customer is the primary reason why a supplier exists*. Its purpose is to identify 'Needs' of the customer and either develop products and services or create new products and services to satisfy customer needs. The focus is customer, not the vendor or production. Thus marketing is a tool to enhance customer satisfaction. It is a mechanism to get feedback from the customer so as to incorporate improvements to enhance the 'benefits to the customer'. It helps the customer to get value for his money.

Maximising Return and Business Growth

Marketing provides the vendor a path to business growth and maximize his returns. Through market research, he can add new business streams to his operation and keep track of his competitor's plan and strategy, and thus enabling him to take timely action. The supplier is encouraged to update technology and optimize cost, which have a positive bearing on his bottom line. It helps him to work out a strategy to enable the customer to differentiate the product offered by the vendor and encourage the vendor to take measures to retain customer loyalty. It also helps the vendor to re-discover his own human resources and deploy them as per their strength and orientation to help in business growth and profitability through better customer appreciation.

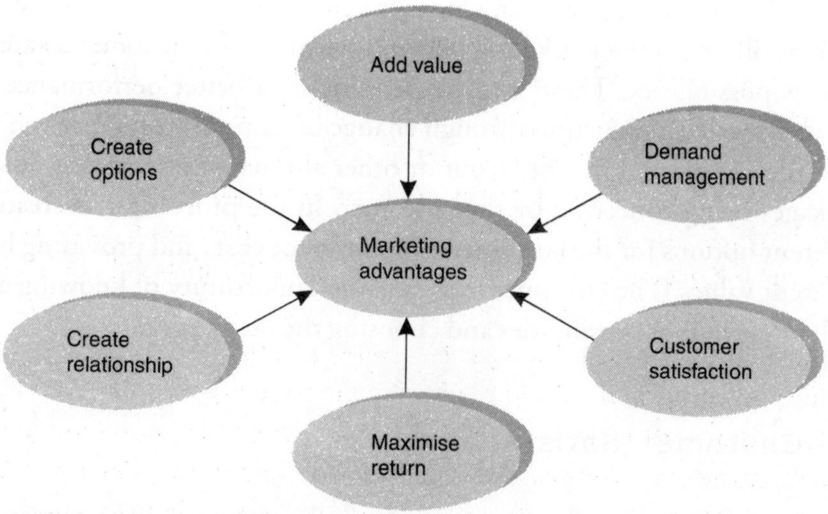

Fig. 1.7 *Advantages of Marketing*

Creating Relationship

Today's business is promoted through relationships. Marketing helps in developing relationship. During marketing, a vendor comes in close contact with customer and his officials. He is able to understand them, learn their requirements and, in the process, build a relationship with them. This relationship is mutually beneficial to both the supplier and the customer. The supplier gets the feedback on his products and services along with information on customer requirement. He gets an opportunity to orient himself and his products and services to meet the market expectations. On the other hand, the customer is able to learn about new development and new options to meet his requirements from the vendor. Thus, marketing creates a relationship that is mutually beneficial. Both the vendor and customer are able to learn from each other. The supplier can closely observe the customer operation to assess his known and hidden needs and develop plans to meet it. He also gets an opportunity to work out various strategies to get a competitive edge.

MARKETING PURPOSE

Most of the marketing books concentrate on customer and customer satisfaction as the main activity or objective of marketing, but this is probably taking it to the other extreme from selling. The basic purpose of why a supplier wants to know customer needs or satisfy the customer or resort to marketing is because in marketing, he finds a way to remain in business and achieve business growth with better profitability. The supplier is in business and he resorts to marketing as this is the only way to prosperity. Thus, the main purpose of marketing is "*Business and Profit growth through customer satisfaction*," i.e. to deliver a product whose benefits exceed its cost and thereby provide net positive value to the customer. Marketing is a tool to provide this value. This is the real aim and purpose of marketing. Thus, an organisation needs to be market-oriented to be successful in business.

It is therefore necessary that in order to have sustained long-term growth in business and profitability of an organisation, its culture and top management, who provide leadership must be market-oriented. It is not only necessary but also essential that the Chairman and other board members must have extensive marketing background. This is a radical change from the 'sixties and the 'seventies when the corporate culture was dominated by production-oriented persons. A marketing person not only thinks of today or tomorrow, but at least ten years ahead. This enables the organisation to have a base to build a position of strength for long-term business prosperity.

DISADVANTAGES OF EXCESSIVE MARKETING

Like any theory and action plan, marketing has its own disadvantages. It shifts the focus from fundamentals to more surface factors which, though successful in the short to medium term, may become obstacles for long-term growth and survival of the supplier. Some of the limitations of marketing are discussed below.

Technological Development

Marketing orientation never promotes fundamental research and development. This is for the simple reason that a market can rarely provide ideas for new products. These ideas basically come from scientists and engineers and not from the market. It is to be noted that long-term business success depends on introduction of radical new technology and development.

In a market-oriented development, efforts are mostly concentrated on product modification, not on fundamental new product development. A customer will rarely be able to conceive ideas about new technology and new products that can substitute the existing product. It is said that "*Eyes do not see what the Mind does not know*". Thus, it will be too much to expect that a customer will be able to conceive innovative and radical ideas on new technology or a new product. His perception will be restricted to his own background. He, at best, can give feedback on modification to be carried out on the existing product to increase its 'value' and consequent benefits to the customer. It must be appreciated that market feedback can provide a basis for Product modification/improvement, but the market cannot provide leadership for innovation. Too much dependence on market forces can lead to introduction and continuation of cheap and second-grade products and services.

Due to the new competitive environment, more money is spent on making a customer aware of product modification rather than on new development.

Misplaced Priorities

In order to secure business and address customer needs, the supplier concentrates on fields that have no relevance to basic engineering and operational requirements. Many suppliers concentrate on offering either an attractive financial package or an equity participation as a tool to secure business rather than on the strength of their products and services.

Such a strategy is a one-time wonder and is not successful in the medium- to long-term. In order to have sustained and consistent success, it is necessary that engineering and operational advantages of the product dominate and become its core strategy. On many occasions, due to specific customer requirements, this takes a back seat.

Recent studies have reinforced the belief that superior and excellent products and services, along with the technological skills, are the best long-term strategy for survival and growth, rather than non-product/non-service based factors. Thus, marketing efforts should concentrate on providing better value to the customer. It should increase the benefits to the customer. Such benefits can only come through sustained improvements introduced through new technological developments and superior products. This is particularly true in the core sector where a lot of emphasis is placed on product quality and technological development. In this business segment, the 'product' itself is the main marketing tool and, hence, the emphasis should be on introducing a product, which provides 'benefits' to the customer exceeding those provided by the competitors.

2

Marketing–Difference Between Consumer Sector and Core Sector

Focused Approach
Segmentation
Financing
Commitment
Critical Decision-Making Parameters
Spares and Services
Deciding Authority and Procedure
Statutory Approvals
Loyalty
Relationship
Product/Project
Market Research
Demand
Addressing the Customer

2

Marketing is a very important part of business management and a lot of literature exists on it. However, this literature basically addresses only the consumer sector. There is a basic difference between the two market sectors and, accordingly, the marketing strategy for them differs totally. The difference between the two business segments can be compared in the same way as the difference between an individual investor in share market and an institutional investor. Some of the major differences between the two segments are summarised in Table 2.1 and are highlighted below.

FOCUSED APPROACH

In the case of infrastructure sector, marketing is focused on the individual customer rather than on customers as a group. Hence, the marketing efforts are more focused and no generalised marketing strategy can be developed; rather it has to be individual based. One has to study the individual customer and his requirement, financial position, project schedule and also understand his overall needs for which the requirement under question will fit to devise a marketing strategy.

In the consumer sector if one has to market and sell a 'dish washer', then initially one has to see whether the 'need' for the product is existing in society or has to be created and whether the creation of this need will be at the cost of some existing product/service and, if so, then the new product, in order to substitute the existing product/service, must offer a better benefit than the existing one. Until this is ensured there can be no market for the new product. This is where the similarities end. The marketing procedure for them is entirely different.

Table 2.1 *Difference between Core Sector and Consumer Sector*

Core Sector	*Consumer Sector*
• Mostly value-driven customers	• Mostly Cost- or Premium-driven customers
• Stress on '*Benefits*'	• Stress on '*Comforts*'
• Market Segmentation based on Industry	• Market Segmentation based on Human being
• Customer's survival may depend on it or it may be his life line	• No such requirement
• Purpose of purchase may be –Production –Expansion –Profitability –Business Growth	• Purpose of purchase may be –Utility –Comforts –Status Symbol –Social Requirement –Changing life style
• They are purchased for business	• They are purchased for personal use
• Major Deciding Factors are: –Business needs –Payback period/IRR –Financing –Life cycle –Ease of operation –Maintenance facility	• Major Deciding Factors are: –Family needs –Fashion –Neighbourhood comparison –Social necessity
• Decision and its procedure for taking is complex and requires approval from appropriate authority. The decision is slow.	• Decision is taken by the family and is very fast. It may be momentary.
• Decisions are taken after due consideration and thorough analysis and evaluation.	• Decisions are more influenced by purchases made by friends and neighbours.
• Statutory requirements and approvals are necessary.	• Statutory approvals are not required.
• Availability of long-term maintenance facility plays a major role in decision making.	• Availability of maintenance facility by the supplier is not essential.
• Marketing approach is based on the organisation and individual customer. Each customer requires a study to identify his buying behaviour and he himself is the focus of attention.	• Marketing approach is mass-based and not individually focused. It can be segmental like based on urban/rural or male/female. Marketing study is based on segmentation.

Contd

Core Sector	*Consumer Sector*
• Advertisement in business magazines can create an image, but marketing is through focused approach, through direct one-to-one presentation and discussion. Presentation can be done to a select group of customers having same business interest	• Advertisement through newspaper/TV/ Radio plays a major role as a marketing tool.
• Pricing is one of the marketing strategies and has to be worked for each and every customer separately. It has a limited role on market share.	• Pricing is a major marketing strategy and can be adopted to modulate market share.
• Very sensitive to technological changes.	• Reasonably sensitive to technological changes.

In the case of a 'dish washer', one has to go through the following marketing methodology:

- Advertisement in newspaper
- Advertisement on TV/Radio
- Demonstration in Trade Fair/Shops and in individual Houses

The advertisement or demonstration will concentrate on the problems with the present product/methods and how the new product addresses it. What are the consumer-friendly features incorporated in the product and how do they benefit the consumers? In advertisements particularly on TV, one has to create a real-life situation. For a dish washer it can be that the housewife is unhappy either with too much time being taken by the maid, or unannounced absence with guests in the house, or her inability to come on time, or the quality of the work she is doing. Even the regular fight between the housewife and the maid can show the problems with the maid and can impress on the husband the necessity of a dish washer, if the wife decides to transfer her anger from maid to husband. While on the other hand, the dishwasher is at your service at any time with any load. You have to just press a button. Its quality does not change with the load. It does not shout or pick up a quarrel with you. It is at your command. No fuss, no disputes, no holidays.

It should be noted that one is concentrating on the 'comforts' of the housewife and removal of her headache. Though the customer is being addressed not as an individual but as a collective one, no distinction is planned between individual customers.

In the core sector, say in a steel plant, which is producing a large amount of flat angles, there is a need to cut them in pieces of different lengths and pack them in fixed number per package for dispatch. There is the need for customers to have an automatic system for measuring length and cutting in pre-measured pieces. There has to be another equipment for counting it in the desired number of pieces. If a vendor who has developed such a system wants to market it, he has to go to the steel plant and make a presentation to them as to how this system could be useful to them and increase their productivity by increasing the efficiency. Increase in return and the savings in cost will result not only in increase in production but in an attractive payback period for the investment. The supplier has to make his proposal attractive by concentrating on the following improvement:

- Increased efficiency
- Business growth
- Ease of operation
- Lesser mistakes—higher accuracy
- More returns
- Attractive payback.

The concentration is not on 'comforts' but on 'benefits', i.e. productivity and profitability. This is the essential difference between the two sectors.

Figure 2.1 shows the difference in the marketing action plan. In both segments one has to begin by identifying the customer needs and developing plans to meet it, but then the change takes place in the action plan for getting the business. In the consumer sector we address as a group the customers whose requirement for purchase and decision making factors are mostly the same. In this segment it may be possible that we may categorise them based on the basis of geographical consideration or sex or based on urban/rural basis but they do not get reduced to an individual identity.

In the core sector, even for the same industrial segment like cement industry, the buying behaviour is entirely different. One strategy may work with one customer, but fail entirely with another customer. Hence, the marketing man has to assess each customer separately by understanding his requirement and priorities and, above all, the purchasing or project investment philosophy of each customer.

SEGMENTATION

In both the consumer sector and core sector, in order to get best results and to optimise resources, customer segmentation is essential. A market segment is a group of present and future customers having some common characteristics in demand that can help in standardising the strategy for them. It can also help in predicting changes in quality and quantity of future demand. The basis of segmentation in both the sectors are entirely different. In the case of consumer sector, the basic segmentation parameters are factors like urban–rural, sex—male/female, age, regional location, habits, etc. If a shampoo is to be marketed, it has to be targeted first at the urban female segment. Similarly, due to different culture and habits , products may have to be marketed on a regional basis. 'Lungi' will eventually find a market in south India.

In the core sector, needs do not show any marked change based on regional location, and the requirements remain the same irrespective of factors like age and sex. The needs can show some similarity if they are coming from the same industry. The steel industry, for example, can show convergence of demand and may help in identifying as a market segment. One of the major differences is that in the consumer sector, the segmentation is mostly based on 'Human Being' as the object generating the demand and all strategies are concentrated on him. In the core sector, the industry becomes the focal point. Normally, the requirements remain the same irrespective of region, and location. Factors that make a difference are naturally not related to the human being, but are project-specific and can make a difference in requirement even in two projects from the same industrial segment located in the same region and even located in the vicinity.

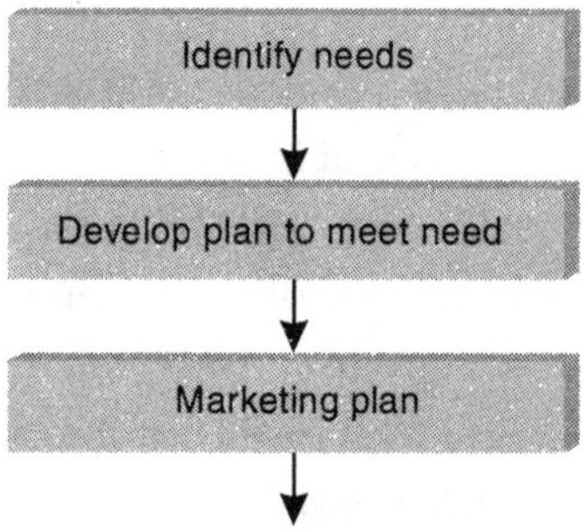

	Core Sector	**Consumer Sector**
Concentration	Benefits	Comforts
Focus	Individual customer	Mass customer
Methodology	Personal visit, Presentation	Advertisement Mass appeal
Factors	• Profitability • Productivity • Payback • Operational ease • Less maintenance	• Utility • Social status • New life style
Strategy	Multi-phased	Price, Utility

Fig. 2.1 *Difference in Marketing Action Plan*

FINANCING

For purchasing capital equipment, one requires money and not many can afford it from their resources. In the consumer sector in most cases, the individual purchaser can afford it while for those who need finances, the financing institutions have a standard evaluation criteria and loans are available easily. The quantum involved is small and financing institutions are also willing to take more risk. In the core sector, the finance requirements are large, and for a long period. So it can rarely be afforded by an individual and therefore assumes an important role in marketing. Investment decisions are not easy. The basic purpose of investment is to have business growth and higher return. Until and unless these two parameters are attractive, there cannot be any investment and demand generation. Secondly, unlike the consumer sector, where a wrong purchase decision has no or negligible effect on the activities of the purchaser, in the core sector, if such decisions later on prove wrong, they can have a catastrophic effect on the operations of the purchaser and can prove a long time drag on his project and total business group and also on the helpless investors. Because of this reason and its long-term effect on investment, arrangement of financial resources is never easy. The cost of borrowing may itself sometime become a major factor in investment. This problem of the purchaser often presents itself as a business opportunity for the supplier. Financing itself can be profitably and productively utilised as a marketing tool in the core sector as discussed in subsequent chapters. The role of financing is very limited as a marketing tool in the consumer sector as arranging finance is not that difficult a proposition. Most of the consumer sector shops that provide financing do so more as a one-stop service rather than as a marketing tool. The mode or kind of financing being provided by the seller rarely plays a role in decision-making in the consumer sector. On the other hand, the type and mode of financing play a major role in the decision-making process and selection of vendor in the infrastructure sector. Many customers in the core sector are known to compromise on other parameters if they are able to get finance on attractive terms.

COMMITMENT

Vendor commitment is another factor that differentiates these two sectors. In consumer sector, the purchase is one-time phenomenon. A customer trying to buy fridge, will do a little market survey, analyse the different brands available and select one. He will then go to the shop keeper/agent/company, which is giving him the best deal and make the purchase. The payment is made and delivery is effected. The contract execution time rarely extends beyond a month and is much smaller than the time taken in decision making process.

On the other hand in the core sector, contract execution time is much more than the time taken in the decision-making process. The delivery is effected in stages. Hence the term 'Vendor Commitment' comes into play. The vendor has to ensure that the supplies are essentially in the manner and sequence as envisaged at the time of deal finalisation and in the project's overall interest. Any deviation from this creates a problem. Non-adherence to time schedule can lead to cost over-run and affect the project viability.

Thus, vendor commitment is very essential in the core sector. Such needs do not arise in the consumer sector.

CRITICAL DECISION-MAKING PARAMETERS

The basic parameters or factors affecting the decisions of the owner are very different in the two sectors and are shown in Figures 2.2 and 2.3, respectively. It can be seen that in the consumer sector the decisions are more driven by family needs and are influenced by purchases made by friends, colleagues and neighbours. In the core sector many times purchase decisions and investment decisions are made just to survive. If a company is having old machinery whose availability is low and maintenance high and its non-availability is affecting business and profitability, then the decision taken to replace it is a decision for survival. Some of the decisions are based on increased profit due to proposed investment.

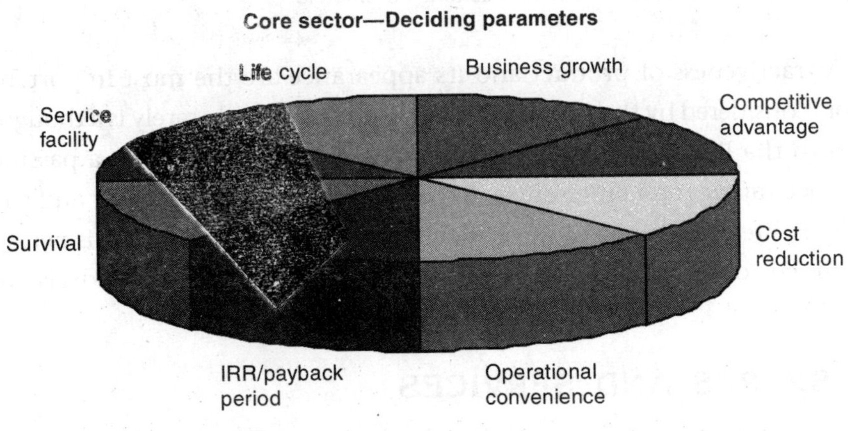

Fig. 2.2 *Core Sector—Critical Deciding Parameters*

Most of the core sector industries like aluminium, cement and steel are power-intensive industries. They require continuous availability of power at reasonable rates. The power available from state and central utilities is costly and not that reliable with power cuts becoming the order of the day. Thus, non-availability of power not only leads to loss of production, but increases its cost also leading to multiple effects contributing to declining profits. Hence, having a captive power plant becomes a question of survival for them. In the case of Indian Railways, power is one of the basic necessities. They have been purchasing power at a very high cost from utilities. Though the Railways have started purchasing power from central utilities at much lower rates, they can still save a lot if they set up their own power plant.

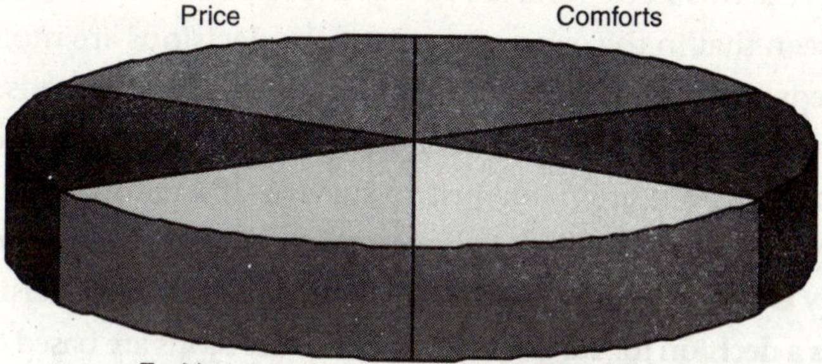

Fig. 2.3 *Consumer Sector—Critical Deciding Parameters*

Attractiveness of product and its appearance are the most important factors considered by the consumer sector purchaser. Only rarely is a thought given to the life cycle of the product. It is considered more as a passing reference rather than an essential factor. In core sector durability and the expected life cycle is one of the critical deciding factors. It is in this period that the customer calculates his return and evaluates his investment decision.

SPARES AND SERVICES

Any equipment requires service to give efficient performance. The service facility required in the consumer sector is mostly to attend to breakdown maintenance. Even in those cases only 15–20 per cent demand is addressed by the main manufacturing company or its authorised service centre. The majority of demand is addressed by the friendly neighbourhood mechanic or repairman.

In the core sector the product is sophisticated and requires trained manpower to operate it. For this the manpower, has to be trained by the supplier. Most of the vendors have observed over the years that if the equipments are operated by the trained personnel, the complaints are reduced drastically and availability of equipment to the customer is increased. This also protects and improves the image of the vendor. The equipment also requires regular overhaul and this needs assistance from the vendor. In case of breakdown or other problems, the customer has to necessarily depend on the vendor and service facilities available with him. It is not possible for the customer to get easily the kind of service facility required at each and every place. Leveraging service facility is an essential part of core sector marketing. The supplier is conscious of the fact that the number of customers is limited and there is always a possibility of repeat business. Hence, reducing the customer complaints and addressing it quickly is very important. It has also been observed that if equipment is operated properly and regular maintenance is done, customer complaints are reduced drastically. Hence, many suppliers themselves do free preventive maintenance. It helps in higher customer satisfaction due to increased availability and better performance from the equipments.

Like service, timely availability of spare parts plays a major role in the core sector. Many important capital equipments lie idle due to non-availability of operational spares. They cannot be just bought at will across the table. Since the life of these equipments is more than twenty years, the customer has to depend on a reputed supplier who will be able to meet the spares needed over such a long period. In fact, in the core sector it becomes the moral responsibility of the vendor to ensure timely and continuous availability of spares. In the consumer sector such a necessity arises rarely and duplicate spare parts are commonly used.

DECIDING AUTHORITY AND PROCEDURE

There is a major difference in the decision-making process and the deciding authority in two sectors. There is no formal decision-making process in the case of consumer sector. The family is the decision-maker. So there are no rules or regulations to be kept in mind and followed. There is no limitation on flexibility of approach. The decision-making process is not important, but the decision is. The decision is therefore quick and easy and there is no manoeuvering or wasted interest.

In the core sector decisions are taken by the appropriate authority or group of people as per the delegation of powers. There is a procedure to be followed and there is due decision-making process. Bids are to be invited. Discussion takes place and bids are to be properly evaluated and, if required, the negotiations are to be carried out by a duly appointed committee. The decision is slow and tedious. There are pulls and counter-pulls. The supplier also becomes part of the process, as some of the manoeuvering is due to him or his other competitors. Vendors are required to have a lot of patience to do business in this segment. A small innocent looking query is sufficient to derail the whole process. Many times the time taken in the decision-making process may itself exceed the contract completion period desired from the vendors. Apart from this the incubation period of the project itself is very high. The cost overrun and financial difficulties during project implementation is a logical fall-out of such situation. In this segment both the decision and decision-making process is important.

STATUTORY APPROVALS

Most of the products required and projects in the core sector are expected to meet pollution and environment norms and other statutory approvals. These norms may differ from place to place and the supplier is expected to incorporate the necessary modification to ensure that they conform to prevailing norms at the site. For example, there are norms of noise level for the operation of equipment that may vary from city to city and place to place. There is one set of norms for equipment to be installed in a hospital, and there will be a different norm for a place other than a hospital. Similarly, there will be norms for pollution that may vary from place to place. The supplier is expected to apply the necessary corrective measures for meeting these norms. Thus, same product will not be suitable until necessary improvements are incorporated to comply with the norms.

In addition to meeting norms, there are a number of approvals specific to the project that need to be taken and complied with. If one is constructing a dam, then one has to ensure that the earthquake co-efficient is taken into consideration. There may be problems associated with resettlement of the existing town and villages, or compensation to be paid to people displaced by the setting up of the project.

LOYALTY

One of the essential ingredients of successful marketing is retaining the loyalty of each and every customer. In the case of core sector monitoring this is essential as there are limited customers and many of them regularly come out with new requirements. Thus, in the core sector, customer loyalty is required to be monitored regularly for each and every customer, and reasons for loss thereof is required to be analysed and addressed properly.

In the consumer sector, customer loyalty is addressed mostly in groups. It is not individual or customer-based. It is studied on market share basis or segment basis.

RELATIONSHIP

In the consumer sector, the customer and supplier do not come in direct contact with each other; hence, there is no bond of personal relationship between them. On the other hand, in the core sector both the customer and the supplier come in close contact with each other during project/product pre-tendering and pre-contract stage. This relationship continues even at the post-contract stage, and it leads to establishment of personal relationship between customer and vendor persons. This relationship slowly matures into a bond of friendship if both parties start liking each other and sentiments and emotional attachment starts developing between them. This bond plays a very important role in business between organisations. As a human beings, we always tend to assist persons, knowingly or unknowingly, with whom we are attached, or for whom we have developed regard and respect. A healthy respect is a prerequisite for business in the core sector.

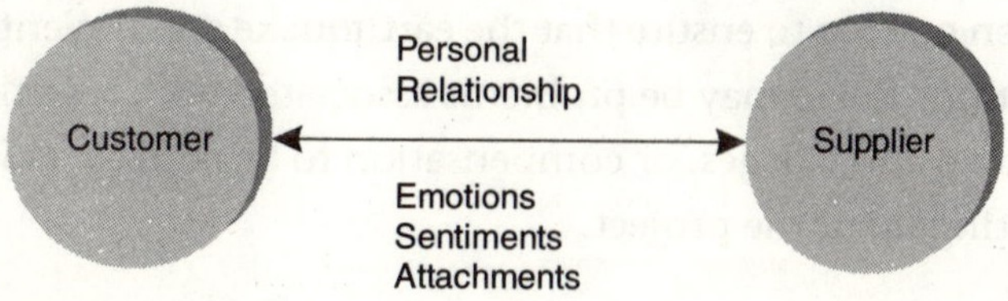

Fig. 2.4 *Relationship Bond in Core Sector*

Illustration

There are many instances where the supplier has just managed business through relationship. Company A had supplied major equipments to company B five years back. During the initial period, the equipments caused major teething problems and resulted in a number of visits of the supplier's personnel to the customer's site. Though the supplier took more than six months to diagnose and solve the problem, the customer's site staff was impressed by the dedication shown by the supplier's staff. After the equipments were set right, they performed well and gave trouble-free service and the performance was better than envisaged in the contract. The customer had, by this time, developed a healthy respect for the supplier and used to consult him regularly whenever required. Five years later, the company again had requirement for equipments, though of a different type and in no way connected to the equipment supplied earlier but manufactured by the supplier. The customer had a natural preference for the supplier and in spite of regular tendering and evaluation process, the old supplier was given the benefit, sometime undue also, so that he could get the business. This justified the oft-repeated remarks of one of my earlier bosses, who used to lay tremendous emphasis on customer relationship, saying that one may have excellent equipments and services and may have submitted most competitive bids, but he gets the business only if customer wants to give the business to him.

If one looks at the above illustration, it is clear that the relationship was established under the most adverse circumstances. As a result of the equipment not working, the customer was suffering, but with determination and dedication, the supplier's team had converted the adversity into an advantage. There are also instances where many suppliers have spoiled or left such opportunities and lost business as a result. Business through such types of relationships is rare in the consumer sector, as the customer and supplier do not get a chance of one-to-one meeting or opportunities where one can judge their tenacity or devotion.

PRODUCT/PROJECT

In the case of the consumer sector, the whole marketing strategy is basically centred on selling the product. One studies the market, identifies the demand and segment which he wants to address and develops a suitable marketing strategy to cater to it. If a supplier is in the business of selling toothpaste, the marketing strategy has to assess the needs of the customer and measure the competitive forces and develop a suitable strategy.

This does not hold good for the core sector. The customer is normally setting up a large project and hence he has to always keep a project approach in mind rather than a product-centric approach. The vendor has to look into the end use of the product. This may make it necessary to incorporate design modifications in the product even if the customer may not have specifically asked for it.

Motors are required everywhere in the core sector application for moving each and every thing. Now, if a customer wants a 500 kW motor, the vendor can simply supply it, but every motor require control so that it can perform the desired function. Hence, the vendor looks on his own to see what kind of control mechanism the customer is intending to use. If the control mechanism is through power electronic device then the vendor knows that his motor will use non-quality dc supply with a lot of harmonics, which may lead to heating and the motor rating will effectively get reduced by about 10–12 per cent. Thus, the motor supplier is required to build this capacity in the motor to ensure that it performs even under these circumstances.

MARKET RESEARCH

Another major difference is in the area of market research. In the consumer sector the focus is on segmental study like rural/urban, etc. It involves collection of details and analysis of culture background, economic background, and habits, perception of segment of society. The research also concentrates on assessing the role of advertisement and publicity on demand generation and in further improving the competitive edge. Product positioning and pricing are determined based on market research. These parameters are fixed after great deal of discussion and evaluation of the collected data and study of the extrapolated results for various combinations. It is to be appreciated that the prices are fixed and they do not vary from customer to customer, as is the case in core sector.

In core sector marketing, one has to concentrate on individual customers. Segmentation study can he misleading. Even customers from the same industry can show different perception. In the cement industry, if a captive power plant is to be set up, some may prefer DG Set, while others may prefer thermal sets. Some may choose one type of boiler; others may, in identical circumstances, go for different type. Even fuel and ambient and operating conditions may vary and the marketing person has to take this into account. Individual choice and perception can be driven by different factors like technology, cost, maintenance expenditure, environmental consideration and past experience. Critical success factors can vastly differ from customer to customer in the same industrial segment.

Table 2.2 *Activity based Difference in the Consumer Sector and Core Sector*

S.No.	*Activity*	*Consumer Sector*	*Core Sector*
1.	Demand behaviour	Slow, smooth and predictable	Fast, abrupt and unpredictable
2.	Demand behaviour stability	Low to medium	Medium to high
3.	Demand generation	Primary demand	Derived demand
4.	Approach	Mass based	Focused, individual customer based
5.	Marketing strategy	Mass based	Focused, individual customer based
6.	Requirement	Product centric	Largely Project centric
7.	Market research	Segmental/community based like Urban–Rural, Rich–Poor, etc.	Industry based with focus on individual customer

DEMAND

Another basic difference between the two sectors comes from the way one defines DEMAND. In the consumer sector it is always defined as a percentage or in large physical number that is generated by statistical projection methods. In the core sector the market demand for at least two financial years is generally based on actual projects, and it is always in actual quantified number. This small change makes substantial change in market research.

The transient behaviour of demand in the two sectors is markedly different as can be seen from Fig. 2.5. In the consumer segment, the changes in demand pattern are slow, smooth and predictable and are generally of long term nature. This is primarily on account of the fact that the demand is generated by the habits of human beings, their culture, their life style. Changes in these factors are slow and smooth. Definitely, time has an effect on such basic behaviour, but it is too slow to cause sudden and unexpected changes. Consumer sector demand also depends upon other economic parameters like GDP growth rate, recession, etc., but it is seen that these parameters do not have a very marked influence on demand pattern of many consumable items and sometimes even do not follow macro-economic parameters. The most important parameter that decides the purchases in the consumer sector is the purchasing capacity of the customer and the need for purchasing it. Most of the time, these factors are not dependent on macro-economic factors. There is increasing tendency for the consumer today to purchase micro-ovens, and the demand is increasing irrespective of ongoing slump in the market. This is due to the buying perception of the consumer.

On the other hand, demand fluctuation in the core sector is dependent on both macro- and micro-economic factors. The perception of the buyer does play a role, but it is negligible compared to the economic factors. Figure 2.6 shows the effect macro and micro factors have on the demand in the core sector and the consumer sector. In the core sector the demand fluctuations are abrupt, fast and unpredictable to a large extent and their life cycle is low. They can reverse very fast. This is primarily due to the fact that demand is derived demand and is influenced by a large number of factors like inflation, industrial growth, country's economic health, investment climate, etc. The demand is also more prone to global changes. The demand is generated by infrastructure projects that have long incubation period before initiation primarily due to requirement of statutory approvals, guarantees, environmental factors, state government and local population mood and attitude, apart from well known economic factors like financing, feasibility, IRR, payback period, etc. Even a small development of sensitive nature can lead to delay/postponement or cancellation of the project affecting the demand.

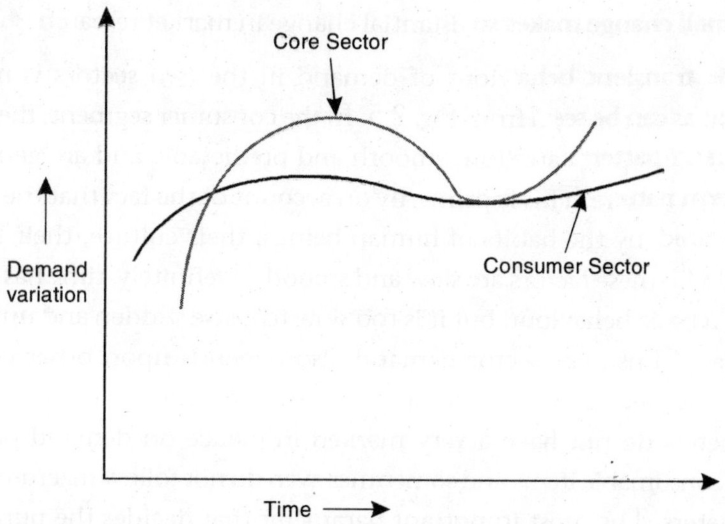

Fig. 2.5 *Transient Behaviour of Demand in Core Sector and Consumer Sector*

Demand in the cement or petroleum sector is not driven by the social status, but by economic growth. Businessmen invest in core sector projects only if they are economically viable. On the other hand, in the consumer sector, customer buy products for fulfilling their needs and for enjoying comforts. They do not buy it to generate further economic value from it. They do not have to run an industry and bother about how to distribute salary to employees or dividend to the shareholders. The picture is entirely different in the core sector. The investment is done to augment production and to generate profits. The revenue generated out of production from this investment will be mainly utilised in paying back the investment. Thus, the demand transient behaviour has a lot to do with economic factors. Depending upon the segment of the core sector, the effect of the economic factors may be felt with a time-lag.

ADDRESSING THE CUSTOMER

In view of major differences in the two sectors highlighted above, the method of addressing the customer is naturally different. In the case of consumer sector, customers are addressed as a group. Advertisement through TV, Newspaper or any other mass target based medium is an important tool. Occasionally, in the consumer sector, one may resort to personal meetings with the customer but this will be limited to very few cases like "sample data research", or sample marketing, or addressing large value customers.

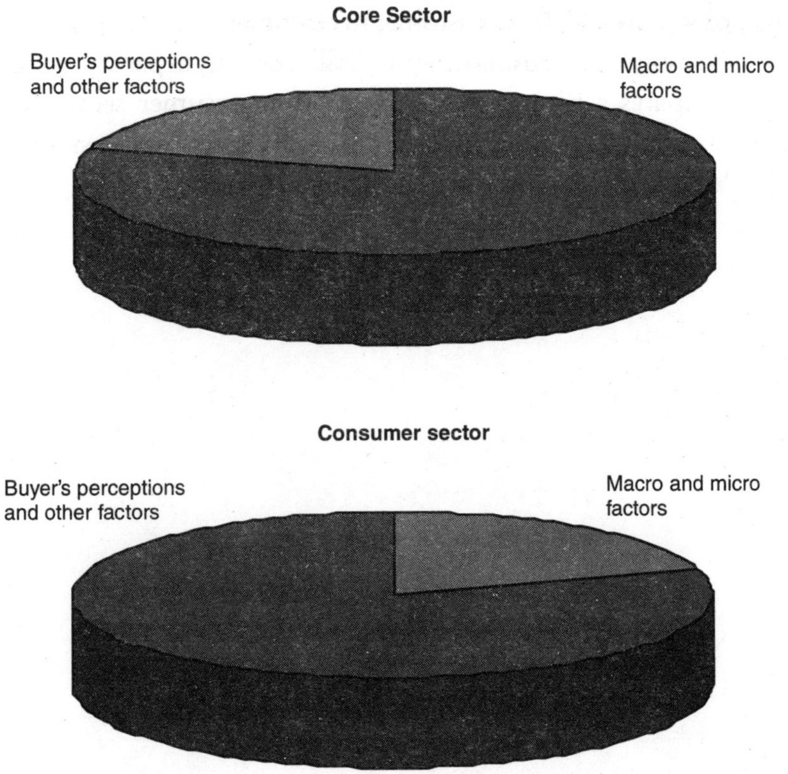

Fig. 2.6 *Effect of Economic Factors on Demand*

Sometimes, it may be followed for promotion of new products also. However, in a majority of cases, the supplier organisation or its top management rarely comes face to face with customers at least to promote the product or secure business. The contact is always through intermediaries like an agent or shopkeeper, etc.

In the case of core sector, direct contact between seller and buyer is a must. Entering into a business is more the beginning of a partnership. It can be compared like entering into a marriage of a son or of a daughter. Naturally all precautions/discussions and enquiries required for entering into the marriage relationship are also undergone here. The role of consultant resembles more the role of intermediaries who will communicate the marriage proposal and furnish necessary clarification/additional information.

Another important aspect is that in the core sector, the USP (Unique selling point) may vary from customer to customer and the supplier's success will lie in identifying and using different USPs correctly as per the requirement. If one compares a business segment of the consumer sector with one corporate identity, then the business will go in American Presidential style to the 'Winner takes All' as there is no partial success.

3

Marketing—What One Must Know

The Classical Four 'U' Theory
Understanding the Individual Customer
Understanding Environment
Understanding Yourselves
Understanding the Competitor

3

THE CLASSICAL FOUR 'U' THEORY

Understanding the task, challenges and assets are very important for successful accomplishment of the result. In marketing also, a marketing executive should understand the four basic principles that are detailed as under before proceeding further. In the core sector it is a fact that a business relationship between supplier and customer is not a one-time relationship between two unknown parties. Here, both the supplier and the customer come face to face with each other and, for a long-term successful business relationship, it is important that they both understand each other, as they are partners and successful project execution depends on both of them. In some countries, especially India, there is a lot of emphasis on matching the thinking of boy and girl before marriage. Some people resort to astrology also for this. The purpose is that marriage should be lasting, peaceful and prosperous. In the core sector also, which is basically a partnership between vendor and customer, this is true. If attitude, approach and other factors between customer and supplier suit each other, the business relationship between the two will be mutually beneficial.

The major constituents of Four 'U' theory are:

- Understanding the Individual Customer
- Understanding the Environment
- Understanding Yourselves (Supplier)
- Understanding the Competitor

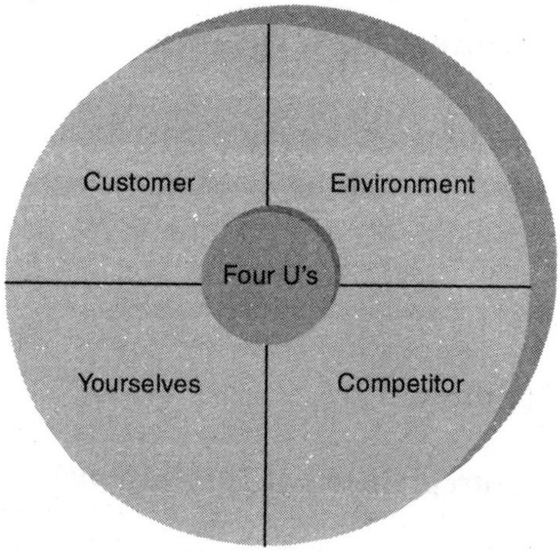

Fig. 3.1 *Four 'U' Theory*

UNDERSTANDING THE INDIVIDUAL CUSTOMER

Why Customer Understanding?

"Understanding the customer" is the first mantra any marketing executive is taught when he or she joins the function. Why is it so important? Marketing, by its very definition, requires that the 'supplier' must satisfy the needs of the customer. For this he must know what the customer is looking forward to. Understanding the requirement and developing a suitable strategy to meet them may itself provide a big competitive advantage. This is like saying that if one identifies the location of the pain and applies balm over there, most of the problem is taken care of. Profitability of the business depends on the customer. Many management experts feel that it is not the product but the customer that gives the profit.

In the core sector, customer understanding assumes added significance as strategy is individual based and it is necessary to find out needs, likes and dislikes of the individual customer and his buying behaviour to develop a focused approach. In many cases the needs may be similar, but the approach may be entirely different due to different likes and dislikes.

What is Customer Understanding?

These are the factors that decide the buying behaviour and **decision of the** customer. The total efforts should be directed to secure info**rmation on** these factors so that a suitable strategy can be developed. Some **of these** factors are:

Type of Customer

A customer can be 'Entrepreneur' or 'Professional' or orthodox, i.e. '*Khandani*' type.

An *entrepreneur type* will be prone to taking more risks. New technology/research will be of interest to him. He may be willing to try them even though they may not have been fully established, but may offer to him certain advantages. He may not indulge too much in finding out '*where it has been used*' or '*where it is operating*' or '*how long it is in service*'. He will evaluate the pros and cons and will take a calculated risk. A customer with such characteristics will be a business leader of vision. He will not tolerate inefficiency and lack of performance even though he may be willing to share business risks involved with the new work. The only way to retain loyalty of such customers is to perform and have a positive attitude towards work. Natural preference of such customers are those suppliers who are professional and whose business approach is driven by technology and who do not leave their clients high and dry on encountering problems during contract execution and operation.

A *professional type* will go in for the systematic and methodical way. He will clearly lay down his requirements and evaluation criteria and will follow a scientific approach. He will be less prone to take risks, but his decisions will be logical. He may not have the ability to take quick decisions compared to the entrepreneur type and may not have that much courage to overrule the advice of his subordinates even though he may personally be convinced. Such type of customers are value seekers.

The '*Khandani*' variety will lay more emphasis on the past performance of the vendor and, especially, the experience they or their group companies have with the vendor. They will not assign any weightage for future potential.

They give great consideration to the past relationship they have with the vendor even though it may not be of any relevance. They are likely to opt for items coming from known hands rather than risk superior products coming from even renowned vendors but with no prior personal experience with them. LOYALTY is at a premium with them. To start business relationship with such a type of customer is really challenging, but once it is established, one can rest assured that it will be more difficult for someone else to throw him or her out. They are the most tolerant class of customers. Relationship is more important to them than the performance. They are a supplier's delight.

Such type of customers show marked adaptability and adjustability with their vendor whom they treat as partners, and are prepared to be even taken for a ride by their beloved vendors. They always like to look for new technologies and products, which provide them additional benefits. They also like new ideas, but they must be proven.

Purpose/Attitude

The attitude of the customer also plays an important role. He can be research-oriented, an amateur or a freelancer. There are customers who spend considerable time in understanding each and every aspect of a transaction. They go in for so much detail that sometimes one may wonder whether they are setting up a project or preparing for their own Ph.D. examination. Naturally, time schedule and cost are of secondary importance to them. One should be prepared to receive and reply to all sorts of questions and information, relevant or irrelevant. Many vendors deliberately misguide them so as to prompt them to ask unrelated question to competitors. They can be easily utilised to collect competitors' most guarded information. They can also be easily confused. Many times they are likely to be frustrated and irritated as they may not be getting the desired results. Their decisions may not be based on logic and objectivity. A vendor should have patience while dealing with them and naturally should be prepared for increased marketing expenditure. While dealing with them most of the marketing executives may end up richer in intellectual inputs, but may not have much to show by way of increase in order book. This research variety takes a very long time in arriving at a decision, if at all they arrive at one.

The amateur or 'Know all' type will be neither methodical nor systematic and may even have no idea why they want to purchase the equipment in question. They are superfluous in nature and will rely on half cooked details. They are unable to understand and appreciate differences and may make decisions on irrelevant factors. Cost is the primary factor with them but at the same time they are eager to show that they have purchased the latest, state-of-the-art equipments. Naturally, with such type of customers, a lot of problems crop up during execution, resulting in delay and malfunctioning of system, and they are very prompt in laying the blame at the doors of vendors though they themselves may be the cause of this situation. It is very necessary to ensure before taking up projects with these types of customers that there are no loose ends and everything is well tied up in everybody's interest.

The 'Freelancer' decides to set up a project because everybody else in the world is putting up one. He is a so-called visionary who lacks the ability to convert an idea into a workable plan and into reality. Great care needs to be exercised before starting a business relationship with freelancers.

The Orientation

A customer can either be cost oriented or value oriented. A *cost-oriented customer* always aims at the lowest cost and, in the process, is willing to compromise on quality, higher efficiency and performance. It would not be advisable to give equipment with better performance and quality to them if it results in extra cost, as it has no value for them. Most of the customers in this category find innovative but suicidal ways of cost reduction. Due to this, when they run into problems, they try to put the blame on their suppliers though they themselves are the reason for this loss.

Illustration

A well-known paper company wanted to augment its existing control system for the process plant and approached a well-known consultant for undertaking the work and advise them about the modification. The consultant quoted a fee of Rs twenty lakhs but the company found the charges too high and awarded the contract to a local

Contd

consultant for Rs five lakhs. Not only did the revised control scheme not work, but the process plant itself developed a problem. The reason for this problem was the local consultant and the customer himself, but they put the blame on the process plant supplier. There was a lot of correspondence between the process plant supplier and the customer on the subject. The supplier was at a loss to understand how a plant, which was operating satisfactorily for the last ten years, could suddenly start giving problems and why the customer was putting the blame on the supplier.

Some other customers have the habit of repairing costly machines and electronic cards locally as it is cheaper and then putting the blame on the original supplier in case of failure. It is to be appreciated that repairing a costly part locally without proper facilities is equivalent to a surgeon performing a serious operation on the roadside. Naturally, the first casualty is the patient and he will catch an infection. It is true in this case also and the machinery and its original supplier have to the price.

A cost-oriented customer will not mind purchasing second-hand equipment and then retrofitting it to perform. Such type of customers are not builders and their basic philosophy is mostly price and not performance. Hence, any supplier whose corporate marketing strategy is driven by efficiency, performance and new technology will not find his chemistry matching with the customer. One will always find the problem of payment with such customers that may result in unnecessary cost over-run for the supplier. Delay in payment to the supplier is also considered as one of the means of reducing project cost.

On the other hand, a *value-oriented customer* will always look for better efficiency and higher performance and may be willing to pay higher initial capital cost provided it results in long-term saving. He will definitely pay a premium if it can lead to lesser maintenance and better economic sense. Such a customer will capitalise on the cost of maintenance, availability, better performance, etc. and work out the differential cost element for deciding the premium to be paid.

There is also a third type who can be ascribed as *technology conscious.* They are always on the look-out to get the best technology and do not mind paying a higher value for state-of-the-art equipment. These types of customers are very good for those vendors who also have improvement as their constant motto. These customers feel comfortable with persons who are having the same zeal as they are having for new technology/innovation and go out of the way to help the vendors. They will also not mind trying out new things and may, in the process, help in creating new references for the supplier that may be useful with other type of customers. It is much easier to develop a common bond with them, which is beneficial to both the parties. Such type of customers can provide a lot of valuable information on new technological innovations. Additionally, they have very good analytical attitude, which may favour a quality-conscious supplier.

Decision Making Process

One of the most important aspects of the customer understanding is to know the *Decision making process* and deciding authority or, rather, authority whose signatures are visible on the decision. There is a misconception in some sectors that higher/top management takes the decision. Nothing can be more incorrect than this. Decision making in a professional organisation is the culmination of organisational thinking and decisions are not taken by a single person. Groundwork for such decisions are made at middle level management, who exercise a major influence in the process. People at the higher level are generally guided by these middle level cadres, and they restrict themselves to the policy matters. Those vendors who try to influence the process from the top and neglect this vital chain do so at a heavy price to themselves. There are customers who prefer frank discussions. They may demand the moon, but they will prefer a supplier who tells them a frank NO rather than one who promises them the moon, but fails to answer how he will do so. In marketing and diplomacy it is often said that the word NO does not exist in dictionary, but at least in marketing, saying a frank NO may give a more positive result with a learned and knowledgeable customer.

However, in the case of companies which are run on the older concept of *Lala*, the decision-making process is concentrated in only one person, namely the Owner and one must concentrate at that level only. There is no use of wasting valuable time at other levels. Of course such '*lalas*' always have their advisors whom they blindly follow, and it may be necessary to have these advisors on the right side.

Market Image and Financial Management Ability

Market image is another factor one should consider seriously as these forces warn a vendor about the environment he is going to face during project execution and the safeguards he must build right now. Many customers take decisions about setting up projects or investments without proper financial tie ups or *financial closer*. Subsequently, not only do they pay a heavy price for this lapse, but their vendor's financiers and shareholders also do so for no fault of theirs. It is therefore necessary to identify such customers and take adequate precautions at the time of business finalisation.

Bargaining Power

One of the major prerequisites in developing a marketing strategy is to understand and judge the bargaining power of the customer. Most of the time suppliers confuse bargaining with price negotiation. Bargaining is a much broader term. It envisages and encompasses the total deal that a customer is getting right from scope, quality, technology, operation and maintenance features as well as performance and efficiency apart from price. Thus, a customer can bargain in any of the following areas:

- Technical scope, system
- Performance and efficiency
- Quality checks and conformation to environment norms, which may be more than required as per the present laws.
- Services both during contract execution and post-contract execution.
- Continuous upgradation of product to the extent feasible, due to changing technology.
- Price
- Completion schedule

We always come across buyers who lay equal emphasis on getting a high performance product and price. There are buyers who do not mind paying extra premium or bonus for getting faster deliveries. Many times, quicker deliveries may not be required by the project schedule, but habit or the challenge set up by the buyer himself to prove to his peers that he can complete project earlier than them, may drive him to pay a bonus or premium to motivate the supplier to try and reduce the completion schedule, or rather than bargaining for price reduction, they may lay more stress on shorter completion schedule.

There may be buyers who are quality conscious and will look for higher availability and reliability of equipments. Many of these customers are those who have made heavy investment in the project, and would like to ensure that the product and services, which go in the project, should have a high degree of reliability and availability as the cost of failure is very high compared to the buying cost of the product.

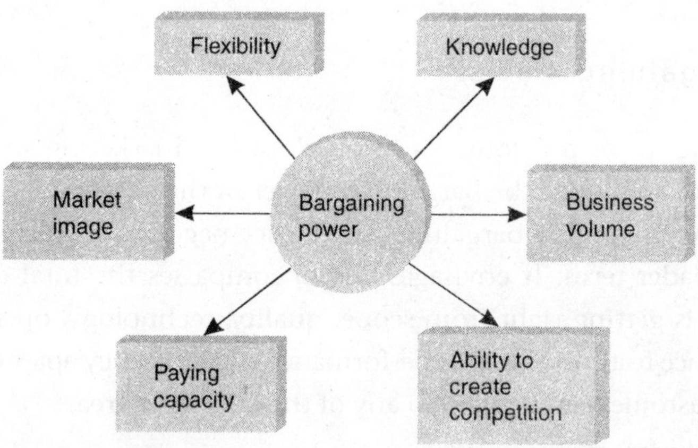

Fig. 3.2 *Buyer's Bargaining Power*

There are buyers who are willing to bargain for improved performance and efficiency to control recurring operating expenditure in comparison to initial cost as they are wedded to the concept of '*total lifetime cost*'. The operating cost may differ widely with the quality and efficiency of the product.

As a general rule, buyers start bargaining for quality and performance. Having settled these parameters, they then bargain for faster completion schedule and only then they start bargaining for price. The tendency is to buy high quality, high performing product at the cost of low quality, low performing product.

Most of the customers derive their bargaining power from the following:

- Ability to create competition.
- Knowledge
- Flexibility of approach
- Paying capacity
- Volume of buying
- Market image

Creating competition is the best way to start bargaining as it puts tremendous pressure on the supplier. A successful person is one who is able to exert more pressure on others than he himself actually gets. Such customers deliberately ensure that at least four to five parties remain in the fray till the last stage, so that he gets the best deal in all respects, i.e. technology, price, performance and delivery schedule.

The competitors also act as information providers. They furnish two types of information, the first pertaining to the technological development taking place in the world and how they are implementing them. The second type is about the status of other vendors on this front and how they are lacking compared to the vendor who is furnishing the information. The vendor also provides information on problems faced by the equipments supplied by other vendors as regards quality, performance, services, etc. The more competition a customer is able to generate, the better return he gets.

Illustration

There was a mining company in Nepal that wished to set up a facility for transfer of ore from a place at a height of 800–2000 feet in a hilly area more easily through a conveyor system. The company floated a tender for the system, but due to inhospitable climate conditions, not many vendors responded. The price proposals were very high. The General Manager of the customer collected the addresses of the suppliers who had not responded and personally visited them to motivate them to participate. He invited them to visit the site and arranged their visit to the site from Kathmandu with his own senior officials accompanying them. As a result of these efforts, he got four more bids and all new bidders were interested due to the positive support and attitude of the customer. With the competition intensifying and suppliers keenly interested in the business, the customer got at

Contd

least 25 per cent price discount along with better terms and better equipment. That is the reward he got for his efforts in creating the competition.

Knowledge empowers the customer and prepares him for bargaining. He is able to have better bargaining power if he collects some information connected with the project. Most of the customers visit similar project executed sites elsewhere and collect relevant technical, performance and cost details on existing projects. Their purpose is not only to collect information about the vendor who had executed the project but also on owner's experience with the operation and maintenance. The customer also collects information with different vendors and after two/three meetings, he has a lot of information to compare terms of different vendors to get the best bargain. But the main question is how many customers are interested in acquiring such knowledge that empowers them to dominate suppliers and force them to give the best bargain. For this the customers have to go into minute technical details and calculations to appreciate the finer points. The effort he puts in here is repaid with interest. It is seen that well-informed buyers are ruthless bargainers. Poorly informed customers tend to be swayed by subjective factors and are not in a position to squeeze the suppliers.

The buyer's bargaining power also depends on flexibility of approach. Many suppliers in the core sector give a heavy discount if some technical emergencies and irritating commercial conditions are diluted. Many customers, who are rigid, stick to their conditions, irrespective of the fact that their project does not require such stringent conditions. By adopting an uncompromising stand, they lose more. Hence, flexibility in approach and openness increases the bargaining ability of the customer.

Paying capacity of the customer is the foremost quality that the supplier looks for in a prospective customer. If he is financially sound and has the ability and habit of releasing timely payment, the supplier prefers to have business dealings with such a customer. The customer also has a larger choice and naturally he can look forward to a better deal.

Though, in the core sector, it is difficult to get large business volume at one time, many of the customers have repetitive requirements and because of this, suppliers pay special attention to such customers and try to give them the best possible deal. The suppliers look forward not only to entry into the group, but they do everything to retain customer loyalty.

Market image is the ultimate thing that decides the customer. It is the sum total of culture, habit, attitude, orientation, business philosophy, financial conditions, payment mode and approach. The customer derives his bargaining power from the image, he enjoys in the market.

Price Sensitivity of Customer

It has been seen in many core sector projects that the buyer is able to pass on the cost of input to the next customer easily. The fertiliser sector is one such example. Prior to dismantling of Administrative Price Mechanism, oil sector was also falling in this category. In such cases, the customer is least bothered about price negotiations. Their bargaining power will be concentrated more on technological and engineering aspects of the project. Price sensitivity of such customers is lowest. Similar is the case with other sectors that either get government subsidy in one form or the other, or where the market competition is not menacing enough to bother them. Most of the suppliers and, particularly, technology-driven suppliers will find such customers to be the ideal choice. They can have handsome deals with them.

But, unfortunately, the reverse is also true. If a customer is operating in an area, which is highly competitive, then it is not possible for him to pass on the increased cost of inputs to the next customer. Such customers are highly sensitive to cost of input and one can expect them to be ruthless negotiators on price. These customers would be basically cost driven and are expected to curtail heavily on state-of-the-art technology, if the cost is not affordable.

Knowledge about the price sensitivity of a customer helps the supplier to decide his marketing strategy. If a customer is in a highly competitive segment, then it will not help the supplier to offer him the latest technology and other frills, as he will not be able to afford them. The supplier will definitely make the customer aware of the positive features of such added equipments. The customer will then pressurise the supplier to absorb the cost of these frills, because with the supplier's laborious explanation, he will be convinced that these extra frills are required in the long run but, at the same time, his purchase budget will not allow it. Hence, either the supplier will have to make a sacrifice or he will be left with an unsatisfied customer. The best solution is to pre-judge the customer and make him an offer according to his requirement and paying capacity. If he cannot afford frills, then it is best to quote him the bare essentials for the safe and meaningful operation of plant.

Buyer's Perception on Cost

In the core sector, a buyer has a different concept of cost. There are buyers who consider cost as the amount they are paying at the time of purchasing. Buyers in the second category are those who consider cost as consisting of two components, namely initial purchase cost plus cost of operation for a prefixed period with net present value reflected on the day of buying. There is a third category of buyers who believe in lifetime cost of the equipment. There is only a slight difference between the second and third categories. The latter one will consider operation cost for the whole life of the plant and will also add cost of maintenance. Thus, while the second category is taking the operation cost as only for the first five to ten years, the third variety will consider it for a minimum twenty-five years.

It is clear from the above that the first type of customer is mainly a cost-driven one and will not give much value to operation or maintenance cost. The basic decision-making will only take into consideration initial cost. Efficiency, performance, ease of operation will have significance only if two bidders are very close in initial cost. The second and third types of customers will quantify the advantages gathered due to high efficiency, high availability, high product life, low maintenance and ease of operation, and will consider them along with the main cost to arrive at total evaluated cost which will become the basis for decision. The supplier has to resort to different type of strategy to meet requirements of these different types of buyers.

Illustration

The following incidents seek to clarify the issue. Though they pertain to the consumer segment, they are reproduced here for their clarity. My friend is running a big electrical/electronic store, selling colour

Contd

TVs. A customer came to the shop while we were talking. My friend talked to him for a few minutes. The customer came in an Opel Astra car, and his wife and he himself were well-dressed. My friend only showed them TVs from the premium segment, which were expensive, but were reliable and better performers compared to other makes. A little later, when another customer came, my friend again spent a few minutes talking to them and then showed them the economy range of TVs and started giving reasons why they were much superior to other expensive models. I was a bit surprised with this change. When the customer departed, I questioned his approach, which was exactly opposite with two different types of customers. My friend replied that he always tried to pre-judge the customer on his preference and paying capacity and then show him the TV model that will fit his choice and budget. Any person alighting from an Opel Astra car, nicely dressed and speaking nicely, would prefer a high performing set and price will not be the main buying criterion. If he shows to this customer the economy model, it will not fit into his requirement and the customer will lose interest in his shop. Later on even if he shows the better model, the first impression is lost and customer will start thinking of alternatives. Hence, he wants to ensure that he judges the customer right the first time itself. Similarly, if he shows the high performing set to the economy buyer, he will immediately like it but he cannot afford it. Then if the economy set is shown to the customer, he will not approve of it as his quality standard had been upgraded but he did not have the means to satisfy it. In both cases, the customer will walk out of the shop. So business is lost and both the customers are also lost.

The two lessons that I learnt from these incidents are:

- Get customer understanding right the first time itself, as there is no second chance.
- Never upgrade expectations of a customer who does not have the means to pay for it.

How to Develop Customer Understanding

Having discussed the importance of customer understanding, the next major question is how to develop it or, as it is said, *how to get under the skin of the customer*. Some of the factors whose studies can help in forming an opinion about the customer are listed below:

- History
- Culture
- Habits
- Beliefs and factors affecting them
- Attitude
- Perception
- Personal approach—Any business finalisation in the core sector requires at least three to four meetings with the customer and during these interactions, a lot of information is available to give an insight into the customer.
- Looking at weak signals collectively to understand the message.
- Analysis of past—If earlier orders were executed with the same customer or same group, then an analysis of reasons for securing or losing the business and experience during execution will be of great help.
- In case of an old customer, the factors leading to his loyalty assume added significance.
- Motivating factors

Should You Choose Customers?

We have already seen that different customers have different perceptions, attitude, approach, culture and different buying habits. Many times customer approach or culture, orientation or business philosophy is totally opposite that of the supplier. This creates problems during contract negotiation and execution and leads to not-so-happy memories, which can have repercussion on other business with different customers. Should a supplier then choose its customers in larger business interest? Will that be in line with the approach and philosophy of marketing? This is the question bothering all top strategic marketing managers of corporates. No supplier is and should be willing to compromise on fundamental core values on which he is making his business strategy. If a supplier is a value or knowledge driven supplier and he wants to enter into business with a cost driven customer, then either he has to compromise with his fundamental values and make himself open to loss of image or loss on the business at a future date, or he will not be able to serve the customer fully. In the end, both the customer and supplier will be unhappy and unsatisfied and irritated with each other. It is common knowledge that a single unsatisfied customer can spoil the well-cultivated market image of the supplier. Thus, many suppliers in the core sector feel that, while entering into business with a customer, one should ensure convergence of business philosophy, attitude, approach and orientation between customer and supplier. Thus '*Customer Selection*' as a marketing strategy is being practised commonly by many suppliers and particularly by those who believe that 'differentiation' of product and service they market is their best strength.

Similarly, big corporates find it difficult to serve small customers. The big organisations operate not on individual working but on systems, and that is their core strength. Small customers do not believe in systems but in individuals. Thus, there is fundamental conflict between the customer and supplier. The customer is unhappy as he will find that individuals are constrained by the system while the supplier is unhappy because a change in mood of an individual at the customer end can tilt the decision or understanding upside down. In the core sector, it is therefore felt that 'Customer Selection' should become an integral part of vendor's marketing strategy.

UNDERSTANDING ENVIRONMENT

Environment plays a significant role in business and business decisions. It can be compared to the 'pitch' and 'playing ground' in a cricket match based on which one selects the team and type of bowlers. In the popular version of a one-day match, this also determines the target one wants to set for the opposition. An understanding of environment can provide similar information. Environment, like the kalchakra of Indian mythology, moves on in an emotionless manner. Those who can understand the signal coming from it and can take necessary pro-active steps, succeed and get better results in the business. They are the managers who are better prepared to handle uncertainty and leave others behind because of advance action taken. Those who do not want to understand environment signals pay a very heavy price and, in a majority of cases, are simply thrown on the wayside. As Fig. 3.3 indicates, the business depends, apart from customer and vendor, on environmental factors as they play a major role in generating and controlling demand. Environment factors analysis can help the vendor to predict the demand behaviour. It can also help him to predict how various core industries will perform in the foreseeable future. The supplier can accordingly plan his strategy.

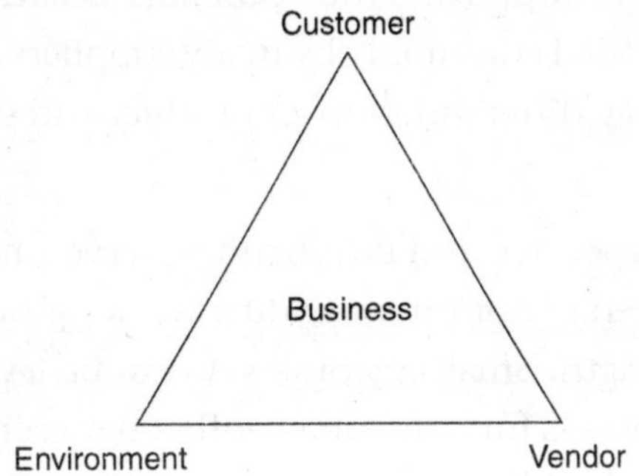

Fig. 3.3 *Environment Effect*

It is therefore essential for a marketing executive to understand the rapidly changing environment and the effect it is bringing on business. It is often said that *forewarned* is *forearmed.* The environment plays a major role in the core sector and any marketing executive should carefully evaluate it before arriving at preliminary conclusions to decide his strategy. Some of the major factors that can be considered are discussed below.

Macro Factors

General Economic Environment

These factors indicate the basic business climate and also give an indication about demand, competition and trends in technology and market orientation. The demand and factors affecting it can be fairly ascertained by analysing GDP projection and growth rates for basic goods, capital goods and index of industrial production. The inflation, bank interest rates, exchange rate and reserve, along with government and RBI policy, also give a major indication of demand forecast. However, it must be remembered that the effect of these factors on demand follows a time-lag, which may vary from nine months to more than a year. Fresh investment for capacity expansion or modernisation generally starts after three to six months of growth in that industry.

Having got a general idea, the executive can look for other factors, which may have a bearing on his target industry. Global factors should also be discounted at this stage. Some of the industries like fertiliser and steel are highly susceptible to government policies and international environment and they should be given due importance while evaluating the environment.

Many times the business climate may be hazy and uncertain and many of us may feel that this may be confusing. However, one must remember that business opportunities are generally presented by such uncertain climate only. Organisations which are able to look beyond this haziness and visualise things to come often walk away with the cake as they are able to respond better and much faster to the changing environment.

The current environment leaves the following clear messages:

- GDP growth will be hovering around 6 per cent.
- The world will become more and more small and one should find global competition anywhere and everywhere and should be prepared for it.
- The perception of India as a supplier of quality and state-of-the-art equipment is improving day by day, and this can be leveraged to give much needed export thrust. This will also act as a cushion to protect/ hedge against the sudden downturn in Indian economy.
- Competition is going to stay and may become more intense. Today's collaborator may become tomorrow's competitor.
- Small is no longer beautiful. The organisation must be large to synergise its strength and address rapidly changing fight for survival. Acquisition and mergers will be the order of the day in the future. It is also possible that later on, in order to address specific focused business niches, the SBU (Strategic Business Unit) concept, more in the mould

of our Panchayati Raj, may become common and be adopted to provide flexibility of operation, while retaining advantages of a bigger organisation.

- Technology will be the major tool for leveraging business. The purchaser will lay more stress on efficiency, losses, performance, maintenance cost and ease of operation. The customer may be willing to pay substantial premium to a vendor for getting better performance and trouble-free operation. The cost of down time, due to breakdown, will be very high and a vendor offering quick and reliable service can look forward to better days.
- Future markets will be knowledge-driven and organisations which are willing to invest in new research and development and regularly upgrade their design, can look forward to premium. Most Indian organisations import technology for two reasons. One, the cost of development is too high to be affordable. Secondly, in their perception, they always feel that they require collaborators' back up and effectively introduce new/upgraded products/systems in the market.

  To some extent their apprehension is correct. Most of the Indian organisations do not enjoy the image of a developer like GE, USA. Nobody seems to ask GE about collaborators' back up or past references to accept or consider their new development. On the other hand, many customers consider it their privilege if they have new or advanced products from this company in their factory, primarily because they consider it a symbol for being advanced or up-to-date. Indians do not have a high reputation for development, but thanks to the software boom, the presence of Indians in a software company even in USA itself is considered a plus point. It is basically a question of market perception and image. Many pharmaceutical companies that have now started giving importance to research can vouch for this theory. One has to set his vision right and start moving to achieve results. The positive transformation will follow on its own.
- Tomorrow's business will be driven by the net. We are in the era of electronic business. This increases the depth of reach and, at the same time, reduces marketing expenditure. The response is both fast and total and information can be provided far more quickly.

If there is recession prevailing in the country and the world, then it is but natural that there would be an adverse effect on the business in general and demand will contract. In order to maintain their business, suppliers will offer more attractive packages and hence both profit and price realisation will come down. On the other hand, if there is economic boom, then the demand will see an upward movement.

There are specific environmental factors that can have major effects on demand. Major earthquakes and wars are followed by massive construction and rehabilitation activity, giving a boost to demand in iron and cement. The anthrax scare in USA led to sudden demand for Ciprofloxacin medicine.

Government Policy

The government policy, especially on taxation, can have a major impact on demand. Fiscal policies can create fresh demand or may lead to change in existing demand. With the government prescribing stringent environment norms to be followed by all industries, the demand for equipments, which can control pollution, has seen an increase. In fact, the Electrostatic Precipitator has been developed especially to cater to pollution from coal-based power plants and dust from cement plants. Further strengthening of such norms have seen the arrival of 'Fabric Filters' in the cement industry for pollution control, which are a substitute for Electrostatic Precipitators.

'Multi point fuel injection engines' have been developed to meet Euro-II pollution norms by automobiles.

Government offers fiscal incentives in the form of tax concessions or cash subsidy to promote certain type of industry. In order to promote the concept of Solid Waste Management and use municipal waste for productive work, the government is offering massive subsidy in this area, thus, generating demand. Fiscal policies can have a long-term effect in generating or reducing the demand in the market and on profitability of the business, particularly in the core sector, which is highly susceptible to them. In the consumer sector nobody will stop drinking tea if the government suddenly doubles the excise duty on it, but in the core sector, if the duty on some equipment is changed, immediately people will start thinking about substitutes.

Development, following formation of oil cartel by OPEC, is a clear pointer in this direction. There is always a substitute for core sector equipment, which will be economically viable with certain taxation policies. Small changes in taxation laws can have major implications for the supplier. If the government reduces customs duty on certain domestically produced items, it will result in increased competition at the domestic level and reduction in price realisation. Customs duty increase, on the other hand, can offer him advantages.

Global Changes

Changes in countries other than the country of supplier can have a serious effect on business. This can happen in two ways. One if the supplier is exporting goods to that country, then changes in that country will have effect on the supplier's business. Secondly, changes in supplier's business segment globally can have an effect on the supplier. Fertiliser prices have shown a substantial dip worldwide in the last three years to the extent that in many countries, imported fertiliser is much cheaper than fertiliser indigenously produced. Steel industry is also reeling under worldwide recession and their problems have been compounded due to higher duties imposed by some of the countries to safeguard the interest of their own industries. The world is becoming smaller and smaller and changes are getting reflected very fast at all the places.

Micro Factors

Having examined the general factors affecting business, it is as well that we focus our attention on specific business segment and evaluate factors, which may drive business in the particular segment. These are direct factors and some of them are discussed below:

Cost

Due to increasing competition, this is the major factor affecting competition. Cost leadership will become increasingly important. Organisation can leverage new development to reduce cost. The design can be made modular and standardisation can be increased though, at the same time, retaining uniqueness. They can also make their raw material procurement cost effective by following new procurement tools like *Reverse Auction*. Procurement process can be upgraded to ensure minimum inventory.

Completion Period

Another important factor, which is now assuming importance, is reduction in completion schedule. This, on the one hand, leads to reduction in interest during completion period and, on the other hand, it helps in realising the gains of investment earlier. Yet another benefit for the customer is that he can delay his decision and to that extent reduce his exposure to uncertainty.

Compactness and Weight

There is increasing tendency for going for equipments which are compact and light as they give major cost and time advantage in transportation, civil work and erection and commissioning without, in any way, compromising on system, or product design, or performance. Space is at a premium today and more so tomorrow and any vendor, who helps in this, is most welcome.

Maintenance

The importance of regular maintenance and cost of it is now much better understood. Any equipment which demands less and easy maintenance will command a premium in the market. Additionally, those vendors who can provide professional regular maintenance/overhauling at reasonable cost, will get automatic preference. Many suppliers are utilising their maintenance offering ability as a marketing tool. Similarly, ease of operation becomes another factor, which can have a bearing on the decision of customers.

Service

The importance of regular maintenance and operation by trained staff is being increasingly felt. It is also being realised that the best maintenance hands are available with the original supplier. Hence, most of the customers want the original equipment supplier to also operate and maintain the equipment. This provides an opportunity to the supplier to increase his business. Service component in the total business of supplier has generally seen an increase of 10–15 per cent. Most of the customers have also realised that even old equipments can be repaired and retrofitted, and their performance and life can be increased. Suppliers can avail this prevailing condition to make use of it.

UNDERSTANDING YOURSELVES

Generally, marketing is defined as understanding the customer needs and developing strategies to meet them to have a satisfied customer. But there is one very important element in the chain, which is the supplier himself, who has to meet the need of the customer and it is equally important that the supplier is clear what he wants to do and what he cannot do. In earlier sections also, it has been discussed that long-term business and customer loyalty in the core sector is only feasible if customer requirements are in line with the business philosophy of the supplier. Otherwise, it may be difficult for the supplier to meet and satisfy the customer. Thus, it is equally necessary to understand oneself to have clarity in the matter.

Some of the important parameters which must be considered are discussed as under:

Vision and Mission of the Company

This outlines the immediate and long-term goals of the company and sets the business direction and approach of the company. Any business activity will be guided by this objective. Additionally, if the company is trying to diversify or add a new business segment, then it will be built around this objective. However, the company's business vision is generally comprehensive enough to cover many possibilities. It generally reflects the company's core competencies and any business has to be built around it.

Values

This has more to do with the culture and the business philosophy of the company. Any marketing activity or the business line pursued by the organisation should be consistent with its value system. Many times there may be conflict between the supplier's and customer's value system. If it is feasible that the relationship can last irrespective of this difference, then the business can be done; otherwise, in a majority of cases, this difference can create avoidable problems in the end.

Organisation Orientation

In a core sector operation, the organisation must identify with the role or the basic strength from which it wants to derive its strategy and dominate. This is sometime also referred as USP (Unique Selling Point). In the core sector a supplier can decide upon a strategy based on any of the following factors:

- Technology leader
- Low cost supplier
- Value supplier

If the company is the technology leader, then it can command a premium in the market as it would always be considered to be the benchmark, which other will achieve with time gap. The knowledge-oriented customer will always consider such vendors as preferred vendors. Such vendors can operate on '*First IN First OUT*' concept. In order to maximise business returns they should constantly upgrade the product or develop new designs. These vendors would be highly successful with a professional technology-conscious purchaser.

There are suppliers who prefer to operate for cost-conscious customers. Their approach is to produce low cost goods. Naturally, product development and innovation with such type of vendors take a back seat. Such type of suppliers should concentrate on those customers who could compromise on technology but price remains their primary concern.

In the case of value suppliers, price and technology are both important and are given justified weightage. A value supplier does not offer the latest technology until and unless it provides commensurate economic benefit to the customer.

As a supplier, one should be sure as to the kind of orientation he is having. If a customer is cost driven and the supplier is value driven, there is no possibility of such type of supplier getting the business, and he will only be wasting his time. Customers will use his bid and hold discussions with him to understand the product, project and essential requirements and will bargain with a cost-oriented supplier to give the same to him. A technology-oriented supplier will be providing free education to the customer in this case. Similar will be the case if a supplier is cost driven and the customer is knowledge driven. The supplier's quotation will be used to beat down the technology-oriented supplier's cost, and there is no way the cost-oriented supplier can get the business.

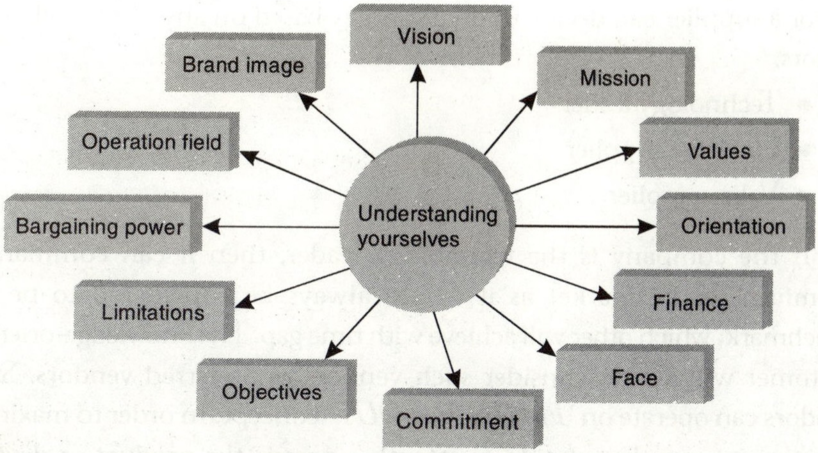

Fig. 3.4 *Understanding Yourselves*

Field of Operation

The organisation can also decide whether it wants to operate in 'High Technology–Low Volume' space or in 'Low Technology–High Volume' space. Naturally, the competition will be more intense in the latter case and price realisation will be less. Figure 3.5 shows the entry barrier in different cases of technology and volume. Wherever the entry barrier is low, the competition will be high and price realisation will be low. High entry barrier will naturally restrict the competition, and hence the price realisation will be high.

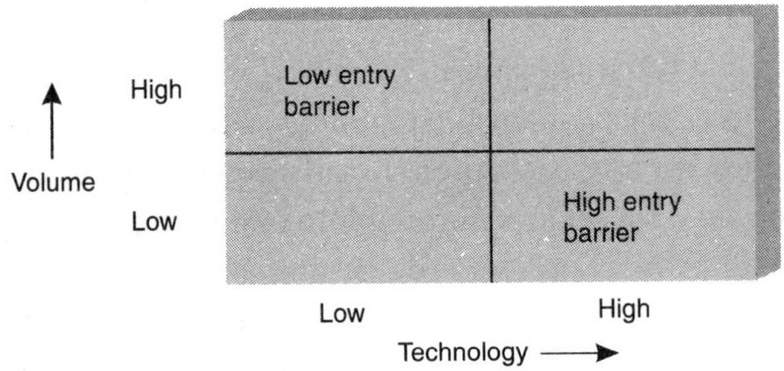

Fig. 3.5 *Technology, Volume and Entry Barrier*

Organisation Objective and its Commitment Towards It

This is very important. The organisation should not render lip service to its professed business objectives. 'Timely delivery', 'customer satisfaction is our motto', etc. are the normal professed business objectives of any business entity, but they fall on the wayside in actual practice when the actual issue of their implementation arrives. The organisation then suddenly discovers all sorts of constraints to honour them. This situation arises because all organisations have their budget, targets, etc. and naturally all efforts are made to achieve them with the result that some of the lofty and professed customer oriented goals become the casualty. Such an approach, to say the least, is suicidal in the long run, particularly in today's environment when the customer has options.

Another important issue which comes to mind is the market expectations from the vendor and how much he is prepared to meet or is capable of meeting it. This expectation can be in terms of technology, price, service, quality and timely deliveries or in any other area.

Brand Image

Not long ago, brand image was given importance only for consumer industries, but this important parameter is equally applicable in the core sector and a good brand image can provide a business edge over the competitor. This is the single mirror through which the market express its considered view on an organisation taking into account all aspects of importance like price, quality, technology, ethics, process knowledge, manpower and their approach, project management, customer relationship, work culture, etc. This decides the premium or discount the market is going to give on your product and services in comparison to other competitors. This is the primary reason why some conscious companies appoint an external consultant to conduct a survey to find out how the market, customers and others who matter perceive them and try to work on weak areas. It would not be out of place to say that in the core sector, where a purchaser looks for a long-term business relationship, brand image plays a major role in decision making.

Organisation Face

Most of the organisations have two faces, one at the time of ordering and the other during execution of work, which are normally exactly opposite or have 180° phase reversal in approach and attitude. The customer notices it very fast and consider it as an important factor in evaluating the organisation at the time of repeat order or future requirement Though it may not be avoidable but it is better to keep it to the minimum. The best is to follow ISO 9000 rule that states, '*Promise only what you can deliver*'.

Finance

The organisation's balance sheet and financial strength is another factor on which the customer judges him. Naturally, a weak financial position becomes a hindrance for business, especially in the core sector, as supplier has to invest his money initially to purchase raw material and mobilise other resources. This also provides an indication about the ability of an organisation to stand and face uncertainties, which may be of negative nature. The supplier with good financial strength can leverage it for getting more business by making some arrangement to finance the project.

Organisation's Limitation

A marketing executive must know the weaknesses or the limitations of his organisation as his competitors are going to develop their marketing strategy on these limitations, and a good marketing executive should either be able to deflect them or explain them or convert them into his strength from weakness. Some of the limitations can arise from basic approach, business philosophy or generic problem that an organisation faces. I still recall a business executive himself opening the subject of repeated failure of certain parts of an equipment supplied by his organisation at many sites and took pains to explain to his prospective customers the reasons for failure, analysis of them and corrective steps being taken by them. This proved to the customer that while failures in some parts are normal and the organisation is not shying away from it, it has the capability to analyse and identify the defect and reasons thereof and is taking corrective action. It has not left its customers high and dry. This increases the comfort level of the purchaser to the organisation in spite of the defect and, on the other hand, the marketing executive has not only preempted the competitor's strategy but has converted a liability into an asset.

Bargaining Power of the Supplier

Like buyers, suppliers can also have their bargaining power. Their bargaining power mainly comes from any of the following assets:

- *Monopoly* If the supplier is the only major source of the equipment in his area, then naturally he can dictate terms. He is under no pressure to reduce cost or improve quality or performance of his product. The delivery period is also decided by him and not by the market.

- *Technological Strength* Many knowledgeable customers prefer a supplier who has technological strength. This ensures that in case of any problem faced by the customer, he can depend on the supplier. Performance and the efficiency of the operation are also ensured. Such type of suppliers always command a premium in the market and their advice is given due respect. They function both as a vendor and advisor to the customer.
- *Market Image* Suppliers can have different type of image in the market and they derive their strength from it. There are suppliers who are known not to compromise with technical performance or quality of the product, irrespective of the price they are getting from the customer. Their approach is decided more by their long time business standing for which they are known in the market and their commitment to not compromise their quality and performance under any circumstances. Such suppliers are preferred by many customers and are in great demand.
- *Service* If a supplier has good service facility and is geared to provide at short notice, then the customer gives him due respect and consideration. In the core sector, the product life is more than twenty years and availability of good and competent service facility is essential. Not only should service be reliable, but it should also be affordable and available at short notice.

UNDERSTANDING THE COMPETITOR

Having discussed three parameters of 4 U Theory, it is time that we discussed and analysed the fourth parameter, i.e. *THE COMPETITOR*. Different factors, which have been considered and analysed for understanding self, are equally applicable here also. However, some of the salient factors are summarised below:

Brand Image

This factor is the most important one as it summarises and presents the ultimate opinion of the market about the competitor. The kind of challenge and competition he is going to pose can be easily ascertained from here. This also highlights his strong attributes giving strength to him and are responsible for the business. It also gives an indication about the premium or discount he can command in the market. In the core sector most of the enquiries/tenders are issued on restricted basis to vendors whom the customer considers worthy for sending enquiries. Image of the company plays a major role in it.

Business Profile

This gives the area of activity of the company and an indication whether the company is product oriented or project oriented and to what extent the business profile of competitor is matching with that of the supplier and whether he is able to derive any benefit due to his profile or carrying any liability on account of this. This not only gives indication on his marketing strategy but can also provide sufficient inputs to decide strategy. The competitor, who can produce more than 50 per cent of required equipments required in a project, will also concentrate on his product expertise in addition to project management capabilities and other services that can be offered.

Finance

This parameter provides information on his financial strength and sustaining ability. Competitors having strong financial strength will leverage it for securing more business. The strong balance sheet provides added confidence and comfort to the customer. Any competitor with strong financial muscle will definitely provide a strong challenge as he may come out with a new strategy.

SWOT Analysis

It is common even for the purchaser to carry out SWOT ANALYSIS (Strength, Weakness, Opportunities and Threat Analysis) and it is all the more necessary for the vendor to carry out such an analysis of likely competitors in the field. Vendors can decide on the basic parameters to be considered for study themselves depending upon the conditions they consider important for their business but some of the suggested parameters are detailed below:

- Image/Market Standing
- Engineering specially system and project engineering capability
- Material Procurement System
- Project Monitoring and Management
- Detail Engineering and Manufacturing system and capability
- Contract Management
- Quality Assurance System
- Top management Commitment and Involvement
- Customer Relationship and Responsiveness and sensitivity to customer complaint
- After Sales service and support
- Response to sudden demand and changes
- Ability of organisation to augment resources to meet emergency
- Ability of organisation to understand, analyse and solve unexpected problems
- Financial Status and strength
- Past References

Above analysis can be done for all the competitors including self-organisation and a rating of 1 to 5 can be assigned to reflect the relative position. Such an analysis and result can then be utilised for working out a suitable business strategy.

Competitor Orientation

Every company has a typical business orientation which can be classified as:

- Technology Orientation
- Cost/Price Orientation
- Value Orientation

Those competitors whose orientation is in line with customer orientation will have the upper hand. If one vendor is evaluating another competitor, then those parties whose orientation is similar to that of the bidder will find commonality in their approach and they will be competing with the same capability tool as far as orientation is concerned. The bidder will have to prepare a suitable strategy to cater to this requirement.

It may also be ascertained whether the competitor has other advantages. If a party has access to continuous upgradation of technology through in-house development or transfer of technology through collaboration agreement, then technology will become his main strategy. Some companies can have a natural advantage in controlling cost because of locational advantage, which may be the result of cheap availability of raw material, cost of transportation. Cost/Price then becomes the main strategy for them.

There are regions where labour productivity is low and unions may be very demanding. Cost of production will be much higher here. At the same time such suppliers will be at a disadvantageous position due to perception of delay due to strikes or go slow and they may not be in a position to offer stiff competition. Similarly, the cost of raw material can vary significantly between places. Fertiliser manufacturers in gulf countries can offer fertiliser at much cheaper rates than Indian companies due to very low rates of feedstock.

A competitor becomes stronger if his orientation suits the customer orientation. Normally, it is difficult though not impossible to change one's orientation frequently, and this sometime becomes a constraint in business development.

Future Competitors and Entry Barrier

Competition is dynamic. Players enter and exit. Thus every vendor, in order to make medium- to long-term strategy of business, has to take a view on the type and intensity of competition and has to consider the possibility of new players coming in and existing players quitting.

New players in a business add to the existing capacity and provide the customer with additional options. In order to make inroads, the new players subsidise cost, improve quality, performance and offer customer-friendly options. This will put added pressure on existing suppliers.

The entry of new players depends upon the 'Entry Barriers' they encounter and their sustainability depends on the reaction of existing players to their entry. If the entry barriers are high, then the chances of entry of new players are relatively less. Similarly, if existing players are strong, then they can offer strong resistance making it difficult for new players to survive.

A new competitor, before he enters into a new area, considers the following factors which play a major role in his decision.

Business Volume

The new player only tries to enter a new business segment and old players only try to remain in that segment, if they envisage sustained business volume for at least seven to ten years or more. In the core sector, developing core competency and competitive edge require both time and resources. The process once initiated cannot be reversed easily. Hence, no supplier will risk his major assets till he is sure of sufficient and sustained business availability. The higher the business prospects, the more would be the attraction for the company to enter. A majority of new companies make entry as part of horizontal or vertical integration or by way of expanding geographical reach.

When India went in for power sector reforms and allowed private sector participation, Enron and other multinational companies entered the market enlarging their geographical reach. On the other hand, entry of Reliance in the petroleum sector was the case of Integration.

Profits

The margin available in the business decides its attraction to new competitors. If the margins available are high, more companies try to enter the business segment. Higher margins are a definite indication of low competition. They indicate that demand is much higher than available supply and provides a catalyst effect for increase in number of players. Some suppliers, in order to make it difficult for new suppliers to enter the segment, deliberately keep the margins low so that the business loses its attractiveness as new potential entrants get a clear message that in spite of low competition, realisation is low and there is not much scope in the business segment.

Technology

If the business segment is such that technology obsolescence rate is high, then it also acts as a barrier to entry of competitors because, in order to survive in the market, one is required to constantly upgrade his technology, which requires both capital resources and high intellectual level of human resources, which cannot be easily afforded by many suppliers. Thus, the higher the technology turnover in the business, lower will be the competition and still lower will be the possibility of new entrants.

Resources and Infrastructural Facility

The entry into a new business segment requires huge resources in the form of capital, machinery, engineering assets and trained human resources. Additionally, all core sector projects require service facility that in turn require proper infrastructure. Hence, new competitors' entry into core sector projects is more in the nature of geographical expansion or through acquisition and mergers. Developing a new business segment from scratch is rare. This approach is also necessitated because, before awarding the contract, customer looks for past references and proven capability of the supplier as he is not only simply awarding the contract to him but in most of the cases putting the future of his business in the supplier's hands. This is a major barrier the entry of fresh suppliers in the segment.

Future competitors can come from any of the following segments:

- Global firms expanding their geographical reach.
- Companies who may find a natural synergy with the new business segments.
- Forward and backward integration by companies.
- Acquisition and Mergers by companies who are interested in entry as part of corporate strategy.

Competitor's Combativeness

The combativeness or the ability of a competitor to have protracted battle decides the type of competition and its tenacity. This also decides the competitor's response to the moves made by other suppliers and thus it becomes an important parameter to judge the competition.

In case the price reduction becomes a marketing strategy (it never pays in the long run as it hurts everybody except the customer), then how long a competitor can sustain it depends on the following factors:

- Ability to cut cost.
- Ability to sustain financial loss for longer periods or recovery of only variable cost till market shows signs of picking up.
- Ability to cross-subsidise from profit earned from other business segments or sale of same product in other regions.

No supplier can sustain a loss for a long period. Those suppliers having more financial muscle and determination can come out winners. Price cut strategies are short-term strategy. Corporates having multi product business are able to fare much better. Global players are also able to sustain competition in one part of the world due to better realisation from the other part.

The second important parameter is the competitor's response to improved product performance and technology being introduced by the supplier. While price reduction decision can be undertaken very quickly, the technological innovation and development is a long-term phenomenon. The ability of the competitor to respond and work in the direction will indicate that he is not a quitter and will give a fight and consider the technological area as his core competency. He will also like to match the moves of other bidders with equal moves from his side. It also indicates his unwillingness to allow other bidders to walk away easily with the product differentiation advantage with market premium associated with it due to better technology.

The companies with large financial strength and multi product profile are in a better position to sustain competition. They can, on the one hand, sustain losses for long-term and, on the other hand, the loss in one of the products does not create a problem of survival for them. In order to throw weak competitors out, such companies can sustain losses in one or two products for quite some time.

Decision Making Process and Response

People like prompt replies. The first impression is created by the speed of response and any company which is good in it ensures a positive image with the customer as he feels the establishment of relationship, recognition of customer message and the importance the supplier is attaching to it. In some way it also gives the impression that the organisation will be quick in decision making as response depends on the decision making process. Suppliers having a professional set-up and matrix form of structure are very decisive and it increases speed of response. Customers give natural preference to those organisations that are quick to respond and this ability gives such suppliers an added edge.

Values

If the value system of the competitor is in line with that of the customer, then he gets an advantage. However, if the value system is different, then there is conflict between them. If there are more competitors, then naturally those competitors, whose value systems are in line with those of the customer, will have an advantage.

Ability to Adapt to Change

The ability of a supplier to adapt to change and the speed at which he does, decides his competitive threat. If the demand is falling, the speed with which he can reorient himself by changing his strategy to safeguard his market share can give him a competitive advantage. Similarly, if demand is increasing, how fast he can gear up to take additional business decides his ability to capture business. In the core sector, it is very difficult to scale up or scale down the capacities. Hence, the flexibility of an organisation to redeploy its resources, according to business environment, provides it with a competitive edge.

The change may also come due to technological changes, which may have the potential of making the competitor obsolete, until he decides to move with the change and continuously upgrade his development.

Human Resources

The type and nature of human resources plays an important part in deciding the fate of the company. Human resource qualification, training and attitude makes a total difference in the quality and speed of response. If people are indifferent and are not committed, no matter how good an organisation may be in technical, performance and financial parameters, it will find it difficult to succeed. The will to succeed and to excel is essential in people for growth of an organisation. If persons are indifferent, then it is a sure sign of a dying organisation, no matter how good its past performance and reputation may be and how superior its facility may be.

For an organisation to succeed, it must be professional and have the ability to allot work to individuals as per their capabilities and the requirement of the work. Such companies will be dynamic, customer oriented and will grow. It will be very adept in adopting to change.

Service

The post-contractual service facilities available with the vendor add to his competitive strength. Core sector equipment requires assured supply of spares and services for next thirty years. The ability to provide quick, reliable and cost-effective service adds to the strength of the vendor. Service business is increasing at a very high rate. Most of the organisations have about 30 per cent business coming in from this fast-growing business segment. The vendor's ability to provide fast, reliable service at reasonable cost, particularly operation and maintenance and annual maintenance, can increase his competitive edge as it ensures trouble-free operation and high availability of equipment.

Marketing Strategy

One must also study past behaviour and experience of the competitor to understand his strategy and both long-term and short-term business objectives. It is often said about human beings that howsoever they may like to disguise themselves, they always leave their footprints behind and these help in identifying and characterising and differentiating them from others. This is equally true about organisations. How best an organisation decides to alter its strategy, it will always be built upon certain basic core building blocks which will be characteristic of it or what a physics professor will tell about these blocks will reveal its typical spectrum. One should be able to analyse messages emanating from these basic building blocks and decipher them to understand the strategy being put into action by the competitor, they will also help in extrapolating the competitor's behaviour under different situations and in formulation of suitable strategy.

It must also be analysed whether the type of business is his main line of business. If it is so then the competitor is going to give him stiff competition; otherwise, the competition will be of routine nature.

Future Plans and Vision

This is futuristic information and is useful to understand medium- to long-term goals of the competitor and to devise a working plan to meet future challenges that he may pose. It may also provide an opportunity to re-validate the expected changes in the future as anticipated by the competitor after its assessment.

In the short term, it gives an indication of his perception of the business and his plan in devising strategy for meeting them and seriousness of his sustained approach. It should be remembered that no organisation runs after a business, which is either of transitory nature or without long-term interest.

Area of Conflict and Synergy

Like politics, there are no permanent friends and enemies in business. In the core sector no single vendor can supply all the equipment or provide total service to the customer. Many times two or more parties have to join hands in total business interest. Hence, it is essential to identify conflict and complementary areas so that one can always examine and optimise the approach in case of joint working.

The other benefit of such an approach is that the problems from government policies and other local bodies, which may be of similar nature, can be put jointly before the concerned authorities for redressal.

4

Technology—The Cutting Edge

The Importance of Technological Development
Future Market Trends—Shift Towards New Technology
Drivers of Technological Change
Technology—The Competitive Advantage
Cost of Non Development
Types of Technological Improvements
Technology Changes and Market Acceptance
Who Pays for Development?
Product Life Cycle
Development and Introduction of New Product/Modification in Existing Product
Marketing of New Products

4

THE IMPORTANCE OF TECHNOLOGICAL DEVELOPMENT

The market place is constantly evolving and is a dynamic place. There are changes due to globalisation, de-regulation, divergence and convergence. Today, in a competitive market, everyone is trying to survive and leave others behind. All commercial parameters like price realisation, completion schedule, market share, bottom line, etc. are under pressure and the customer is wanting more and more in the form of higher performance, better facilities and operational feature at lower cost and in the least possible completion time. Organisations are resorting to cost-cutting, reduction in cycle time, quality improvement, better equipment performance, etc. to not only retain their existing position, but to improve upon it.

Technology is a tool which can contribute a lot to the above. In fact, an organisation, without concentrating on technology, can only achieve incremental improvement in the cost or performance of the equipment. Revolutionary and drastic changes can only come through technology improvement. Examples are many. In the automobile industry, the arrival of MPFI engine led to drastic changes. Similar changes can be expected with changed fuel. It can be mixing of ethanol in petrol or, at a later date, introduction of fuel cell in the car. In a sugar industry, sugar production is no longer the main business. The profitability now comes from efficient generation of power from bagasse (cane left over after juice extraction) and its sale to utilities. Today, 2 MT of bagasse generates one MW of power. With new technological development and production of bio-oil, only 1.2 MT of bagasse would be required to generate the same one MW of power. This is one example of positive effect on the profitability due to technology changes. Thus, the effect and relevance of technology in today's environment cannot be underestimated. The future market is going to be knowledge-driven.

FUTURE MARKET TRENDS— SHIFT TOWARDS NEW TECHNOLOGY

The environment is showing definite trends towards a 'Knowledge driven market'. Ten years back, the majority of customers believed that technology did not play as significant a role as cost in business finalisation. Hence, the majority of suppliers were concentrating on means to reduce cost rather than improve performance, quality and efficiency. The concept of consumer or operation-friendly product did not exist; the focus was more on the cost of the product. As far as it was reasonably priced, the customer was willing to compromise on other performance parameters. Increased maintenance and breakdowns were considered normal. The cost of poor performance was low. The world has changed a lot since then. Intense global competition and new stress on profitability and productivity has made suppliers look for means to improve them and not the cost alone. The cost of achieving excellence is much lower than the benefits that accrue due to improved efficiency and performance. In the years to come, this trend is going to get more strengthened and the market is going to be more technology-driven.

DRIVERS OF TECHNOLOGICAL CHANGE

Technological changes can be initiated or conceptualised by any of the following agencies:

- Customer
- Supplier
- Scientist/Engineers/Thinkers

A customer normally narrates his unfulfilled needs or the operational and maintenance problems troubling him to the supplier. He wants the supplier to ensure that availability of equipment is increased and maintenance frequency is reduced. Some of the problems faced by him may be due to reduced flexibility in the system. The supplier can evaluate the need of the customer and may introduce changes in design and process to cater to the customer's requirement.

Most of the time such efforts lead to improvement in product performance through design, or through improved process during production and installation to address the concerns of the customer. This may also result in improvement in quality of raw material and even in quality procedure itself. But only rarely does the customer act as a driver of the major technological changes and his suggestion lead to engineering and design changes.

Illustration

A well known Hospital wanted to set up a small power plant to cater to its own emergency power requirements. The hospital was in the silent zone and the noise level was required to be very low, around 50–55 dB. But the ambient noise level itself was 70 dB. Considering that the equipment would also generate some noise, it was difficult to contemplate meeting the environmental requirements. The supplier however worked on his civil design for power plant equipment building to take care of the acoustic requirements. This development was a result of customer need.

Pet coke is now available in abundance and at relatively cheaper price from refineries. This fuel has high calorific value but much lower cost compared to other normally available fuels. However, due to its peculiar characteristics, it is difficult to burn in normal boilers. But since it is a cost-effective fuel, the customer wanted to take advantage of the option available, this forced the boiler designers to develop a design so that the boiler could easily burn pet coke.

Marketing executives have an important role to play in new product development as they are the link between customers and their organisation, and they must convey customer's expectations and suggestions to the concerned persons in their organisation. The supplier, who can address the customer's requirements and develop technology to meet it, gets due recognition and preference from the customer during future business finalisation.

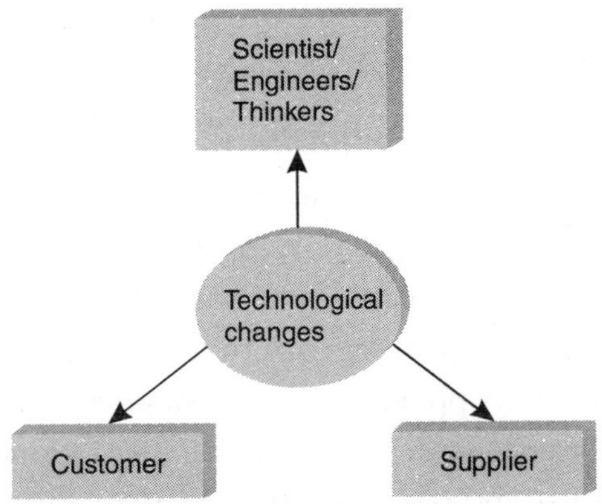

Fig. 4.1 *Drivers of Technological Change*

Technological changes also take place due to initiatives taken by the supplier himself. The supplier tries to introduce improved versions of the existing products to give the customer more benefits. Such improved versions will definitely include more user-friendly facilities. The main driving force is the supplier's inclination to provide more benefits/value to the customer for the money he is spending. Some of the improvement may thus relate to providing total information to operating personnel in the control room of the process plant on a real time basis and to give the operator the suggested course of action during emergency depending upon various possibilities. Installation of 'Fly-by-Wire' system by Airbus Industries falls into this category. Transportation of fuel and gas were earlier done by Railways/by Roads. Now laying pipelines are common for such transportation.

Many corporates make it a strategy to encourage successful new product development. They plan business growth through new internal developments and the company's policy is oriented to create environment to promote/ encourage acceptance of new products. Such companies create market expectations in such a way that the customers start looking forward to introduction of new products.

However, revolutionary technological changes which either change the way people think or their life style, generally come from the scientist/ engineers and thinkers. Examples are numerous. 'Internet' is the most commonly cited example. This has revolutionised the whole world. Nobody thought before its advent that one could do shopping, banking, bill collection and payment through the click of a small mouse, without even moving from one's house.

There has always been conflict as to whether an organisation's development should be customer driven or technologically driven. The die-hard marketing experts feel that development of technology without customer needs is a waste of talent and resources. In Chapter 1, we have seen that most of the customers cannot be considered as leaders of technological change. If a supplier is going to wait for directions from them, then he is going to be a laggard. Technological revolutions are heralded by engineers and scientists and not by customers, who are the benefactors of such developments. The basic aim of any organisation should be to anticipate customer needs and find out better ways of fulfilling it through new development. There are products for which need and necessity only arise as they unfold in the market. Any development, which is aimed at providing 'benefits' to the customer, will find a ready market as the customer only buys benefits and not the products. Hence, if a company wants to be a business leader, it must concentrate on finding ways and means to enhance customer benefits and developing products, or improving them to achieve it. Needs and demand will automatically follow.

In road construction, wherever overbridges (flyovers) are constructed on existing roads, the necessity is that the work should be completed as fast as possible. Casting the flyover at the site is a time consuming procedure and space requirement for construction is also very high. Hence, in order to meet market requirements, the companies developed pre-fabricated methodology of construction, which reduces the construction time drastically.

In all industrial functions, the performance improves tremendously, if controlling parameters are monitored regularly and information is available quickly and processed immediately. This helps the control system to take fast action. Keeping the need of the customer in mind, various digital control systems have been developed to monitor critical parameters, analyse them, identify discrepancies and trigger corrective action immediately.

TECHNOLOGY—THE COMPETITIVE ADVANTAGE

In a highly competitive market, technology provides the distinctive marketing edge in a number of ways, namely:

- Cost optimisation
- Process Improvement
- Performance Improvement giving Evaluation benefits
- Premium and increased Profitability
- Operational and Maintenance benefits
- Increased Customer Satisfaction

Cost Optimisation

The price of a product is the major deciding parameter. Every customer looks forward to getting the best product at the lowest cost. Most of the technological improvements are aimed at reducing cost. The cost reduction can come from new design, or from modification in the design, or substitution of the material. Design tolerances and redundancy can be re-examined and optimised. The other aspects which can contribute to cost reduction include "Value Purchasing" of raw material and component. New tools like "Reverse Auction" should be used for re-discovery of purchase prices and value buying.

Process Improvements

The second aspect where technology plays a major part is 'Process Improvement'. This improvement can result in optimisation of resources, reduction of wastage and reutilisation of waste. Cycle time reduction can be the other outcome of process improvement, resulting in lesser requirement of working capital and fast rolling over of it.

One of the examples that immediately comes to mind is the use of washery rejects at collieries for power generation using new development in boiler technology, i.e. Fluidised bed combustion. Similarly, the same boiler technology has helped in bringing down unburnt carbon percentage in ash (obtained of fuel burning), making it suitable to be used as raw material for the manufacture of cement. Process Improvement can also lead to reduction in rejection rate.

Performance Improvement and Evaluation Benefit

Most of the business in the core sector is decided through formal enquiry process, where price alone is not the deciding criterion. Products from different suppliers give different performance parameters, offering different benefits to the customer. New/modified technology can enhance efficiency of the system and it may also lead to reduced maintenance and ease of operation. It can also lead to increased availability of equipment, which may give additional value to the client. Attempts can be made to reduce auxiliary losses and utility requirement.

Table 4.1 *Increased Value through Technology Innovation*

Schedule	*Cost Optimisation*	*Process Improvement*	*Performance Improvement*
Activity	• Innovation in Design • Innovation in material specification • Value purchasing of raw material and component • Resource optimisation and waste utilisation • Cycle time reduction	• Lesser rejection • Waste utilisation • Cycle time optimisation • Multi-activity approach	• Higher efficiency • Increased availability • Lesser losses and utility consumption • Ease of operation • Lesser pollution • Low maintenance
Benefits	• Lower Cost • Value for money • Customer Satisfaction • Business Growth	• Cost Reduction • Reduced Completion schedule	• Valued and improved equipment

In order to access suitability and competitiveness of the proposal, the customer assigns a monetary value to the performance and other intangible benefits being given by various suppliers. In case a supplier is offering 'negative benefits', i.e. liabilities, like higher utility consumption, then negative monetary weightage can be assigned to it. The loading assigned to each proposal is called "Evaluation Weightage" and can be added or subtracted from the quoted price to arrive at final evaluated price. Thus, technological improvement provides evaluation benefits to the supplier and makes it easier for him to secure business.

Table 4.1 indicates various activities and benefits through cost optimisation, process improvement and performance betterment.

Differentiation

New technology can add special features to the product, which can increase its 'value' in the eyes of the customer. This value addition can come in the form of:

- Increased Performance
- Higher Efficiency
- Lower Maintenance Requirement
- Higher Availability
- Good Aesthetics
- Higher Life Cycle

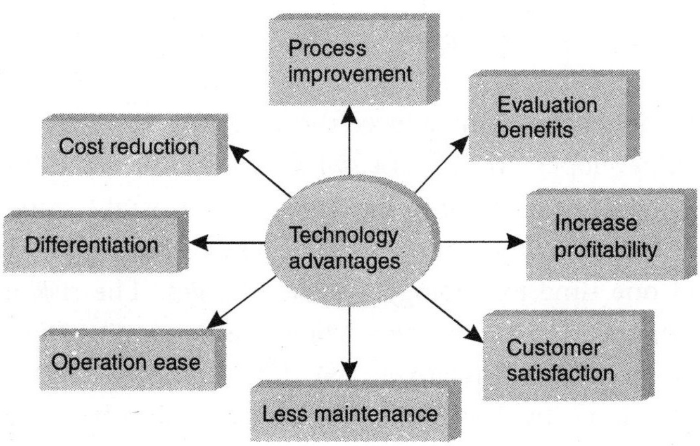

Fig. 4.2 *Technology—Competitive Benefits*

Differentiation helps the product and supplier to make a niche for him in the market, thereby providing a competitive edge.

Increased Profitability

One of the major reasons for introduction of new product/technology is to improve the profitability. Customers, as a rule, are willing to pay more for specific features, which are not available in other contemporary products. "State of Art/Advanced Class", are the most important words, which along with supplier's image, can easily fetch 5–10 per cent premium from the customer.

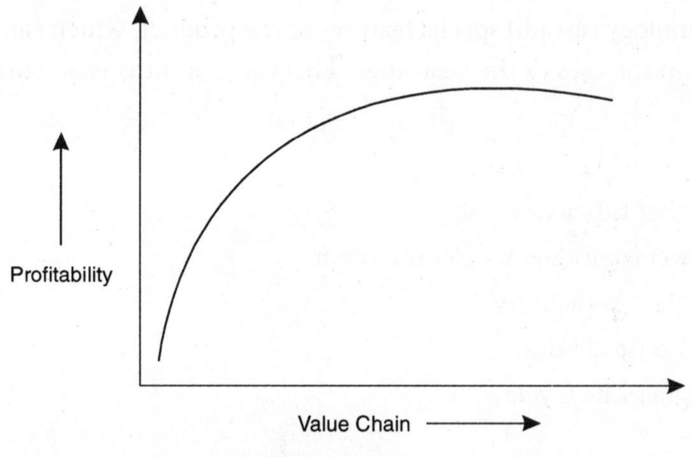

Fig. 4.3 *Value Chain and Profitability*

A new product can be introduced through transfer of technology from the original developer. In this case, while the supplier does not have to spend the money for developing, testing and establishing the new development, he can enjoy the returns of new technology by paying the royalty and one time technology transfer charges. The risk involved is negligible compared to the situation when he is developing the technology himself but the return is relatively low. On the other hand, if the new product is developed by the supplier himself through in-house efforts, then the resources required are substantial and the supplier has to develop, test and commercialise the product. Though the risk is very high, returns are equally high, as the competition will be less, and by the time competitors will catch up with the development, the supplier can move ahead to the next development, thereby always keeping himself ahead of the others. Companies like GE, USA, successfully follow this principle of 'First In–First Out' to maintain high profitability. Any organisation, which can continuously upgrade its products and introduce a new one, will face lesser competition in the market and have higher profitability. Such type of companies always works on the high end of the value chain, which is the reason for their profitability.

New development can lead to '*Repositioning of Product*' or can also result in addition to existing product lines. Repositioning can increase the tactical value of the product and hence profitability. Similarly, additions in existing product line can fulfill gaps in existing product range and result in not only increased business volume, but also additional customer satisfaction, as the supplier is in a better position to meet customer requirements. Many times the supplier feels handicapped due to non-availability of product in particular rating in his product range and has to offer his regrets to the customer. Completion of product range removes this handicap and enables the company to retain its customer base.

Operational and Maintenance Benefits

The supplier, based on operational feedback, introduces most of the technological improvements in existing products. Such improvements are generally aimed at removing operational difficulties. Thus, the improved products are more customers-friendly and are preferred by the customers. In core sector projects, the customer does not simply look at the cost of the product but more to the utility value of the product. The utility value of the product can be many times more than the cost as it may jeopardise the complete project. In all such cases, the customer is willing to pay a much higher price for the product if it ensures higher availability and reduced operational problems. No customer will want his Rs 500 crore project to remain idle for a product of Rs 5 crore value. For such a customer, technological improvement providing him comforts towards product working and improved performance and higher availability will be worth buying.

Customer Satisfaction

Most of the technological innovations are introduced to either meet the market needs, or are based on feedback from the customers. The supplier undertakes developments to provide more value and benefits to the customer. Even changes of fundamental nature are introduced, keeping the customer in mind. Thus, the net effect of technological development is to provide more satisfaction to the customer.

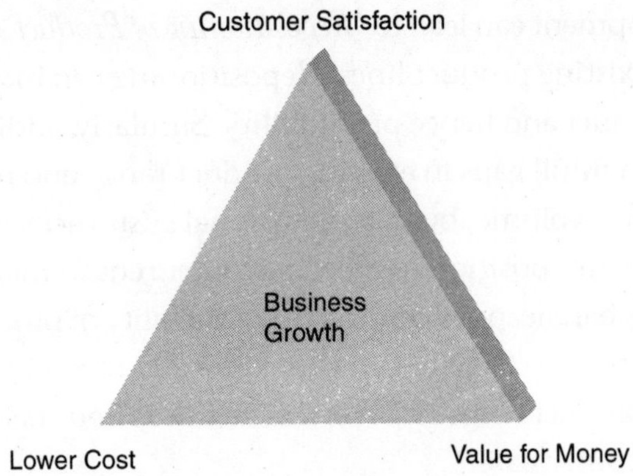

Fig. 4.4 *Business growth through Technology*

Lower cost, along with additional features, improved performance and ease of operation, can lead to increased customer satisfaction and result in higher business growth and market share of supplier as shown in Fig. 4.4.

To Protect Business Share

In a fiercely competitive environment, suppliers are forced to develop new technology or acquire it through transfer of technology, as otherwise they start losing their market share to those competitors who have already introduced new technology/modifications. Even if left unchallenged, such competitors walk away with higher price realisation. Thus the loss to the vendor, who is not up-to-date as far as technology is concerned, is double, namely, falling market share and higher realisation for other peers.

COST OF NON-DEVELOPMENT

We have already discussed in earlier sections that development can be of two types, i.e. fundamental development and work connected with modification and improvement of the product to meet changing market needs and improved life cycle. The fundamental development takes place mostly in developed nations or in those industries and institutions that have the resources and will to do it as it requires capital, patience, determination and ability to face failures. The success rate of fundamental development is not very encouraging. Hence, the majority of industries enter into agreement with the developers for technology transfer by paying a one time fee and royalty on sale volume. In such cases it is often seen that technology transfer takes place only once and the industry entering into such an arrangement is having access to 'State of Art Technology' only on the date of agreement for such transfer of technology. Slowly, this technology starts becoming old and in the next ten to fifteen years it becomes a liability until and unless the recipient organisation has taken care during this period to constantly upgrade the technology through modification and in-house development to keep in tune with the times. The second alternative is to re-purchase the technology again. In today's environment, where knowledge is available at a premium, it is not possible to get new technology at those terms, at which it was feasible about ten to fifteen years back. Hence, it is necessary that companies start concentrating on in-house development also. The cost of non-development is very high as detailed hereunder.

Loss of Competitive Edge

When the company starts losing its competitive edge and business, it is not able to meet new market needs in the form of performance parameters, cost, efficiency, quality and operation and maintenance requirement. As the business volume dips, the fixed cost of production starts getting distributed over a smaller volume, thereby increasing the cost per unit further, setting a chain reaction. For any company it is a double blow or 'Loss–Loss Situation'. On the one hand, it is not able to meet market requirements and expectations and, on the other hand, the cost goes on increasing, resulting in further loss of business. This chain reaction results many times in either the company itself abandoning the product, or it goes out of business until corrective measures are taken in the mean time.

Illustration

One of the well-known corporate houses in India, having a large number of engineering, production and service centres throughout the country, acquired technology from foreign manufacturers for producing two different products at two different units of the company. The technology was one of the best available at that time and was well adopted at both the plants and that resulted in good business. The engineering management at one of the places constantly tried to improve upon the available technology and added new major variations in two decades to ensure that they remained uptodate on the technology front to the extent feasible; the other engineering department and the unit management simply concentrated on production.

The results were visible twenty years later. The group, which also concentrated on engineering upgradation, still operates at 90–100 per cent shop capacity in an otherwise recessionary scenario and manages to earn an average return of about 5 per cent, though the price realisation has come down by 50 per cent due to recession and reduced customs duty, contributing to increased competition with demand coming down. The greater the competition, the more innovation was done by this unit's engineers to increase performance and reduce cost there by increasing the value to the customer. No doubt while undertaking development, there were failures, some even at the site making the affected customer very unhappy, but they saw to it that every problem was examined, analysed and remedial action taken immediately. The equipment after initial teething problems had worked well and customer confidence returned not only because of sound working of equipment but with the knowledge that the supplier had the ability to meet any technical eventuality. The customer was proud of the engineering skills of the supplier's engineers and was certain that even if a problem arose in future, he would be able to depend on the technical skill of the supplier. He was a typical core sector customer who derived more comfort from the supplier's ability to identify the problem and solve it. Every company and every product faces problems, but it is the ability of the supplier to solve them, which gives confidence to the customer.

Contd

The other unit, which only concentrated on production and gave engineering development stepmotherly treatment, now operates at 50 per cent shop capacity and is not in a position to recover the full cost. The division is not even in a position to serve those customers who want improved design, as the division does not have the ability to do it, as it has never bothered to develop this capability. They are looking forward to another collaboration agreement for technology transfer, which will bring them up to date. But twenty years is a long time. Today, technology is not available as cheaply as it used to be at that time. Reasons are simple. Twenty years back outsiders were not able to bid in India freely, so the best way to do business was to pass on the technology to a reputed local supplier and earn royalty and part of business through him. Today, there are no such restrictions in India. Foreign parties can easily do business in India and get premium for their technological skill, so why should they pass on hard earned technological development at throwaway price.

Management Attention

Uncompetitive products and plants eat away a very high percentage of the management's time. Since the product is generating a loss and business share is decreasing, management attention is always on the plan to salvage the business, improve the competitiveness and capacity utilisation.

It is also seen that in such circumstances, middle management time is wasted in preparing an explanation note for the top management and board, explaining reasons for such a state of affairs and in suggesting and analysing salvation plans rather than in actually putting them into action.

The board and top management also, at this time, concentrate mainly on short-term cosmetic retrieval plan. Rarely does the management put into action long-term revival plans, probably due to the fact that the risk involved is much higher and results trickle in slowly.

Effect on Company Image

Continuous loss, operation below rated capacity and performance problems in outdated products can tarnish the company's overall image in the market and may have a detrimental effect on the business of other successful products. It is often seen that the damage caused by one failure is very high compared to the benefits accruing to ten successful events.

TYPES OF TECHNOLOGICAL IMPROVEMENTS

Technology improvement can basically be classified in three categories as under:

- Modification/Incremental Improvement
- Multi-use/Convergence
- Conceptual/Revolutionary

Modification/Incremental Improvement

These are the changes which fundamentally lead to incremental improvement in the product. Some of them also may be cosmetic in nature. Some examples, which can be categorised here, are:

- Tube based radio to Transistors
- Carburettor to MPFI system in the car
- Black and White TV to Colour TV to Multi channel TV with added functions and internet
- Telephones with added functions

Though such development leads to continuous upgradation of the product, they do not lead to path-breaking changes which can bring a quantum change in the market.

Multi-use/Convergence

These changes primarily originate from the supermarket concept, where the same product can also incorporate features of other related products, thereby increasing the utility and appeal of the existing product and thereby increasing the business. Some examples are:

- Two in One/Three in one
- Internet and Internet telephony
- Mobile with e-mail/alarm/calculator and SMS

Conceptual/Revolutionary Changes

These are the technological developments which set the market on fire as they are of a fundamental nature. Some of them are:

- Electric driven cars with solar or chemical fuel cell
- Internet, e-mail, e-banking, e-business
- Changes leading to doubling of efficiency like new bio oil process, increasing the electric power generation from the same quantity of fuel by 70 per cent

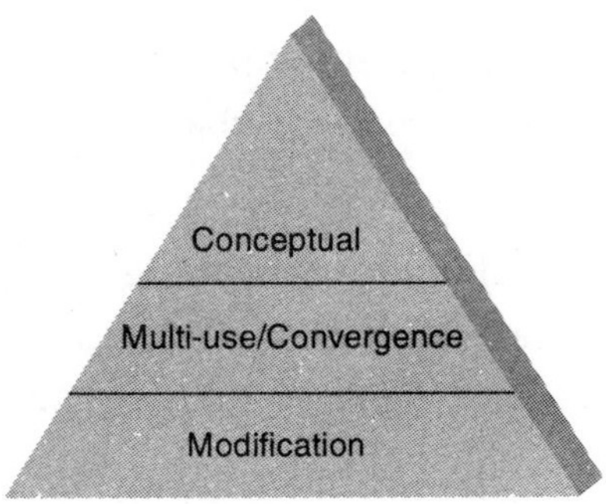

Fig. 4.5 *Levels of Technology Innovation*

Such type of fundamental changes has profound effect and can lead to growth in the business and bottom line at double-digit rates. One example, which immediately comes to mind, is power generation in sugar mills. The cane left over after extraction of juice is called bagasse and earlier it was not considered to have any commercial value. In fact, it was considered to be a hazard as it was inflammable and could lead to fire in the factory. However, during the 1990s, it was realised that it had the potential to generate energy. Now, the steam generated from it is not only utilised to generate electric power, but is also used for process application. The surplus electrical energy is now supplied to Electricity Board and the revenue from it has become a main source of profitability for sugar industries. Having realised the potential of bagasse as an attractive revenue source, attempts are continuously being made to further develop the system and generate additional returns. Presently, the bagasse is fired in a conventional stoker fired boiler and about 2.1 MT of bagasse generates one MW of electrical energy. But now some companies have developed better methodology by using fuel gasification route and converting bagasse in Bio oil. As a result same 2.1 MT of bagasse can now generate much higher power. Such are the revolutionary changes where technology can change the total process concept and fuel double digit growth. Digital camera, Internet telephony are the other examples of similar changes.

TECHNOLOGY CHANGES AND MARKET ACCEPTANCE

It is often said that recognition is more important than the concept. Similarly, technological revolutions or new developments can only get importance if the market accepts it. Some of the factors that can help in market acceptance of new ideas are as under:

1. The market is looking forward to development in the field, i.e. demand has already been created or exists.
2. Development is preceded by substantial field trial establishing the concept and the benefits are widely publicised.
3. User/customer gets substantial benefit in terms of cost reduction, better performance, ease of operation, maintenance, quality and, not the least, increase in bottom line.
4. Developer has a brand image of successful technology developer and improver. (A new product from GE is easily accepted in the market and becomes a status symbol, while a similar product from less known companies may have to cross a number of obstacles before gaining acceptability in the market).

It may however be appreciated that long-term survival of a new development is only determined by factors listed at S. No. 3 above, otherwise new development will fade away as soon as it is introduced. It is a hard fact that like any commodity, a new development, or new product, or new technology has to be self-sustaining.

WHO PAYS FOR DEVELOPMENT?

Any type of research and development is costly and requires a lot of resources in terms of money and time. It is therefore important to discuss the sources that can provide them.

Many organisations like GE follow the principle of "*FIRST IN and FIRST OUT*", which essentially means that such companies keep themselves at least 4–5 years ahead in technology. They also have a brand image of technology leaders and customers look forward to them for new development and consider it a prestige to have the latest state-of-the-art product from them. With such a situation, a new product comes with a hefty price tag and a developing company is able to recover its cost of development and reasonable return on it in 3–4 years. By the time their competitors catch up with them, they are already thinking of new developments.

PRODUCT LIFE CYCLE

Like any human being, a product (here by the word 'product', we mean either an entirely new equipment, or improved version of it, or a sufficiently modified version of a product having an entirely new look) has its life cycle and it passes through different phases like birth, learning, maturity, and decline before becoming redundant. For a marketing executive it is very important to identify the stage of the product evolution to work out the proper marketing strategy. Table 4.2 shows the following five different stages (phases) of product life cycle. They are:

- Introduction/Birth
- Establishment/Learning
- Maturity
- Life Support/Old Age
- Retirement/Redundancy

Table 4.2 *Phases of Product Life Cycle*

Phase–1 *Introduction/Birth*	*Phase–2* *Establishment/Learning*	*Phase–3* *Maturity*	*Phase–4* *Life Support/Old Age*	*Phase–5* *Retirement/Redundancy*
• Customer Apprehension • Lack of Reference • Teething Problem • Modification and Relaunch • Lower Price	• Time for Customer to look at positive side of development • Build up of Reference List • Demand Build up • Identification of long-term operational problems • Customer feedback and improvement • Operation establishment • Price pick up	• Fully Established • Healthy Reference List • Demand at peak • Profit Time • Customer Loyalty	• Product Technology start • Lagging Market requirement • Unable to compete with new products • Product re-powered to face competition • Can increase life cycle, performance with modification/touch up	• Falling Price Realisation • Decreasing Market Share • Empty shop capacity • Time for graceful exit

Introduction/Birth

This is the phase in which the product has just come into existence either due to suggestion from the customer or due to development undertaken by the supplier to meet the market need. In either case the product is untried and there are apprehensions in the mind of the customer about its utility or its meeting its objectives. The demand and the price realisation are low and it is feasible that the supplier is not able to recover the complete cost of the product. The phase is also characterised by teething problems and frequent modifications in the product based on the actual site experience. However, as the product starts overcoming initial hiccups and starts working satisfactorily, the news spreads from one customer to the other. The supplier can also help in this by making personalised presentations to target customers, highlighting the trial phase, problems faced and how they were overcome. These help in generating demand and increasing price realisation.

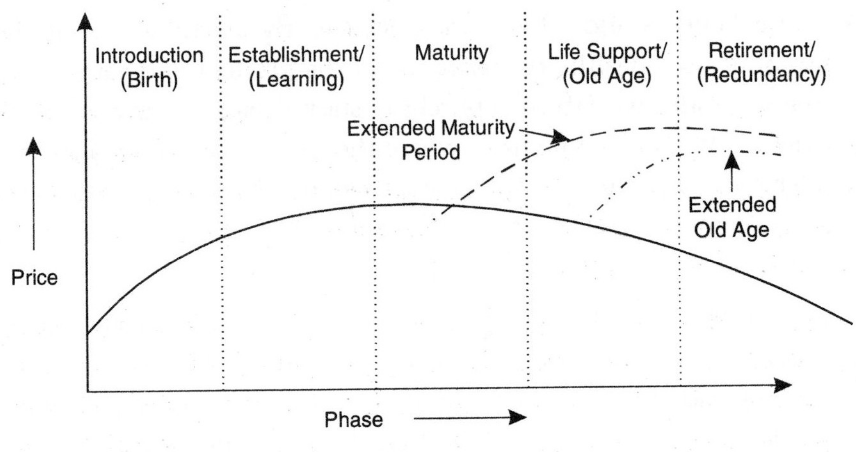

Fig. 4.6 *Product Life Cycle and Price Realisation*

Establishment (Learning)

During this phase both the customer and the supplier become familiar with the product. If the product starts working suitably, the market acceptance increases and with that the demand and price realisation also goes up. The supplier also gets an opportunity to optimise the cost and, with increasing price realisation, he also starts earning profit. The supplier's reference list also starts building up and the product slowly starts making a niche for itself. However some latent problems, which might not have come to his notice during the introductory phase, starts appearing and keeps the supplier occupied with them. But if the supplier addresses these problems, the product and the supplier both get positive weightage for it. However, there is only one disadvantage, which is that the competitor also starts taking note of it and either improves the product or introduces a new similar product. Thus, the competition sets in.

Maturity Period

In this phase, the product is at its peak and market share and profitability is maximum. As the product becomes fully established, competition starts building up, the supplier starts thinking and implementing improvement in the product to enhance its performance, efficiency and quality and tries to increase 'benefits' and value to the customer. By this time, the supplier has also built up a healthy reference list of the product and some of the customers, satisfied with the first purchase, start placing repeat business on the vendor. This is the time from where the supplier must keep track of customer loyalty and business lost to other vendors. Each business loss must be examined and analysed for the reason for the loss, and corrective action must be taken to arrest the decline.

The supplier, by now having mastered the new product and having established it, must now start working on major improvements in it, which may become necessary due to competition, or which may give it extended competitive advantage by increasing the span of maturity period. As can be seen from Fig. 4.6, such modification helps in maintaining a competitive edge and profitability for a longer period. It is also seen that technical improvement at this stage, when the product has achieved market confidence, helps in creating "*Differentiation*" in the market and thereby getting a premium from the market, resulting in enhanced profitability. It is also seen that regular improvement in the product, leading to its enhanced value to customers, helps significantly in elongating the maturity period. This was what the first unit, under case study, (*refer* Loss of Competitive Edge) did and successfully reaped the benefits.

Life Support Period (Old Age)

This is the start of decline. If the supplier is negligent and does not undertake upgradation of product technology, this period can start very early. A product life cycle is similar to the human life cycle in many ways. If human beings, during their youthful days, do not take adequate care of their health by regular exercise, they age fast, pick up number of diseases and require a good amount of regular medication to remain in shape. Similar is the case with products. If they are neglected, not updated, they become old fast and become a '*Problematic Child*' for the supplier, as has been the case with the second unit discussed in the case study (*refer* Loss of Competitive Edge).

This is the period during which the product technology starts lagging behind the market expectation. Performance, quality and other parameters are unable to meet customer needs. Market share starts falling and shop floors are half empty. The morale of supplier's human resources also comes down and profit, along with price realisation, starts falling. At the fag end of the phase, the product becomes a management and boardroom problem and starts eating into the profits of the other products and divisions.

This is the time serious retrieval plans are made by the management to cut costs on one side and to increase its appeal to the customer on the other side by whatever improvement that can be incorporated at this stage. If improvements are substantial in nature and speed of action is fast and the product is re-powered, it rediscovers its competitive edge and gets a new lease of life as shown in Fig. 4.6 by having an extended old age.

Retirement

This is the time when the product should be given a graceful exit or, what in management language is called, 'Withdrawn' because if the supplier does not do so, the other competitors will do it. The decision is never easy. The organisation has emotional attachment to it as once it had served it and had contributed to the organisation's growth, prosperity and achievement. The human officers associated with the product also oppose such decisions and delay it to the maximum extent possible. However, an organisation needs to be pragmatic and should take timely decisions, no matter how painful and unpleasant that may be, because the cost of not taking the decision is always very heavy. Every organisation needs to develop transparent criteria to decide when to move out of a particular product or business segment. This can be based on following:

- The product has lost its competitive edge and in spite of all the measures taken to re-power it, has shown no sign of retrieval.
- Continuous declining Price realisation compared to Peers
- Declining Market Share
- The organisation is booking a loss year after year on the product and the financial drain has started affecting profitability and business in other segment and products.
- Human Resources in the declining product are idling and are slowly becoming accustomed to it. Indifferent and idling human resources are the biggest liability of the organisation and should be checked immediately. If left unattended, they spread like a cancerous cell in the organisation, spoiling the work culture of the company.
- Starts requiring disproportionately high attention and time of top management.

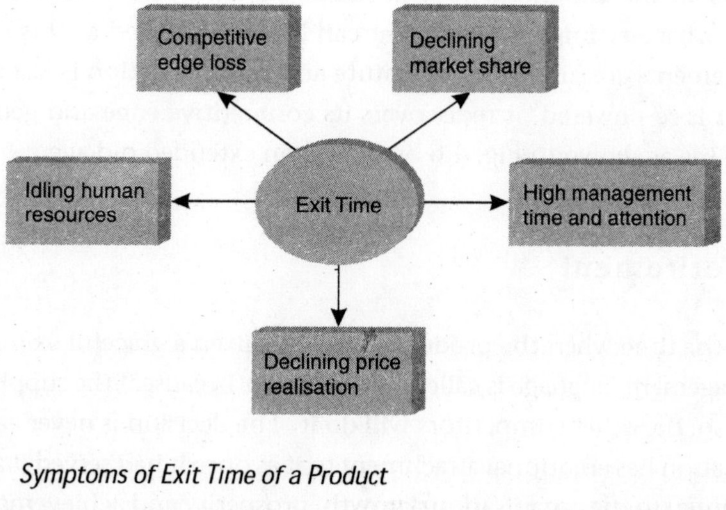

Fig. 4.7 *Symptoms of Exit Time of a Product*

In the core sector it is never easy to decide about the retirement of a product, but if the product meets the above criteria, then it should be phased out smoothly and capital and human resources should be redeployed. The management must explain to loyal customers the reasons for such decision and should create an environment so that all can accept the decision. It helps to retain customer loyalty in other products.

DEVELOPMENT AND INTRODUCTION OF NEW PRODUCT/MODIFICATION IN EXISTING PRODUCT

A lot of care needs to be taken before introduction of a new product or substantial modification in the existing product, because the repercussion of failure has a major fall out like:

- Serious doubts about the other new products/modifications even leading to continuous abandonment of the idea/no acceptability in the future.
- Financial strain due to analysis of reasons for failure, identification of corrections and incorporating it.
- Diversion of resources (Financial, Technical, Human) leading to loss of production.
- Effect on other activities due to loss of confidence.
- Financial loss to the customer due to non-performance and diversion of resources.
- Customer dissatisfaction and loss of image in the market. This may have effect on future development and acceptability of other products in the market.
- Demoralisation of the human resources at supplier organisation, which can have a far more damaging effect than the product failure itself.

In view of the foregoing, it is necessary that new product/substantial modifications are introduced in the market after total check up and examination. The process of introduction of new product or major modification is shown in Fig. 4.8 along with major activities.

Conceptualisation

The idea for modification can come from the customer/consultant, site staff and marketing executives or from the designer/scientist/engineer. The idea is mainly generated to cater to unfulfilled needs of the customer or to overcome installation/performance/operational problems. It can also be to get a competitive edge by reducing cost, improving performance or reducing contract completion schedule. The fundamental change idea may come from researchers, thinkers or scientists, which may be suggesting the development of the new product to meet the demand which may not be visible today, but may be in the horizon in the next five to six years like 'Fuel Cell'.

Analysis and Evaluation

The suggestions are discussed and analysed at this stage to evaluate their potential to contribute to the business and profitability of the company. The evaluation consist of:

- Consistency of new product to the long-term goal of the organisation and its compatibility with the vision, mission and market segment area chosen by the company for the operation.
- The second factor is market acceptability. What are the issues that a supplier may have to address to create market acceptability and whether it is possible to achieve it? What are the environment and other statutory norms that the product will be required to meet and whether the product has the capability to meet them?
- What are the benefits in the critical performance factors that can be achieved over similar products in the market? In case of substantial modification and part substitution in existing products, the implication of such change on performance and efficiency needs to be ascertained and benefits that may accrue need to be analysed and compared with the efforts made and the competitive edge that may be created for the supplier.
- The other competitive advantage that may accrue in the form of cost reduction or early completion of the project.

- An evaluation of likely reaction from the competitors must be done along with the strategy formulation for suitable response in the matter. If the competitor is likely to neutralise this advantage fast, then the concept should be revisited to explore the possibility of making it unique so that it can create differentiation in the market.
- The supplier should also consider the perceived impression of the customer on the new development. This will help in incorporating his views and opinion at the development stage itself. This also helps in generating demand.

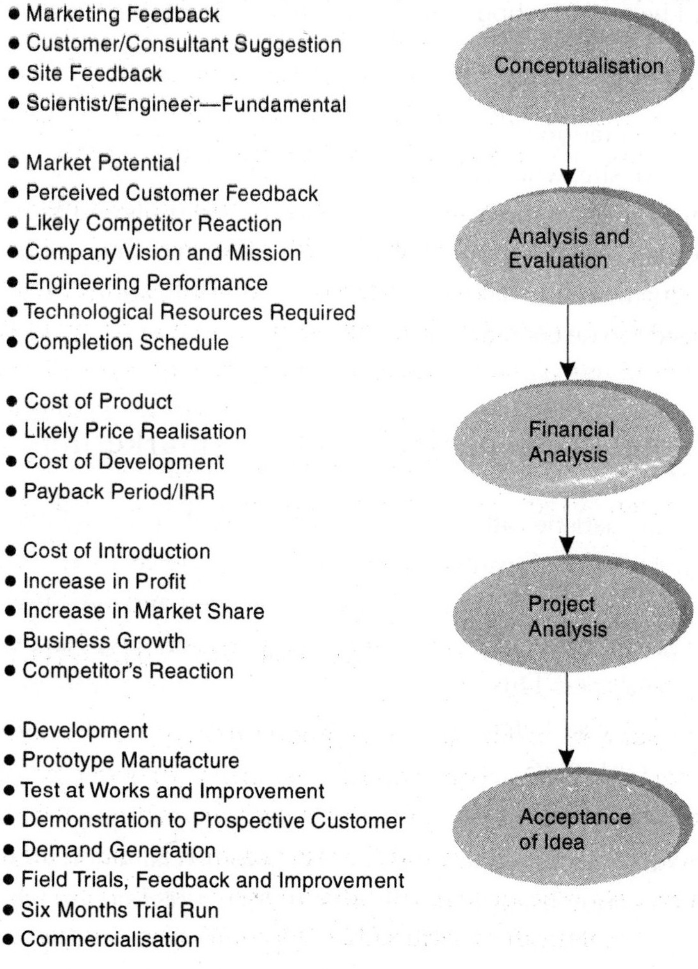

Fig. 4.8 *New Product Introduction*

Financial Analysis

Financial analysis includes the cost of development, cost of new tools, machines and infrastructure facilities required and cost of re-training and redeployment of manpower. Likely price realisation, market potential and market share has to be quantified along with present demand and likely forecast of future demand. Based on this basic data, the likely payback period and Internal Rate of Return (IRR) must be calculated to check financial viability of new product/modification. No new product can be launched or major product modification should be undertaken unless it is financially justified. The analysis should also take into consideration the development cost and the expenditure likely to be incurred in marketing the product. Initial marketing expenditure will be substantial, as the supplier has to make extensive presentation to the customer and arrange visits of interested parties to his works or site, where field trial is undertaken. He may also be required to present a report on problems faced during field trials and modifications that may have been incorporated due to this. Performance parameters achieved during field trial and their financial implications on the project will also need to be considered.

Product Development and Pre-marketing

If the product satisfies all the above parameters then actual development work is undertaken. Simultaneously marketing department should start pre-marketing activity to generate customer interest and demand. This may consist of presentation to prospective customers, contribution of articles in business magazines. This helps the supplier to evaluate customer interest. Many times it also helps in identifying site for field trials. Some of the enthusiastic customers may also come forward to offer their works for field trial of equipments.

Some suppliers undertake marketing at commercialisation stage thinking that it will surprise the competitors with sudden introduction and they will have a substantial head start over them. However, any product in the core sector has a long life span and initial head start will be a very small part of it to have any competitive advantage. The main requirement is that the product should be strong enough to face competition, which will catch up with it in any case. By getting the views of the customers and their likely reaction along with strategic reaction of the competitors at the development stage itself, the supplier can incorporate necessary changes very quickly at the initial stage itself at less cost and utilise this time in demand generation. These reactions also help in strategy formulation.

Field Trial

Every new product or major modification should be subjected to extensive tests at works and six months field trials. During this period the supplier gets an opportunity to identify operational problems and to rectify them before commercialisation. Some of the suppliers skip this phase in product development. This deprives them of valuable experience about the operational behaviour of the product. Direct commercialisation without field trial is an avoidable risk. In such cases the customer suffers and the supplier carries out the test and modification at great inconvenience to the customer. Additionally, the reputation and image of the supplier also takes a beating and it has an effect on his other business and product.

It is thus better to conduct the field trial at a site, which may be offered by an enterprising customer. It may also be advisable to leave the product with the customer as a goodwill gesture or sell it him at a discounted cost. It helps the supplier to get continuous feedback from the place and even failures do not have a serious effect. Apart from this, it helps in creating customer loyalty.

Once the product has successfully passed through all these stages, it is ready for commercialisation.

Failure of Development

In spite of all the precautions taken, a product or modification can fail. This may be due to any of the following reasons:

- Shortcuts by avoiding vital stages of developments like commercialisation without proper test and field trials.

- Inadequacies during engineering
- Inadequate Marketing
- Lack of proper understanding of customer/market needs
- Lack of understanding of effect of working in a system simultaneously with other equipments.
- High cost
- Strong Competitor's response

In core sector projects, it has been seen that most of the failures take place due to engineering reasons. This takes place mostly in not predicting the performance of the product in a total system when operational. The other possibility is introduction of the product without adequate field trials. It is to be appreciated that technical deficiencies in the product noticed after commercialisation are the biggest handicap in successful launch and continuation of development.

Managerial reasons of failure to use development include inadequate data on demand and lack of efforts in making prospective customers aware of positive side of new development. The failure to create interest and demand for products developed for substitution also result in non-acceptance of new product by the market.

MARKETING OF NEW PRODUCTS

New product marketing requires focused and extra efforts. The marketing man must understand customer needs and guide his company to develop a suitable product to meet it. He has to predict the demand and market price. Once the product is in an advanced stage of development, he has to do pre-marketing with prospective customers. If the product is a substitute product, then also the marketing executive has to create demand by highlighting the differentiation in the new product and the additional benefits that may accrue from its usage by the customer.

The biggest work of the marketing executive is to identify the customer who will accept the new product and will help the supplier in future in refining the product. Not all customers will meet this requirement. Most of the customers who accept new products will generally have the following qualities:

- They are entrepreneurs and knowledge driven.
- They follow the principle that taking an calculated risk is essential for sound business growth.
- They believe in capabilities of the organisation introducing the product rather than on the product itself.
- They have strong faith and confidence in themselves and in their own abilities.

5

Customer Relationship Management

What is Customer Relationship Management (CRM)?
Facets of CRM
Importance of CRM
Re-discovering the Customer
Customer Response
Customer Satisfaction
Customer Loyalty
Customer Complaint Management
Service
Organisation Set Up
Psychology of CRM
Sample Case Study on CRM
Survey Result Analysis
Action Plan
Tracking the Change

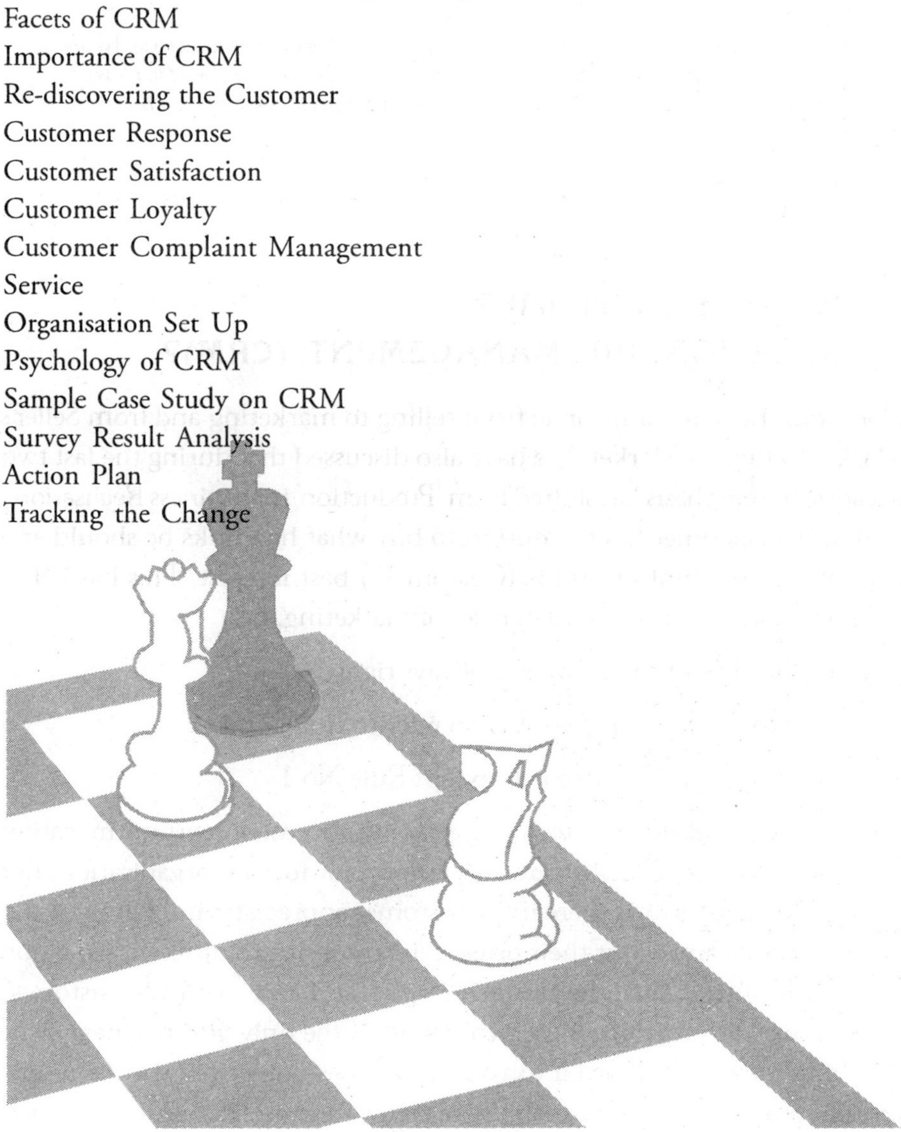

5

A customer is the most important visitor in our premises. He is not dependent on us. We are dependent on him. He is not an interruption in our work. He is the purpose of it. He is not an outsider on our business. He is part of it. We are not doing him a favour but he is doing us a favour by giving us an opportunity to do so.

Mahatma Gandhi
Father of Nation and Father of CRM

WHAT IS CUSTOMER RELATIONSHIP MANAGEMENT (CRM)?

The world has come full circle from selling to marketing and from Seller's Market to Buyer's Market. We have also discussed that during the last two decades, the emphasis has shifted from 'Production' to 'Business Realisation'. Today, the customer has the option to buy what he thinks he should and from whom he thinks is in his (Customer's) best interest. This has led to the formulation of three golden rules of marketing, i.e.

Rule No 1—The Customer is always right.

Rule No 2—In case of confusion refer to Rule No 1

Rule No 3—There is no rule except Rule No 1

Product development, technological improvement, cost optimisation and excellent service facility are very important for any organisation, but their importance is only there if the customer appreciates it. Diamond and Coal are both carbon but their price is different due to different valuation by the customer. Thus, the business begins and ends with the customer. One of my Directors often used to tell us, "One only gets business if the customer intends to award it to you". If he does not wish it, he has ample manoeuvering facility and capability to throw the supplier out. These words have been repeatedly proved irrespective of the tendering process and evaluation process. The importance of CRM cannot be put in better words than this.

A Chairman of a renowned Indian Corporate House had once told to a financial institution, "the money I am spending on the project is my money and it is my right to choose a supplier in whom I have confidence, because my long-term profitability and operation and hence survival of business depends on him. The financial institution can restrict their role to lending; they can lend me or refuse me but cannot influence my right to choose the vendor I want."

The whole business is revolving around the customer and he has become the key to business growth and profitability. That is why every company today wants to be customer-focused and customer-oriented. Business in the infrastructure sector is as much done by brain as by heart. It is often said in politics and international relations that for relations between two countries to be normal, one of the essential conditions is that the relation between the leadership of two countries must be excellent. It is true in business in the core sector where one has to meet the customer face-to-face, at least twenty times for the same project. Until and unless the chemistry of relationship is not ensured, the project may lend up in petty roadblocks.

The business is between two organisations and it is necessary that all the personnel, from top management up to worker level, enjoy enviable relationship which can solve complicated problems in a spirit of give and take, otherwise non problems can become major stumbling blocks. To put it more as a culture phenomena, business relationship in the core sector is like a marriage and all possible respect, regards and convention, as it is necessary in a marriage relationship, is required to be observed here from both the parties. Transfer of Title of equipment can be compared with the migration of a daughter from her parental house to her in-laws house. Any equipment supplied in the infrastructure sector normally has a life span of 25–30 years and during this service period how it perform and give service to customer reflect on the vendor organisation and his image in the same way as the performance of a daughter in her in-laws house will reflect on her father's house and will play a major role in the marriage of her sister and brother. Hence, a vendor company should ensure good performance of its equipment and excellent relationship to not only get repeat business but also business from other customers on the strength of good image.

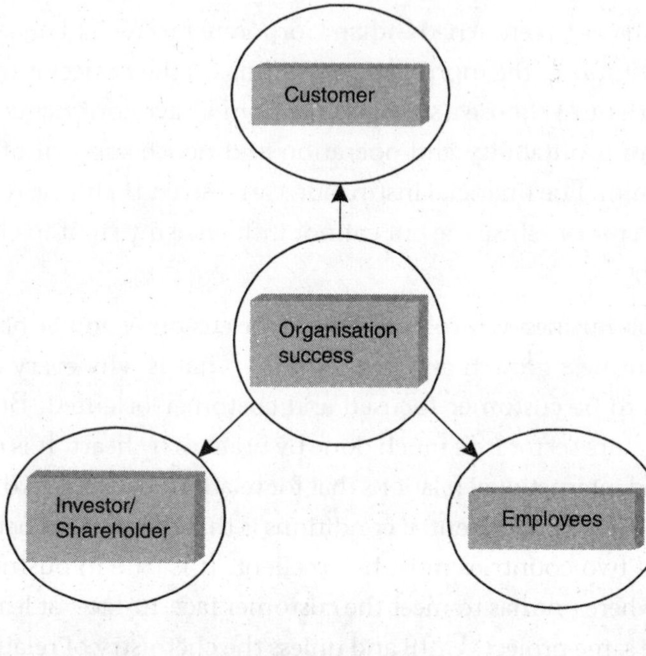

Fig. 5.1 *Important Agencies for Business Success*

The customer relationship is something beyond business. It envisages a emotional and personal bond between the people. Until and unless one develops this type of attachment, the work is incomplete. It is this linkage more than anything else which drives the business. The kind of relationship and attachment should be such that individual officials from the customer should feel free to share their happiness, sorrow, problems at office and home, their internal relationship with their superiors and subordinates, anxiety and other general issues affecting their day-to-day life in office and at home in the same way as it is shared between two close friends.

The principle of Echo is equally applicable in a relationship with the customer. "*Life returns what one gives it. Similarly, the Customer returns what the Supplier gives it.*" There are other similar views like, "What you are is your Customer's gift to you; what you become is your gift to your Customer."

For any business success there are three important agencies, as indicated in Fig. 5.1, whose benefits need to be looked after by the Supplier's organisation. These are:

- Customer
- Investor/Shareholder
- Employees

An organisation, in order to become globally competitive/excellent, needs to provide benefits and enhance values to all the three parties referred to above. However, we will restrict our discussion to enrichment of values and benefits to the customer in the present chapter.

The total integrated activity, which helps the company achieve its objective of becoming customer focused, is referred as "*Customer Relationship Management*" or CRM. This maximises the value of company's customer portfolio through convergence of marketing, project management, service and complaint redressal. CRM is a comprehensive approach which provides integration of every area of business like marketing, design, system engineering, project and site management, installation, field engineering, service, complaint management, etc. through integration of technology, human resources, process and equipment. CRM creates a mutually beneficial relationship with the customer.

FACETS OF CRM

CRM is a methodology to achieve global excellence through customer satisfaction. It tracks the customer's history, needs and coordinates the Company's multipronged interaction with its customer for business excellence. CRM's tentacles reach every area of business. These are:

- Customer Needs
- Customer Response and Influence
- Customer Satisfaction
- Customer Loyalty
- Reclaiming Lost Customer

- Customer Complaint
- Customer Service

In subsequent sections we will discuss each of these issues in detail.

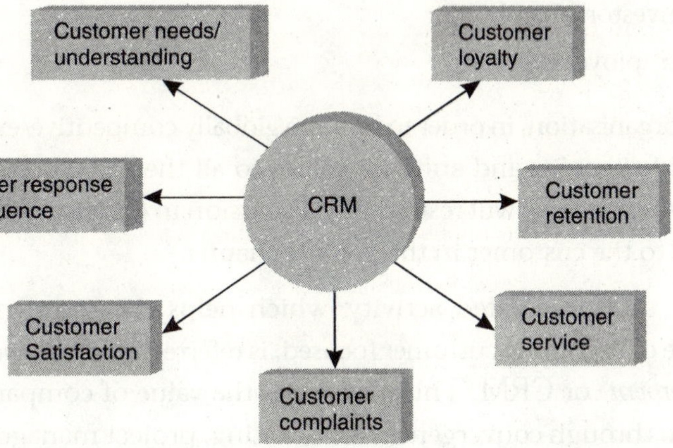

Fig. 5.2 *Facets of CRM*

IMPORTANCE OF CRM

CRM helps the organisation to identify the customer's needs and re-focus its strategy to serve him better. It helps the company to achieve business growth through development of its competitive edge and excellence. Some of the major issues it addresses are:

- Identify Customer Needs.
- Help in rediscovering the Customer and understanding him.
- Identify untapped business potential.
- Identify fields requiring new technology and development.
- Identify strong and weak points of supplier.
- Provide feedback to the Supplier on his total operation.
- Provide feedback and new information on Competitors.
- Benchmarking to achieve global excellence.
- Details on the work portion on which customer is happy with the Supplier and on those where he feels that improvement needs to be incorporated.

- Action plan to make organisation Customer Centric.

CRM helps in providing uniqueness to the organisation to help it build up differentiation from its competitors. This is achieved through:

- Comprehensive approach tailored to meet customer's specific needs.
- To build up customer focused operating environment and culture.
- To prepare and implement result-oriented action plan.
- Continuous upgradation of competencies to provide enhanced benefits and satisfaction to customer.

CRM is a strategic business and process issue. The principles of CRM are developed out of market/customer focus, methodology involving the understanding of need based segments, the development of segment based proposition and the management of delivery against those propositions to maximise the customer value. CRM is the understanding of this segmental relationship and the ability to generate an action plan to help staff working in different segments to devise a plan to maximise benefits to the customer. An effective CRM results in maximising business and profits throughout the customer life cycle.

The best CRM strategy should aim at making the customer interested in the growth and development of the competitive edge of the supplier. The success of CRM is in making '*Customer as Supplier's Marketing Office*'. This amounts to customer becoming an equity holder in the supplier's organisation. Thus, CRM should help in creating customer's equity in the supplier's company. The customer's interest in supplier's organisation is derived from the expertise the organisation possesses in the eyes of the customer and the benefits it can provide to the customer. There are many cases when a supplier got business from other customers because of the recommendation of the first customer. There are also a large number of instances where a customer had gone out of the way to help the supplier in getting the business against all odds.

Illustration

There is a famous case of a capital goods organisation which re-floated tenders three times just to ensure that a particular supplier got the business. The move was not driven by any unethical objective

Contd

but was borne out of strong recommendation of operating staff of the company showing preference for this supplier because of the excellent service offered by its equipments in the past and the technical expertise the supplier was having for which the customer personnel were having high respect. There was another case where a supplier picked up a running battle with his financier to award business to a party well known for quality and performance, but it was not the lowest one. The customer had argued with the financier that he is only taking loan from the company and will repay it with interest. He would prefer to change a financier rather than purchase equipment from a vendor other than the chosen one. The argument was simple. The loan gets paid with interest in 5–7 years, but the equipment has to work for about 25 years and he needed the continuous support of a reputed supplier to ensure uninterrupted and trouble-free operation of the equipment for its life time.

There was another customer who ensured that the supplier got orders from the other fellow customers known to him. He went out of the way to inform other customers about the advantages of getting the equipment from the supplier he was recommending. So impressed was he that he went to the extent of marketing the product of the supplier unknowingly during his visits abroad. Why did he do all this? He was a first-time entrepreneur and decided to award the contract to a very renowned but big supplier. The customer released the order after a lot of deliberation as many of his advisors had mentioned to him that, for his small requirement, the big supplier he was choosing would not give proper attention as the business was of small value. But his apprehensions proved wrong. The supplier gave him all the attention and respect that he was giving to any other big customer. Even when the system did not perform correctly at site, the supplier deputed his experts on priority to the site to attend to the problem. The customer was naturally impressed and delighted with the attention he got that he placed the next order on the party without any tender and became interested in the supplier's company and even promoting their business. Thus, in a real sense he picked up equity in the supplier's organisation.

REDISCOVERING THE CUSTOMER

The first and foremost starting point of CRM is 'Understanding the Customer'. We have, in Chapter 3, discussed in detail the importance of customer understanding and have also presented some of the tools that help in developing customer understanding. Here we will discuss the front-line sensors that provide first hand authentic information on the customer, his needs and behaviour and dynamics of it. These sources are detailed in Table 5.1 and can be broadly classified in two categories, namely:

- Internal
- External

The Internal agencies include all those arms of the supplier which come in direct contact with customers. They include agencies like Marketing, Project Management, Contract Department, Engineering and Service Department. Similarly, external agencies that can provide customer-related information are Consultant and Financiers. Even sharing the information and discussion with Competitors can also throw useful light on the subject. The supplier can either conduct direct feedback meets with customers or can hire a professional agency to elucidate his opinion on the supplier. This can provide information about his needs, likes, dislikes and attitude of customer. This has been dealt with in detail through a case study (*refer* Survey Result Analysis). Their opinion must be evaluated and analysed to generate the profile of the customer. The information so collected can be supplemented through the historical information available on the customer with the supplier. The supplier must prepare a customer profile of each and every important customer and should regularly update it. In the core sector there are not many customers, and hence each one of them should be tracked.

Table 5.1 *Customer Understanding—Frontline Sources/Sensors*

Internal Agencies	*External Agencies*
• Marketing Department	• Consultant
• Project Management Group	• Financier
• Contract Management	• Competitor
• Project Engineering Coordinator	• Customer Meet
• Site Staff	• Customer Perception Survey
• Field Engineering Staff	
• Service Department	

CUSTOMER RESPONSE

The first impression a customer makes about the supplier is from the response he receives from the supplier. This gives him an indication about how valued he is by the supplier. The more value and attention he receives, the more inclined he is towards the supplier. If the response is fast, courteous, supporting and caring, the supplier has started on the right track. Response has both behavioural and efficiency aspects and is an indicator of the type of company and its culture. Some of the situations that make a difference are described under the first part of the sample case study on Customer Perception which is an essential part of CRM. The sample case study had been carried out by a company XYZ through an external agency. The reason for selection of the external agency and methodology of conducting Customer Perception Survey are discussed in more detail subsequently (*refer* 'Why Customer Survey?'). Here we will just restrict ourselves to the Response part of the Survey.

We have also included Benchmark in the survey. *Benchmarking* refers to the practice of looking for corporations worldwide for the best practice methods followed by them and incorporating the same suitably at the time of formulating action plan for course correction based on the results of the survey. These are the companies most preferred by the customer. It is natural that a company becomes most preferred because of any one attribute or a combination of them. For example, one company may be known for 'Engineering Skill', while another company may excel for the 'Service' it provides. The significance of this is that these are the highest parameters achieved by different companies in different segments, but if a company wants to become globally competitive and excel, then it must set its target on exceeding these parameters. This is the significance of Benchmarking. They become the quantitative targets for an organisation to achieve and exceed in order to become a globally excellent company. Benchmarking also helps in assessing the gap between the company and the best in the field.

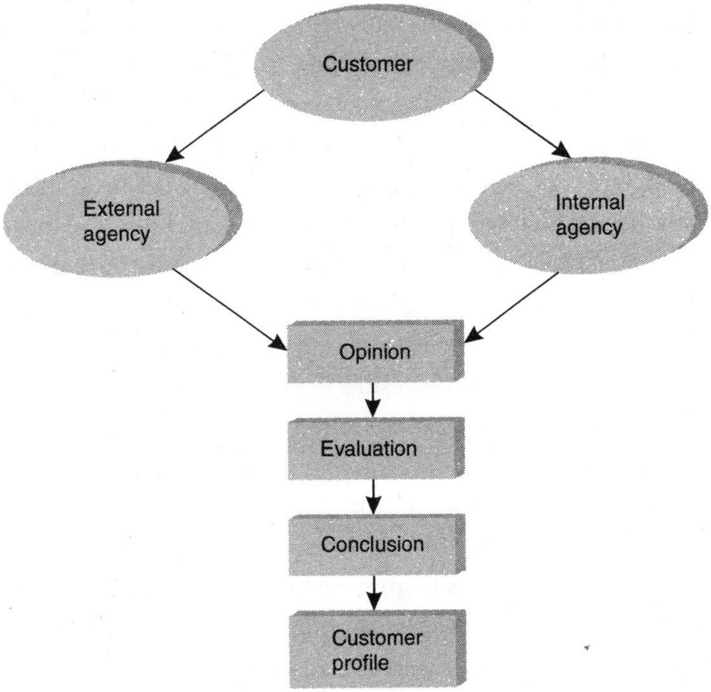

Fig. 5.3 *Customer-Analysis and Profiling*

CUSTOMER SATISFACTION

In a Buyer's market where the Customer is the King, business begins and ends with the customer. The business growth, profitability, liquidity and image of an organisation depends upon the customer. It is therefore essential that a supplier meets the customer's expectations fully and ensures that he is satisfied. To evaluate the image the supplier enjoys with the customer, he needs reliable information. He needs to know what comes to the mind of the customer on hearing the name of the supplier. Does it sound Efficient? Innovator? Modern? Quality Supplier? Reliable or not trustworthy? One who keeps commitment? Does the customer understand and appreciate why the supplier's company is different from others and how it provides better value to the customer?

It is therefore necessary for the supplier to measure Customer Satisfaction and take appropriate actions to improve it. Any business requires quantitative measures to run it. It is often said that what is not measurable is not authentic. Can a business be run without knowing in quantitative terns the actual turnover, profitability, inventory or cash position? Customers are the most important assets of business, and without them there cannot be any business. No customer will buy or recommend a supplier until he is fully satisfied with the product and services offered by the supplier. Thus, the measurement of customer satisfaction provides to the supplier quantitative feedback. If such measurement is done at regular intervals, as in the case of other business parameters like turnover and profits, the supplier also gets a feedback whether his efforts have produced positive results or there is need for course correction. In fact it is expected that in future, like targets for turnover and profits, similar targets would be set for achievement of different parameters of customer satisfaction to drive the company toward it. The objective of the supplier should not end at customer satisfaction, but should aim at '*Customer Enrichment*'. The road to this begins with sincerity and integrity followed by hard work and dedication. Some of the specific reasons for customer satisfaction measurement are summarised as under:

- A satisfied Customer acts as an extended marketing arm of the Supplier.
- A Customer is unsatisfied as the Supplier has either not come to his expectation or not honoured his commitment. It hurts the customer more as somewhere his own profitability and image is also getting affected due to supplier's delay. Some of the customers may make it a point to share their negative unfortunate experiences with other fellow customers, which may affect the business of the supplier.
- Due to human psychology an unsatisfied customer is more likely to speak often on the subject than a satisfied customer. A single unsatisfied customer could outdo the effects of three satisfied customer.
- Only a portion of the unsatisfied customer complains while the balance simply switches to other competitors. They are simply lost without the supplier coming to know of it or getting an opportunity to undo the damage.
- Loss of a customer is loss of an opportunity for business and profitability.
- Loss of business of the supplier is the gain of the competitor.

- Measurement of customer satisfaction allows the supplier to get feedback both on his strength and weakness and also on that of his competitors. It acts as a mirror reflecting his actual position in comparison to other participants.
- Measurement of customer satisfaction allows the supplier to identify his core competencies as perceived by the market on which future business strategy can be developed by the supplier.
- It helps the Supplier in identifying his weak areas needing improvement. Feedback from the customer helps him in arresting this trend and reclaiming lost customers.
- It helps the Supplier in identifying reasons for loss of customers and in taking preventive measures. Cost of acquiring new customer is many times higher than retaining an old customer.
- It helps the Supplier find out the value the customer assigns to products and services being rendered by him.

Customer Satisfaction Index (CSI)

This is the measure of the overall satisfaction the Customer is getting from the Supplier in meeting his expectations. This can be defined as:

$$\text{CSI} = \frac{\text{Total Marks obtained by Supplier based on Customer Feedback}}{\text{Total Marks expected by the Customer for Supplier to Obtain}}$$

CSI helps a Supplier to find out that how much he is able to come close to meeting Customer's needs and expectation. It can be assigned as a performance-measuring parameter by the organisation for measuring the effectiveness of its work force. Companies can also use this index for overall monitoring of its progress in becoming customer centric.

Excellence Index (EI)/Competitive Index (CI)

This is the measure of standing of the Supplier in comparison to individual best targets against different activities. This also indicates the gap which a Supplier has to cover to achieve excellence. It is defined as:

$$EI = \frac{\text{Total Marks obtained by Supplier based on Customer Feedback}}{\text{Total Marks based on Benchmark for Excellence}}$$

Like CSI, Companies can use EI for overall monitoring of its progress in achieving excellence. This factor has more relevance than CSI as it indicates the competitive edge the company has or lacks, as the case may be. The business growth or differentiality and hence customer preference that a company can have in the market, depends on this factor. CSI is after all an expectation of the customer, but EI or CI is a reality and it can have a bearing on CSI. It can actually decide the business direction.

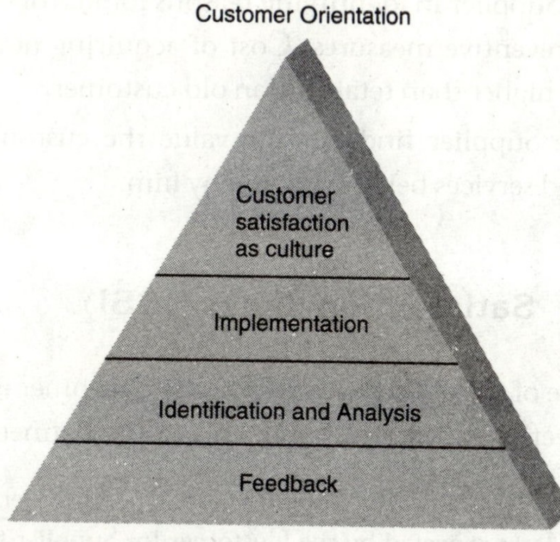

Fig. 5.4 *Promotion of Customer Satisfaction*

How to Promote Customer Satisfaction?

There are four major activities involved in promotion of Customer Satisfaction. These are:

- Listening to Customer
- Identifying factors needing attention and developing action plan
- Striving to make organisation trusted by the Customer
- Developing Customer Satisfaction as Corporate culture.

Table 5.2 *Customer Feedback Methods—Relative Merits and Demerits*

Area	*Frontline Agencies*	*One to One Meeting*	*Complaint/ Appreciation Letter*	*Customer Meet*	*Customer Survey*
Coverage	Local Issues	Burning/ Immediate Issues	Burning/ Immediate Issues	Serious Issue	Comprehensive/ Holistic
Systematic	Unstructured	Unstructured	Unstructured	Semi-structured	Structured
Objectivity and Honesty	Subjective	Subjective	Subjective	Part Objective	Objective/Honest
Relative Expenditure	Low	Low	Low	Medium	High
Time Schedule	Low	Low	Low	Medium	High
Uniformity	Poor	Poor	Poor	Excellent	Excellent

Listening to Customer/Customer Feedback

Listening to a customer and getting his feedback is like an investigation done to identify diseases in medical science. It can be done to diagnose the diseases, i.e. falling market share and loss of business or it can be used as a preventive check-up so that the organisation remains healthy.

There are a number of ways to get to listen to the voice of the customer. Some of them are:

- Feedback through frontline agencies
- Feedback during one to one meeting
- Complaint/Appreciation letters
- Customer Meets
- Customer Perception/Satisfaction Survey

Why Customer Survey?

We have already discussed in earlier parts of this chapter that various functional departments of a Supplier, who are front-end agencies, are the best agencies to listen to the customer and provide feedback. But it is seen that such feedback is not structured, systematic and comprehensive. It requires a full feedback integrator department in the Supplier's office to assemble, analyse and supplement other findings. It is therefore essential that a focused and comprehensive exercise be done to systematically get customer feedback. Further, the feedback collected by Supplier's frontline agencies reflects more the impressions of the customer on a particular project rather than reflecting his views on the organisation in totality.

Similarly, feedback through one to one meeting and Complaint/ Appreciation letter are more towards burning/immediate issues and not holistic. Since in such meetings different sets of questions are addressed to different customers, the feedback uniformity is lost and it cannot be used for analysing the relative position of different competitors and benchmarking them. Though the cost of getting customer feedback is low and time required is small, this method does not produce satisfactory results.

Thus, the best way to listen to the customer and get feedback from him is through a properly designed Customer Survey through a structured questionnaire to a well-selected sample of customers, and results are extrapolated to arrive at overall conclusions. This is discussed in detail in Chapter 6, *Market Research.*

Surveys can be carried out over the telephone, by post, Internet or through face-to-face interviews. The relative merits and demerits will be discussed in Chapter 6. Telephone and Internet surveys are cheap but lack the advantage of face-to-face interviews by reading and appreciating the intensity of customer feeling. It also prevents supplementary questions or further clarifications, if required to elucidate the subject.

The surveys can be done by the Supplier himself or through external agency. Surveys through external agencies are helpful as no human elements/ feeling is involved. It is human nature that while giving feedback to the person concerned, we tend to highlight more the positive aspect and less the negative aspect and hence the result can go tangential. Thus, it is better to engage a professional agency that can provide additional benefits. The reasons for choosing an external agency can be summarised as:

- Designing questionnaire, selecting samples, data collection and analysis can have a major impact on final result and professional help should be resorted to for better results.
- Customer finds it hard to give honest feedback to supplier's representative, especially if it is negative. Similarly Supplier's representative will find it hard to ask uncomfortable questions reflecting on the Supplier's own performance.
- Suppliers tend to devote time to their main line of activity and will not be able to do justice with this activity.
- The questionnaire should have both quantitative and qualitative questions that many times need to be indirect and psychologically designed to allow the reality to surface.
- The selection of customer representative is equally important. A professional external agency can help the supplier in proper selection of such persons.

How to Conduct Customer Perception Survey?

Some preliminary precautions are necessary before actually undertaking the survey. They are:

- Defining the objective of the Survey.
- Identifying the major issues to be addressed.
- *Deciding the frequency of the Survey* It should not be too short as such surveys are costly and consume a lot of time. Too short a period also makes them rituals rather than a serious exercise. An extended period of time will not allow the Supplier to apply timely course correction in his action plan. Normal frequency is two to three years.
- *Budget* The Supplier's budget will decide the sample size and the error in the survey. It will also have a bearing on the frequency of the survey.
- *Methodology of Survey and targeted customer segments* The survey is normally done through a pre-decided questionnaire so as to ensure that it is comprehensive, uniform and structured and the results reflect the views of the majority of customers on the same issue. But in order to have wider perception of the customer feeling, it is better to have an unstructured discussion with the customer after he has filled up the questionnaire. This helps in getting the additional feedback and help in identifying fields on which he feels very strongly. It can also help in identifying those areas that have not been considered in the questionnaire and also helps in getting suggestions from the customers.

In a survey, only a selected number of customers are considered. These customers should be carefully chosen as wrong sample selection can result in error in the ultimate result. The sample must cover those business segments of the company that are contributing substantially to the company's business. They should also include those customers who are market movers.

Preparation of Questionnaire

The design of questionnaire is very important, as it should cover all major aspects of the business. Questions must be so designed as to encourage the customer to reply in a natural way. The questions should be both qualitative and quantitative and their answers should add value to the information already available with the supplier. Some of the questions have been included in a sample case study covered later in the chapter.

CUSTOMER LOYALTY

One of the essential parameters which can measure the success of an organisation is the "LOYALTY" it enjoys with the customers, i.e. amount of repeat business it has got. There cannot be a better parameter to judge customer satisfaction than getting repeat business. This is the primary aim of CRM. One cannot expect loyalty from dissatisfied customers but sometimes even a reasonably satisfied customer also switches sides as he sees better benefits in going to other suppliers. *Thus, the key to business is not only having a satisfied customer or delighting him by exceeding his expectations, but also achieving business excellence.*

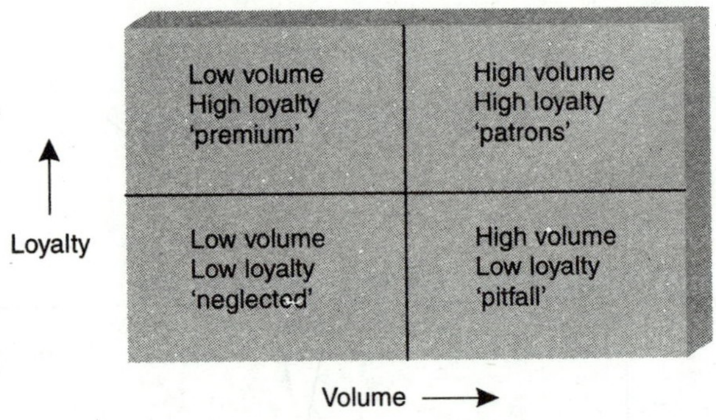

Fig. 5.5 *Loyalty–Business Volume Matrix*

Thus, the company must monitor the business volume and loyalty of at least high volume customers. The importance of this has been shown in Fig. 5.5. The customers who fall in the first quadrant of 'High Loyalty–High Volume' are the Patrons as they are really contributing to the success of the organisation. At the same time customers who are falling in the second quadrant of 'High Volume–Low Loyalty' need to be studied and analysed to take them to the first quadrant. As they have high volume, there is need to concentrate one's efforts here and convert them to the Loyal customers. This is discussed in more detail later (*refer* How to Retain Customer Loyalty). The third quadrant is 'Low Volume–Low Loyalty'. This is a neglected lot as not many suppliers concentrate on this segment until absolutely necessary. The company really needs to take a decision on the efforts required here and the return expected, and takes corrective action accordingly. The fourth quadrant belongs to the customers who have 'Low Volume but High Loyalty'. The company can revisit its marketing strategy for this segment, as this is the premium segment and can add value to the company's bottom line.

Tracking Customer Loyalty

Figure 5.6 tracks the business of a customer along with his loyalty. The figure indicates the transient behaviour and the period at which the corrective measures are required.

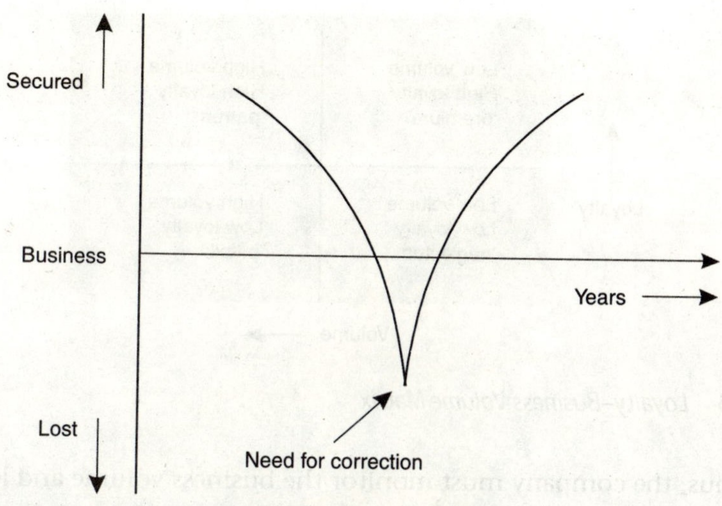

Fig. 5.6 *Tracking Customer Loyalty*

How to Retain Customer Loyalty

Some of the Do's for retaining customer loyalty are enumerated below:

- *Empathy* One of the main reasons for loss of business is the supplier's inability to understand and appreciate reasons behind a particular position taken by a customer and respond accordingly. It is therefore necessary for the supplier to put himself in his customer's shoes and find out where it pinches, and what efforts need to be made to make it comfortable. Such an approach would not only bring immediate business, but would result in the beginning of a lasting relationship of mutual benefit.
- *Transparency* Batting with a straight bat always help. Most complicated problems on the earth look easy or the persons are able to forget and forgive if the offending person opens his heart to explain why he took a particular action, which in retrospect appears to be a catastrophe. In an infrastructure project one of the main reasons why a customer gets annoyed is because of slow progress or delay or deficient performance. At the onset, it is to be appreciated that delays in a large project are not uncommon. What is required is that one takes the customer into confidence and explains to him why the delay has taken place and what corrective action is being taken to either eliminate it or bring it to the barest minimum level. In most of the cases there would be delay from the owner's side also and he, in most of the cases, will not be unreasonable.

  Similarly, in case of deficient performance, it would be advisable to share with the customer why this is happening and what action is being taken to ensure that performance is restored to the guaranteed level.
- *Comfort and Confidence* In all the approaches one must ensure that the customer derives comfort and confidence. There may be occasions when there may be disputes between the customer and the vendor or the vendor may be looking for a new approach, which may be making the customer anxious. It is our responsibility to explain things to the customer and address his concern.
- *Differentiation* If products and services offered by a supplier are unique and create differentiation from those offered by other suppliers, then it helps in retaining the customer.
- *Service* Products having a high service component lead to high loyalty from the customer.

- *Positioning* Products positioned at the high end of the value chain display high customer loyalty, as they are relatively insensitive to other business factors. Similarly, if a company is having multi product profile, then it is in a better position to retain customer loyalty.

How to Reclaim Lost Customers?

It is often said that the cost of adding a new customer is many times more than retaining an old customer and hence there is a need to retain loyalty of existing customers, particularly where the business volume is high. It is therefore necessary to examine the reasons for loss of customer loyalty and take appropriate corrective measures. The loss could be due to price, performance (contractual/technical or both), wrong information, lack of proper service, lack of communication, personal factors or perception.

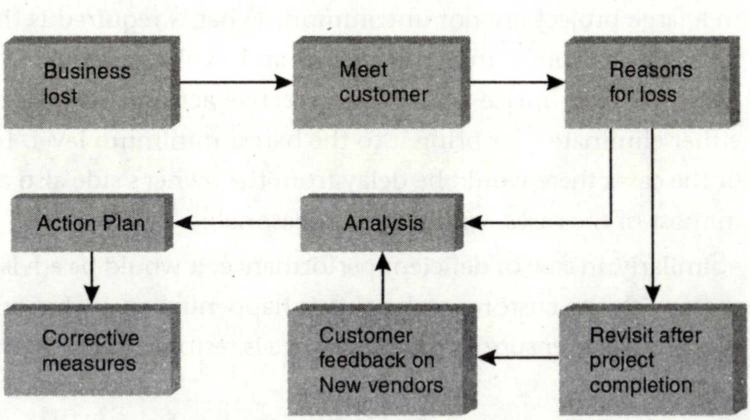

Fig. 5.7 *Reclaiming Lost Customer*

Figure 5.7 shows a road map for analysing the lost business and customer and to bring him back. It is advisable to call on the customer after a time gap of two to four weeks to find out why he has gone to another vendor. The intervening period is important as it is the cooling period required for the customer to be a little frank in telling reasons for his decision and will be a little rational and pragmatic. This feedback can be analysed and corrective action can be taken. It should also be ensured that the Supplier visits the customer again after the competitor has completed the work to collect the feedback about the work he has done and the customer's opinion regarding post contract execution which, in any case, is more important and take appropriate corrective action. It is often seen that many times the customer will feel more dissatisfied with the new vendor and it would be easy to win him back. In case our competitor friend has done good work, the message is clear—'Improve or Perish'.

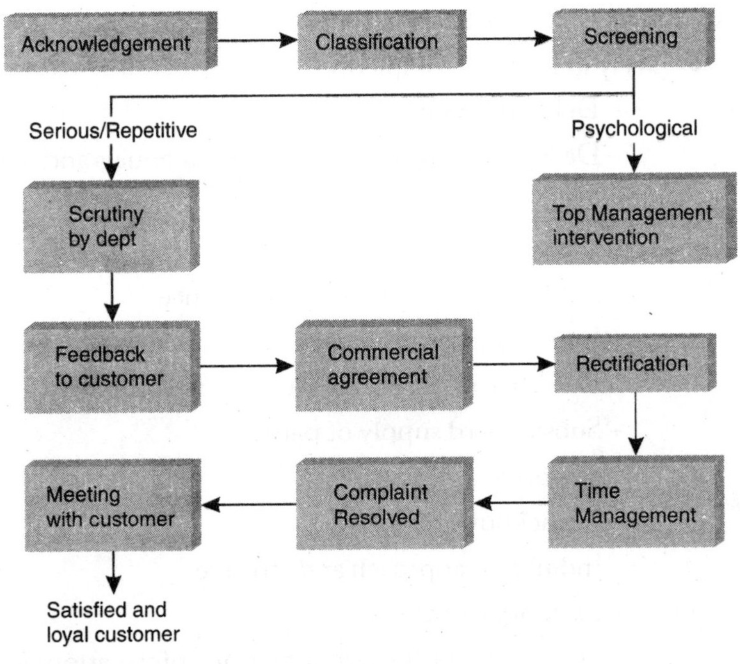

Fig. 5.8 *Complaint Redressal Mechanism*

CUSTOMER COMPLAINT MANAGEMENT

It is commonly said in human psychology that one who works will commit mistakes. The same is true in business. If there are business transactions, there are bound to be complaints. Many suppliers are allergic to receiving complaints from customers. They must realise that this is an essential part of business as they are the source of feedback from the customer and provide an opportunity to the supplier to improve upon his existing operation. If addressed properly and comprehensively, complaints provide an ideal opportunity to a supplier to enhance customer satisfaction and customer loyalty. There is need for every company to have a structured complaint redressal system that can analyse every complaint, find out the cause of it, devise and implement rectification work. The positive part of complaints is that, if handled properly, they can enhance customer satisfaction and help in retaining customer loyalty. The Supplier needs to have a specific department for this with the following functions:

- Acknowledgement of Customer Complaint
- Analysis and Classification in following categories:
  - Delay in Project Completion
    - Delayed Supply
    - Delay in furnishing of operation manuals and drawings
    - Non-sequential supply
  - Non Achievement of Performance
    - Equipment guaranteed performance
    - Individual performance of equipment
    - Defective or abnormal working of equipment
    - Substandard supply of parts.
  - Non Response
    - No acknowledgment
    - Indifferent approach and attitude
    - Lack of priority
    - Delay in furnishing of quotation/information/action
  - Service
    - Frequent breakdowns
    - Delay in supply of spares
    - Delay in deputation of service personnel
    - Lack of co-ordination between man and material
    - Delay in undertaking work
    - Lack of priority even in emergency cases
    - High prices
  - Warranty Obligation
    - Performance not in conformity to contract
    - Breakdowns and failure

– Substandard material

– Substandard workmanship

Figure 5.8 depicts the flow chart for complaint addressing mechanism. After acknowledgement the complaint should be classified under serious and superfluous categories. Screening of complaints helps in better-focused action and optimisation of resources. Many customers are habitual complainers. Most of the complaints originate because of the anxiety of customers to complete the project on time with excellent quality as the stakes involved are high. In the process some of them make suggestions that are not workable in the total project interest and as these suggestions are not implemented, the customers become edgy. The best way to address such complaints is managerial. An anxious customer needs to be provided with comforts and confidence to calm him down. This should be followed by counselling to convince him that the action plan followed by the supplier is the best. Next, visible action should be taken on the project front to convince the customer that his project is being given top priority. Such customers are to be handled at a fairly senior level, as their problem is more psychological than technical.

The serious problem needs to be referred to the concerned division for redressal. The concerned division, after examination of the complaint, must offer the following advice to the customer:

- Cause of the problem
- Likely solution
- Cost and time required for attending to the problem
- Any other investigation or details required

The customer may require more details, which should be provided to him. After an agreement has been reached with the customer on commercial issues, the supplier must start rectification work. The complaint redressal cell must monitor the progress of action and should keep the customer posted of the progress on a regular basis. In case further action/investigation is required, the cell should act as a project monitoring group to ensure co-ordination and completion of activity. The cell should activate appropriate authorities in case of delay to ensure that timely corrective action is taken.

Once the complaint is resolved, the supplier's representative should call on the customer to ensure that his problems are being taken care of and they are fully satisfied. The meeting is very important as it conveys the concern and significance the supplier attaches to customer complaints. This helps in retaining customer loyalty.

The complaint redressal cell can render other important functions for increasing the supplier's competitive edge. They are:

- Identification of products and components having generic problems. Such issues need to be brought to the notice of top management so that proper priority and importance can be given for their analysis and resolution. Similarly, complaints of repetitive nature need to be analysed and resolved. If the problem is of generic nature, then the supplier should, of his own accord, call on all those customers who have purchased but not complained, and incorporate necessary corrections. This helps in creating a positive impression on these customers and getting their loyalty.
- Yearly analysis of complaints, their cause, remedial action taken and time consumed in resolving help the company in targeted approach in improving response time in complaint management. It can help in identifying those fields that are taking an unreasonably long time. Chronic complaints also get identified. This can also lead to development of standard checks to help both the customer and supplier to get early warning signals.
- The cell can offer valuable suggestions on customer training and even on supplier's employee training to enable them to meet customer expectations better.
- The group can provide authentic first-hand information on customer needs and changes that are taking place in it. It can also provide valuable inputs on priorities being assigned by the customer in different areas like quality, performance, etc. to enable the company to work on it and leverage it to add to its competitiveness and business growth.
- The cell can provide valuable direction to product engineers and R&D department of the company about where they should put their money and efforts.

Complaint redressal is an important part of business. In business, mistakes are bound to happen, but how one responds to them is more important. The original mistakes are forgotten and are replaced by admiration of supplier's approach in resolving it. When complaints are addressed properly, they help in not only making a customer loyal but also becoming a supplier's marketing official. It is therefore essential that we exceed the customer's expectation while attending to his complaints. The driving strategy should be 'Give more than the customer expects. Do not simply satisfy him, have him delighted'. *Convert a complainer into a Business Ambassador.*

SERVICE

Service segment is an important part of core sector business. Products used in core sector are having a life span of 25 years and they require regular maintenance and repair to keep them in operation. As they grow older, they may be retrofitted and re-powered to extend their life further. Earlier, most of the products supplies in core and consumer sectors had restricted their role to supply of main equipment and spares. The service part was left to other agencies, which were mostly local. Majority of customers had preferred this arrangement, as repairs were cheap and quick. However, slowly, the disadvantages of such type of working became visible to both supplier and customer. Repairs undertaken by untrained and unprofessional persons created more problems rather than solving them. Both equipment life and performance got negatively affected. The customer also realised that repairs undertaken by unprofessional people were not after all cheap.

Suppliers also noticed an increase in equipment performance complaints after repairs undertaken by such casual workers. They realised that their own image was also getting affected due to their not providing professional service. With both supplier and customer converging on the need for professional service, this sector got the well-deserved boost. The supplier also realised that he could get more advantages like:

- New business segment for growth. The profitability in this segment is higher than in main equipment business.

- As a guideline, most of the core sector suppliers realised that at least 25 per cent of their business and 35–40 per cent of the profits should come from service segment.
- Providing genuine spares and professional service drastically reduces customer complaints and improves equipment performance. It also increases equipment life. Thus, on the one hand, it increases customer satisfaction and on the other hand, it adds to the supplier's image.

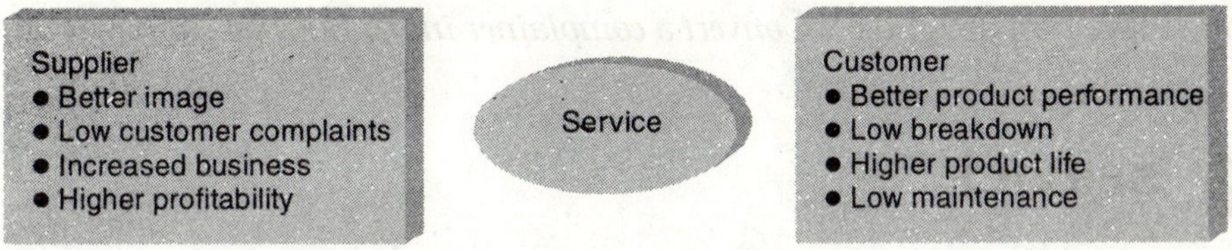

Fig. 5.9 *Service—Twin Benefits for Supplier and Customer*

More and more decision makers are striving to leverage service component of business as a key competitive differentiator. Many customers have also made it clear that they will forego everything, including price, to do business with companies who place 'Service' at the top of their corporate culture. The preparedness of the supplier to service even the most demanding customer is the key to business success. The importance of this business segment has thus been recognised and, today, it is one of the fastest growing business segments.

Types of Service Business

Service Business can come from any of the following areas:

- *Call Centers* These centers can be located on regional/zonal or country basis. They are like primary health centers, where the customer can make the first call. They can either attend to the problem themselves or can refer it to their expert center for further investigation and advice. The center has the advantage of being close to the customer. Suppliers can also connect these call centers on the net so that customers can approach them through the web also. In time to come, the concept of call centers is expected to grow at a rapid pace.

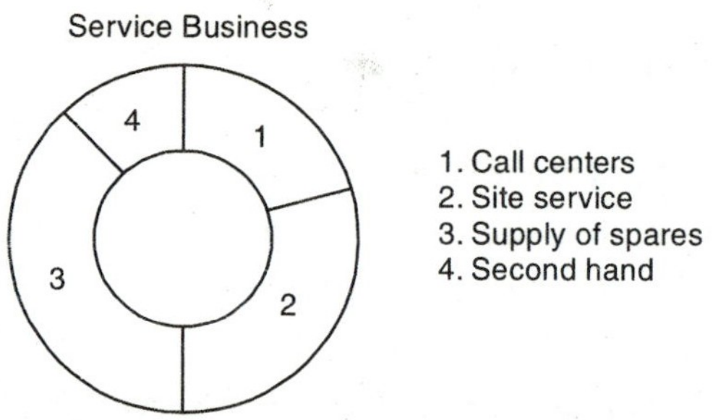

Fig. 5.10 *Service Business Segments*

These centers can provide expert guidance to customers about their problems and offer solutions on chargeable basis. This is a highly profitable segment and the need for it has been felt for a long time. This concept can be extended to provide diagnostic facilities.

- *Supply* Supply can include the following activities:
  - Spares for operation and maintenance.
  - Replacement of damaged or worn-out components.
  - Change of components with new technological upgraded one.
- *Site Service* Site service can include the following activities:
  - Installation of main equipments.
  - Annual maintenance and overhauling of equipments.
  - Operation contract with or without workers.
  - Life assessment study.
  - Retrofitting and re-powering of old equipments.
  - Repair of damages sustained due to accidents and fire.
- *Second-hand Segments* There can be business opportunities in the following areas:
  - Assessment of fair value of old equipments for purchase by customers.
  - Repair and refurbishment of second-hand equipments.
  - Total service for dismantling, transportation and installation and commissioning of old equipments at new location.
  - Operation and maintenance of second-hand equipments, once they are purchased and installed by the new customer.

Management of Services

In order to achieve the twin objective of customer satisfaction and business growth with profitability, the current management of services needs to undergo total change. Most of the companies still treat service as "Add on Business" and not as frontline business. As a result it gets priority, human resources and top management attention reserved for second category business. The time has come to recognise that 'Service' is as much a main line business as selling the main product. In fact, marketing a service is a more difficult job than marketing main equipments as it requires more creativity and determination to create an opportunity and utilise it.

To begin with, companies should accord the status of "Mainline Business segment" to the service department, which should be entirely independent of main supply business. They should have separate marketing, production, purchase and finance departments. It is seen that if these activities are combined with main product department, then the service department will always suffer particularly during the last months of the financial year or quarter.

Companies should post their best marketing personnel in service department in addition to main product department, if they want to generate double-digit growth in business. Most of the service department officials in the core sector are still living in "Supplier's Market Syndrome". They are still accustomed to customer sending them an enquiry for spares, telephoning them and visiting them frequently to get a proposal. With such a situation, one can imagine the follow up required to expedite supply. These gentlemen and their employers are not aware of the quantum of business they are losing because of such an approach and the amount of customer dissatisfaction they are generating.

What is required is that service-marketing department keeps track of places, where they have supplied new equipments and installed them. They should approach such customers on their own at regular intervals advising them about the type and quantity of spares and checks they must do based on the operating hours the equipment has performed. This will help the customer generate both goodwill and business for the supplier. The service department of a supplier may regularly like to send messages like the following to their customers.

Illustration

Dear Mr Customer,

We thank you for being a privileged and proud owner of the products of XYZ company. The equipment has now completed four years in operation and we hope that they are performing as per your requirements and giving you trouble-free service. In order to ensure that you continue to get the same efficient and trouble-free operation from the equipment, it is necessary that we check them for you and replace parts that may be worn out. We are attaching a list of spare parts along with their prices and delivery schedule for your consideration. These are the parts that generally need replacement after four years of operation. Our technical experts, based on their expertise and experience, had prepared the list. You may like to procure them to ensure the smooth operation of your equipments.

The equipment will also become due for regular service after three months. You may like to consider our proposal and advise us per return of your intention to avail services of our experts for this. We are also enclosing charges of our experts for attending such type of work.

Thanking you and assuring you of our best attention

The letter may be followed by a personal visit by the marketing executive. This type of pro-active approach can, on the one hand, build an emotional bond between supplier and customer. (In fact in the earlier section, we had compared business in the core sector to marriage relationship. This pro-active approach is in line and in consistency with that similarity). On the other hand, it will convince him about the importance and value a supplier attaches to him. This will enhance his liking for the supplier. Business is bound to grow.

At the cost of repetition, it would not be bad to reiterate that marketing function of service should not be attached along with marketing of main equipment. Service will never get priority. Many corporates think that the main marketing department had already made inroads in customer organisation by negotiating and securing main product business and their relationship can be leveraged to secure service business. There cannot be a greater myth than this. In such an arrangement, service will remain neglected. Main product group will always give priority to marketing of main equipments. Marketing is a specialised field and marketing of main equipment and spares and services require different skills and attitude.

Similarly, the service departments should make standard packages for offering "Annual Maintenance Contract" and regular operation service. They can start their marketing as soon as the business of main equipment is received. Today, the world is shifting towards professionalism and many customers would prefer to utilise the supplier's professional service and keep them free to concentrate on their main business activity. But for all this to happen, the supplier should not only follow a pro-active approach but also create proper infrastructure to take up these activities. Many customers will prefer to hand over operation and annual maintenance, or at least regular maintenance to the supplier as this will free his people from the bother of arranging timely spares and experts from the supplier as and when the necessity arises. He need not even purchase and store spares and block his capital. He does not even have to worry about purchasing the quantity of spares and damage that may occur due to long storage.

Any main line product supplier does not like the second-hand business segment as it eats into his main business. But the world over, a good number of the customers are preferring it and there exists a substantial market for this. Thus, it would be unwise not to take advantage of this opportunity. The service department can offer a number of value-added services in this segment. These are:

- Assessing the condition of the old equipment.
- Conducting residual life assessment studies.
- Preparing reports on refurbishment required.
- Re-powering and retrofitting of equipments.
- Dismantling at present site, transportation and re-installation at new site.
- Operation and maintenance of main equipments.

This area has a lot of potential because some customers may be interested in selling the equipments to other parties. Some other customers, who may be having similar units at different places, may like to utilise their resources in the optimum way by shifting capital equipments from one place to another to augment its usefulness. A professional hand is of great help to them.

Structure of Service Business

The service department can have its main unit or headquarters at only one or two places in the region depending on the quantum of business and availability of resources, but it must have skeleton staff at regional centers, the strength of which can be 5 to 6. Marketing staff should be located at these centers and from here they should do pro-active marketing. They should advise the customers in advance about regular services that are falling due and furnish quotations to them for spares and other requirements based on the operating time of the equipments They should visit customers regularly. This will enable the organisation to capture a large part of service and spare business that is presently being lost to other people.

ORGANISATION SET UP

Today's market is customer driven and it is necessary that we have an organisation set up which caters to the need of the market. CRM is the core around which organisational set up should be webbed. Basically, we should be having an "*Extrovert Looking*" organisation or *Customer Centric Organisation Structure*. The customer should find it easy to access the person required.

Some organisations also believe in appointing "*Business Ambassadors*" for individual customers on the line of "*Single Window Concept*" of government. There is a lot of positive benefit with this arrangement as can be seen from details listed below:

- Better access to customer who is also provided with a permanent contact in the organisation. In large companies many middle level customers feel uneasy, as they do not know whom to approach in case of problems and often feel lost in the process, which is not good from the vendor's perspective.
- Frequent contacts lead to not only better understanding but also develop into personal rapport with the customer on one to one basis, which is very important. This personal bond leads to an emotional relationship and is useful in leveraging business and can play a major

role in influencing business decisions. Many times it is said that large business decisions are as much a game of business relation as of technical specification, price, evaluation criteria and commercial conditions.

- Such business ambassadors can utilise the European concept of dating to build up a long-term relationship.
- Such type of arrangement can help in providing early and reliable market intelligence on company's short- and long-term business plans and it can be useful in deciding the marketing strategy.
- In a business no person wants arbitration or protracted disputes with the customer. At the same time in large projects, some difference of opinion or minor disputes are unavoidable. Business Ambassadors can help in ensuring that such disputes are not allowed to reach flash points and are resolved in the best tradition of 'give and take'.

Table 5.3 clarifies the differences between Traditional and Customer Centric Organisations.

Table 5.3 *Comparison of Traditional and Customer Centric Organisations*

Activity	*Traditional*	*Customer Centric*
Product and Service	Short-term focus Reactionary Approach	Long-term focus Pro-active Approach
Planning	Management by Objective	Customer driven
Performance	Bottom line Return to Investor	Customer Satisfaction Market Share Long-term profitability Quality Orientation
Attitude	• Customers are irrational and a pain in the neck • Customers are a bottleneck to Profitability • Take it or Leave it attitude	• Voice of customer is important • Customers are the means to Profitability • Courteous and responsive • Empathy and respect

PSYCHOLOGY OF CRM

During marketing and business development in the core sector, there are face-to-face meetings with the customer and the way a person responds can create a different impression on the customer and affect business decisions. People at the senior level want things in a particular way. Same information presented to them in a way they prefer will create positive results, while if it is presented in a way they dislike, it can create negative results. Hence, it is suggested that we study the personality of the customer and present the reply/information in the way he wants it to get better results. As a general rule one must devote adequate time for a first time customer to understand his likes, dislikes and habits to modulate response. This study is required both for first time customer and his officials.

The Supplier should also ensure that the customer has enough options to choose from and take business decisions. It may be a different matter that a knowledgeable vendor may have made an important contribution in his esteemed customer reaching the decision.

It should be remembered that market driven organisations are those which provide excellent quality and competitive product and services to satisfy the needs of a well-defined market segment.

SAMPLE CASE STUDY ON CRM

This case study has been conducted for a company 'XYZ' operating in the core sector. The questionnaire and sample replies received are as under:

Qualitative

S.No.	Question	Response
1.	What does the company's name XYZ bring to your mind?	• Timely Work Completion • Quality • High Performance
2.	Are you fully aware of the company's product profile and range of services it offers?	• Partially
3.	Do you associate any uniqueness with the Company? If so, please list them in order of priority.	• Timely Work Completion • Quality • Price
4.	Name the three most important prerequisites that a supplier should have and rate company XYZ and two other leading companies you feel are the best.	• Timely Project Completion • Technology Company XYZ is good on Timely Project completion but needs to improve in the other two areas. Company 'A' is excellent in Technology but is not up to the mark on the other two fronts. Company 'B' gives competitive prices but lags in technology. Its performance on the delivery front is better than 'A' but inferior to Company 'XYZ'
5.	How will you rate company XYZ on the following? • Technology • Price/Cost • Value Supplier	• Technology and Price—It needs to improve to provide value to Customers for the money they are paying.

Contd

<table>
<tr><th>S.No.</th><th>Question</th><th>Response</th></tr>
<tr><td>6.</td><td>How much importance do you accord to following factors while selecting vendor? Do you think that company XYZ meets your expectation? Is there any other company, which in your opinion, meets these requirements?
1. Price
2. Performance
3. Product and Service Quality
4. Engineering capability
5. Technology
6. Project Management
7. Timely Project Execution
8. Service
9. Ability to identify problems and offer solutions</td><td>C denotes the priority assigned by Customer. Companies are ranked on a 5 point scale, 1 indicating poor and 5 indicating an excellent rating. There are three companies, namely XYZ, A, B.
Item C XYZ A B
1 2 4 3 1
2 4 1 4 5
3 5 1 1 4
4 1 3 4 4
5 3 3 1 4
6 8 1 3 2
7 6 1 3 2
8 7 5 1 3
9 9 4 1 4</td></tr>
<tr><td>7.</td><td>What mode of buying do you think is best and will prefer:
1. Informal discussion and negotiation
2. Formal Tendering with Negotiation
3. Two Part Tendering (Technical and Price) with negotiations
4. Two Parts or Single part tendering without negotiations.
5. Formal Tendering with Reverse Auction through Net.</td><td>1. 10%
2. 30%
3. 25%
4. 25%
5. 10%</td></tr>
</table>

Contd

S.No.	Question	Response
8.	What percentage of market will be transacted in your business segment through net-based transactions five years from now?	• 25%
9.	What is the orientation of the company?	
	1. Product Orientation	1. 30%
	2. Project Orientation	2. 40%
	3. System Orientation	3. 30%
10.	Has the company been prompt in accepting mistakes and arranging replacements?	Only partially. This is the area in which the company needs to improve.

Engineering

The marks are assigned on a 10 point scale with 1 indicating poor and 10 indicating best.

S.No.	*Question*	*Customer Expectation (CE)*	*Customer Opinion on Supplier (S)*	*Benchmark (BM)*	*Difference Marks S – CE*	*Difference Marks S – BM*
1.	How do you rate the knowledge base in the company?	6	6	6	0	0
2.	Do you feel that Company XYZ is up-to-date on technology?	5	2	6	–3	–4
3.	Do you feel that the company gives priority to regular development work?	3	2	7	–1	–5
4.	Do you recall instances of the company's positive development?	3	2	7	–1	–5
5.	How do you rate the system engineering ability of XYZ?	8	5	6	–3	–1
6.	How do you feel about the company's project engineering ability?	7	6	8	–1	–2
7.	Does the company seek engineering deviations from contract after agreement?	9	3	8	–6	–5
8.	Do you feel that the company has adequate engineering staff?	4	2	6	–2	–4
9.	Does the company adhere to international standards?	7	5	9	–2	–4
10.	Does the company resolve technical issues on priority?	5	2	8	–3	–6
11.	Does the company submit drawings/documents and other calculations on time?	5	5	6	0	–1
12.	Total	62	40	77	–22	–37
13.	Total in percentage	56.36%	36.36%	70%	–35.48%	–48.05%

Response

S.No.	Question	Customer Expectation (CE)	Customer Opinion on Supplier (S)	Benchmark (BM)	Difference Marks S – CE	Difference Marks S – BM
1.	If the Customer gave a telephone ring, was the Receiver courteous and interested?	4	2	5	–2	–3
2.	If the Customer gave a telephone ring, and the Receiver was not present, did he return the call and enquire the reason for it?	3	2	5	–1	–3
3.	In the absence of the call the person who attended it, was he/she friendly and helpful or indifferent. Did they make an attempt to provide the information the caller was looking forward to?	3	2	3	–1	–1
4.	If the receiver was present, was he enthusiastic and positive? If not, which of the following course did he choose? • Simply informed that he was not dealing and hung up. • Informed the name and contact phone number/e-mail of concerned person. • Informed the name and contact detail of concerned person and offered to ensure that the caller receive the return call from him.	5	2	6	–3	–4
5.	Were the letters acknowledged promptly?	5	2	6	–3	–4
6.	Was the information provided in totality promptly?	4	3	3	–1	0

Contd

S.No.	Question	Customer Expectation (CE)	Customer Opinion on Supplier (S)	Benchmark (BM)	Difference Marks S – CE	Difference Marks S – BM
7.	Was the customer required to call higher up to expedite routine details?	4	2	4	–2	–2
8.	Has the supplier provided requisite priority?	8	3	7	–5	–4
9.	Was there a difference in attitude and response between Supplier's Marketing, Contract execution and Service Department (Many organisations suffer from this 180° change in approach between the departments)	6	3	5	–3	–2
10.	Were the calls made to top management officials in Supplier's organisation taken?	8	3	8	–5	–5
11.	Did the senior management of supplier spend reasonable time with their counterparts during their visit to supplier's office?	6	3	5	–3	–2
12.	Were the service experts sent on priority?	9	3	5	–6	–2
13.	Did the Supplier make an attempt to go out of the way to help the customer in SOS conditions by arranging man and material?	8	9	9	1	0
14.	During your visit to Supplier's works, were you required to arrange security passes? Was supplier's representative present at the reception to receive you?	5	4	7	–1	–3
15.	Were the engineering details and service manuals provided in time without follow up?	4	2	5	–2	–3
16.	Total	82	45	83	–37	–38
17.	Total in percentage	54.7%	30%	55.3%	–45.12%	–45.78%

Price

S.No.	Question	Customer Expectation (CE)	Customer Opinion on Supplier (S)	Benchmark (BM)	Difference Marks S – CE	Difference Marks S – BM
1.	Do you feel that the price charged by the company was reasonable?	9	3	6	–6	–3
2.	In your opinion how much premium company's product is worth based on the overall value it provided to you?	5	3	4	–2	–1
3.	Do you think that the company has done enough to optimise cost?	5	2	4	–3	–2
4.	Total	19	8	14	–11	–6
5.	Total in percentage	63.33%	26.66%	46.66%	–57.89%	–42.85%

Project Management and Timely Completion

S.No.	Question	Customer Expectation (CE)	Customer Opinion on Supplier (S)	Benchmark (BM)	Difference Marks S – CE	Difference Marks S – BM
1.	Has the company been able to meet its delivery commitment?	7	7	7	0	0
2.	Does the company need customer's follow up to meet its contractual commitment to timely completion?	5	7	7	2	0
3.	Does the company understand and appreciate the importance of timely project completion?	5	7	7	2	0
4.	Is there sufficient authority and empowerment at the working level to take timely decision?	4	7	7	3	0
5.	Does the company have effective project management system?	4	7	7	3	0
6.	How far is the company successful in implementing the single point concept?	3	8	8	4	0
7.	How effective is company's project co-ordination?	5	7	7	2	0
8.	Is the attitude of the company's official positive?	4	4	6	0	–2
9.	Total	37	54	56	17	–2
10.	Total in percentage	46.25%	67.50%	70.0%	+45.94%	–3.57%

Service

S.No.	Question	Customer Expectation (CE)	Customer Opinion on Supplier (S)	Benchmark (BM)	Difference Marks S – CE	Difference Marks S – BM
1.	How reasonable is the price of spares?	6	2	3	–4	–3
2.	Is the company prompt in supplying spares?	5	7	7	2	0
3.	Does the company respond positively to SOS messages from the Customer?	7	5	6	–2	–1
4.	Does the service department have adequate manpower?	5	3	7	–2	–4
5.	Are the service personnel well trained?	5	3	7	–2	–4
6.	Is the service department time conscious?	5	7	7	2	0
7.	Is the company fair and reasonable in meeting its warranty obligation?	5	4	8	–1	–4
8.	Are the service personnel having a positive attitude?	4	3	6	–1	–3
9.	Total	42	34	51	–8	–17
10.	Total in percentage	52.5%	42.5%	63.75%	–19.05%	–33.33%

Quality

S.No.	Question	Customer Expectation (CE)	Customer Opinion on Supplier (S)	Benchmark (BM)	Difference Marks S – CE	Difference Marks S – BM
1.	How do you rate the quality of engineering drawings?	5	4	7	–1	–3
2.	How is the quality of workmanship?	4	3	6	–1	–3
3.	How is the quality of manpower?	5	3	7	–2	–4
4.	How is the quality of tools and tackle?	4	3	6	–1	–3
5.	How is the quality of packing?	5	2	6	–3	–4
6.	How is the quality of site work?	4	3	5	–1	–2
7.	How is the aesthetics?	4	6	7	2	–1
8.	Does the company have International level Quality Assurance System?	5	5	7	0	–2
9.	Is the company complying with International Standards?	4	4	8	0	–4
10.	Total	40	33	59	–7	–26
11.	Total in percentage	44.44%	36.66%	65.55%	–17.5%	–44.06%

Customer Complaints

S.No.	Question	Customer Expectation (CE)	Customer Opinion on Supplier (S)	Benchmark (BM)	Difference Marks S – CE	Difference Marks S – BM
1.	Does the Company have an established mechanism to address customer complaints?	5	4	7	–1	–3
2.	Were the company officials serious and sincere in their approach?	4	5	8	1	–3
3.	How far has the company succeeded in resolving the issue?	6	4	8	–2	–4
4.	What was the time taken by the company for resolving the issue?	4	2	6	–2	–4
5.	Has the company kept monetary interest in mind while resolving the issue?	4	1	6	–3	–5
6.	Has the company capability to address and solve the problem?	5	2	7	–3	–5
7.	Were you satisfied with the equipment performance after the complaint had been attended to?	6	3	8	–3	–5
8.	Total	34	21	50	–13	–29
9.	Total in percentage	48.58%	30%	71.43%	–38.23%	–58%

Performance

S.No.	Question	Customer Expectation (CE)	Customer Opinion on Supplier (S)	Benchmark (BM)	Difference Marks S – CE	Difference Marks S – BM
1.	Had the equipment performed as per the contract?	6	6	8	0	–2
2.	Was the equipment performance better than the contract?	3	4	6	1	–2
3.	Was the performance deficient but promptly corrected by the vendor?	5	4	5	–1	–1
4.	Was the equipment performance deficient and could not be corrected by vendor, but rectified by other party?	4	3	6	–1	–3
5.	Was the performance deficient but corrected by the vendor by prompt replacement?	5	3	6	–2	–3
6.	Total	23	20	31	–3	–11
7.	Total in percentage	46.0%	40.0%	62.0%	–13.04%	–35.48%

Loyalty

S.No.	Question	Customer Response	
1.	If you have requirement of similar equipments earlier purchased by you from company XYZ, then which of the following alternatives will you opt for?		
	• Place order on XYZ company on negotiated basis?	• Totally Loyal	7%
	• Opt for tendering, but ultimately prefer to place order on Company XYZ?	• Mostly Loyal	15%
	• Opt for tendering, but give preference to Company XYZ?	• Marginally Loyal	16%
	• Strictly go by tendering and evaluation?	• Neutral	40%
	• Not like to go to Company XYZ at any cost?	• Lost	12%
	• Go to Company XYZ as there is no better option?	• Trapped	10%

SURVEY RESULT ANALYSIS

Customer Expectation and Behaviour

As per Quantitative analysis, customer gives the following priorities to various parameters:

Price	15%
Engineering	14%
Response	13%
Project Management and Time Consciousness	11%
Service	13%
Quality	11%
Complaint Redressal	12%
Performance	11%

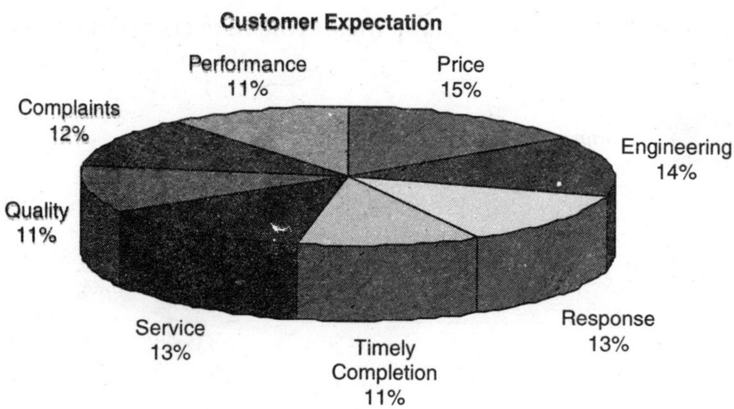

Fig. 5. 11 *Customer Expectation*

The above results are shown in Fig. 5.11 and are not very different from the qualitative opinion expressed by the same customers. The deviations can be between mark obtained by the company and customer expectations classified in the following three different categories. These are:

Excellent Deviations > –10%
Acceptable Deviations < –10% but > –20%
Moderate Deviations < –20% but > –30%
Serious Deviations < –30%

The summaries of deviations for the company are given in Table 5.4. This gives at a glance how close the company is in meeting customer expectations. In one case of timely completion of supply, it had really 'delighted' the customer by handsomely exceeding his expectations. The table also indicates the gap in various fields to become globally competitive.

The *Customer Satisfaction Index CSI* is 75.48 per cent which, by all accounts is very good. This is primarily due to the company exceeding customer expectation in Timely Project Completion and coming very close to meeting it in Service, Quality and Performance.

The Excellence Index or the Competitive Index is 61.58 per cent.

A good 40 per cent of the customers are inclined to settle business through negotiations after evaluating the market. This indicates that their perception of the supplier is going to play a major role in decision making process.

Table 5.4 *Summary of Results*

S.No.	*Question*	*Customer Expectation (CE) in %*	*Customer Opinion on Supplier (S) in %*	*Benchmark (BM) in %*	*Difference Marks – CE in %*	*Difference Marks – BM in %*
1.	Engineering	56.36%	36.36%	70%	–35.48%	–48.05%
2.	Response	54.7%	30.0%	55.3%	–45.12%	–45.78%
3.	Price	63.33%	26.66%	46.66%	–57.89%	–42.85%
4.	Project Management and Timely Completion	46.25%	67.50%	70%	+45.94%	–3.57%
5.	Service	52.5%	42.5%	63.75%	–19.05%	–33.33%
6.	Quality	44.44%	36.66%	65.55%	–17.5%	–44.06%
7.	Customer Complaints	48.58%	30%	71.43%	–38.23%	–58%
8.	Performance	46%	40%	62%	–13.04%	–35.48%

Company Image

The qualitative analysis reflects that the company enjoys the image of timely supplier of quality and high performance products. This image is revalidated by quantitative results as summarised in Table 5.4. The company's performance on Service front is also reasonable. The company had high image for time consciousness

Summary at a Glance

Figures 5.12 to 5.16 show at a glance the relative position of the company in various fields in comparison to customer expectation and Benchmark.

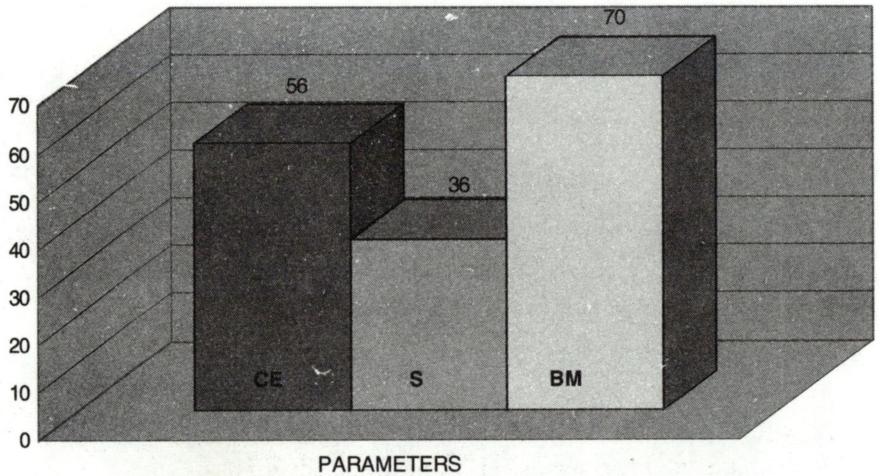

Fig. 5.12 *Engineering*

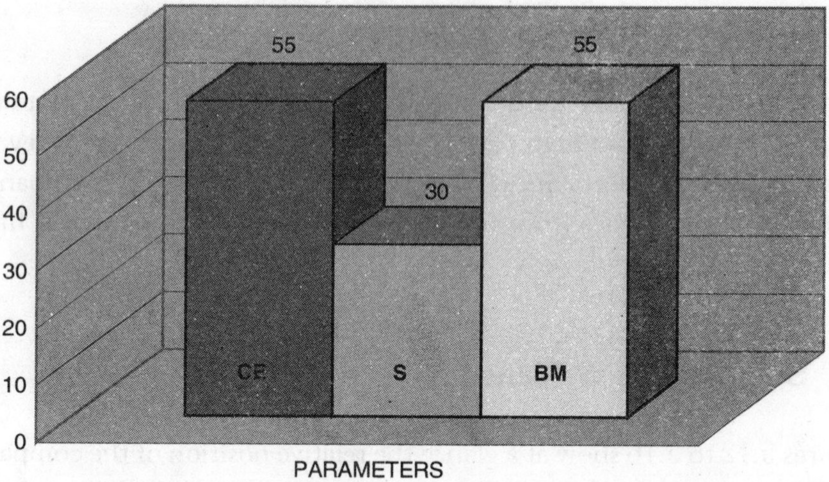

Fig. 5.13 *Response*

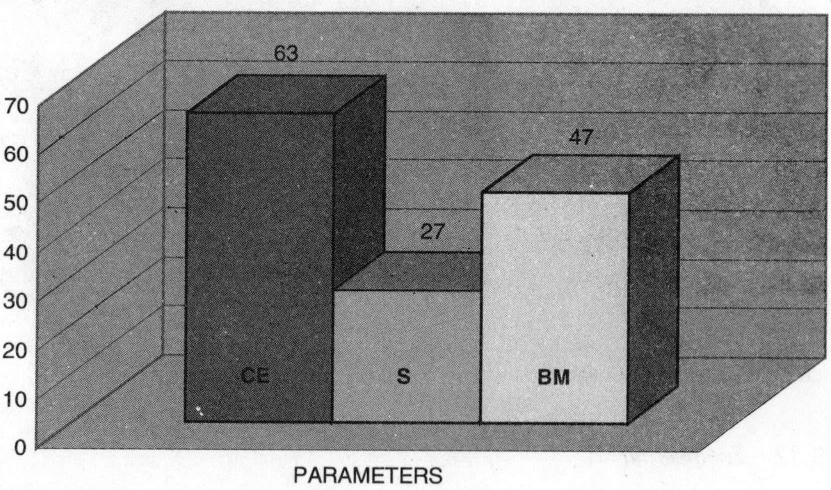

Fig. 5.14 *Price*

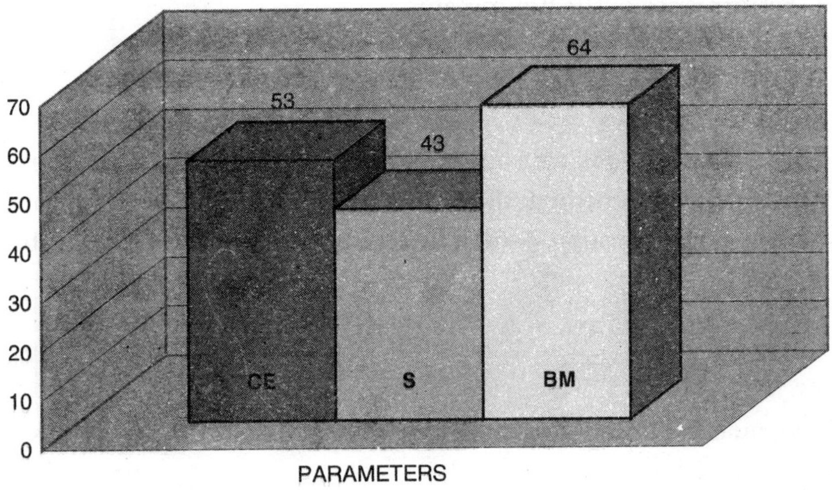

Fig. 5.15 *Service*

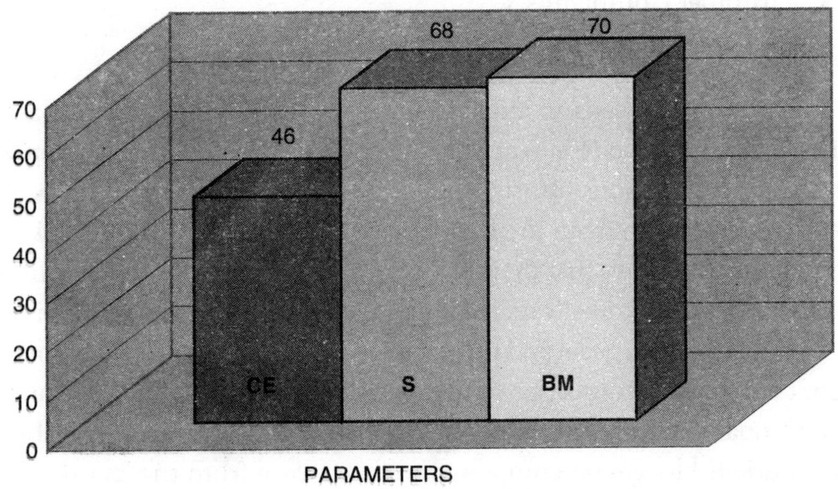

Fig. 5.16 *Timely Completion*

Strength

The qualitative and quantitative feedback clearly bring out the company's strength and weakness. The strong fields are:

- Project Management and Timely Supply

- Performance of the Equipments
- Quality of equipment
- Service

These strong points can be leveraged to provide competitive edge/ additional premium through differentiation. The Company is one of the best globally in timely supply and is uniformly recognised for this attribute.

Weakness

Both the qualitative and quantitative analyses bring out the weaknesses of the company. They are:

- Price
- Response
- Customer Complaints
- Engineering

The company needs to make serious efforts in this direction as its deviation is beyond moderate capacity. It appears that company management had not devoted serious efforts in this direction in the past. This is also reflected in deviation from the Benchmark as can be seen from Table 5.4. This table also indicates that though the company is within acceptable limits of deviation from customer expectation in Quality, Performance and Service, but it is far behind its peers and until it takes corrective measures, it can fast lose out to its peers. It must be remembered that customer expectation is a dynamic quantity and can change very fast depending upon the availability in the market. Hence, no company can take solace from the fact that it is within acceptable limits of customer expectation.

CUSTOMER LOYALTY PROFILE

Figure 5.17 shows the loyalty profile of the customer. Only 7 per cent of the customers are totally loyal against 12 per cent lost and another 10 per cent who, in any case, are feeling suffocated. Sixteen per cent of the customers in the marginally loyal category will give company preference or first right of rejection of counter offer. But what the company should really worry about is that there is a large segment of 40 per cent customers, who are going to choose the supplier on merit and the company must meet their expectations and must excel compared to other competitors. The company must worry about customers in the 10 per cent segment that are feeling trapped or suffocated. It must identify reasons for their feeling and address them. It is much easier to retrieve their lost faith and loyalty than those 12 per cent who have been lost.

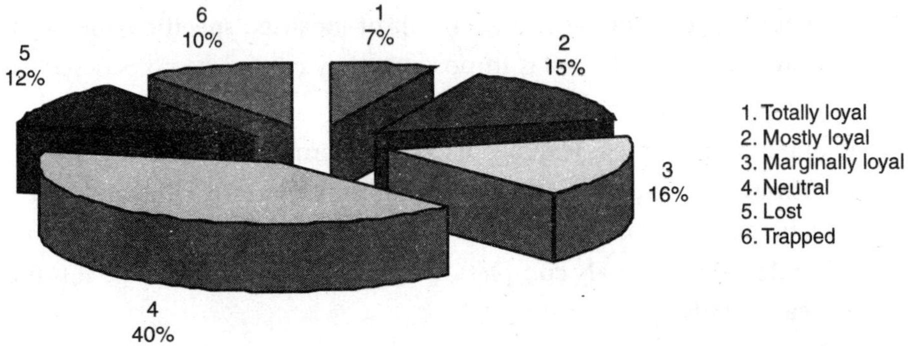

Fig. 5.17 *Customer Loyalty Profile*

ACTION PLAN

The above analysis clearly brings out the company's strong and weak points and deviation from the customer expectation and the best in the area. The company must chart out its action plan that should consider the following:

- Identify reasons responsible for deficient performance in the weak areas and prepare a plan for improvement. In case the company had already put into operation its action plan based on earlier similar survey, then it must identify reasons for failure of the action plan and take corrective measures to rectify the deficiencies of its earlier action plan.
- It should identify grey areas where it is either close to Benchmark or Customer Satisfaction but deviation is high in relation to other parameter, as this is an early warning signal for future problems. The

large deviation from Customer Satisfaction indicates a potential unsatisfied demand and business prospect for a Competitor who can meet it. Deviation from Benchmark indicates loss of competitive edge and business leveraging capability.

- Evaluation of specific comments and suggestions by different customers.
- Meeting with a customer who has given strong negative comments on a subject or where his comments are not in line with the opinion expressed by majority of customers. Most of the time it is seen that such abstract comments are a result of localised specific issues and though their resolution is important, they cannot be considered as reflecting the general trend.
- The company must leverage its strong competencies to expand its business and retain Market accepted differentiation. This can lead to higher business share and profits. The current survey gives the company a major plus in timely completion of delivery and project and it is no mean strength.

Human Aspect of Action Plan

The biggest challenge to change in any field is to convince human assets of the need to change. It require herculean efforts to convince the people that what they are doing over the years needs to be changed in order to create more value to the customer and bring more returns to the company and them. The customer dissatisfaction and complaints occur due to the actions of organisation and people working with it. They need to change their thinking and behaviour to bring changes in product, project and service. Thus, the first and foremost requirement is to convince people to accept change. It is to be appreciated that people in every organisation are busy with their allotted normal work and "Need to Change for Better Customer Satisfaction", will put that much extra burden on them. Thus, in order to achieve best results, it is necessary that they are convinced first and are made drivers of change. The company can involve them in finding creative solutions to customer satisfaction problems. It can appoint Cross Functional Teams (CFTs) to deliberate on various aspects and suggest creative solutions.

The situation may demand training and reorientation of employees to impress upon them the positive aspects and benefits that may accrue. These efforts are necessary to make an organisation 'Customer Oriented' and to develop a culture of 'Customer Satisfaction' within the organisation. The cultural change is essential because this alone ensures the success of the action plan.

TRACKING THE CHANGE

It is necessary that such surveys are done regularly, maybe at intervals of three years. It is then advisable to compare the current feedback with earlier surveys as they can provide in-depth dynamic information on different aspects like:

- Changing customer needs and perception.
- Effectiveness of earlier action plans.
- Information on strategy being adopted by competitors and their effectiveness.
- Reassessment of relative competitive edge of different suppliers.

Table 5.5 details the results of the customer survey done earlier and now and the relative change in the position of various parameters. This table indicates some interesting results that can be summarised as under:

- *Customer Needs* These have increased in the area of engineering, quality, equipment performance and service with the last one showing a steep increase. This is natural as the market is becoming more technology and performance-driven and professionalism in the service sector is increasing. This indicates a growing business opportunity in this sector. The massive positive jump indicates that the trend is likely to continue. There is reduction in the expectation on price and time consciousness, indicating that customer today gives more preference to technology and service and is willing to compromise on price and delivery time to have good performing equipment and a supplier who can provide long-term reliable service. With the change in time, customers are demanding faster service.

Table 5.5 *Customer Needs—Changing Trends and Performance of Company XYZ and other Competitors*

S.No.	Parameter	Survey–2			Survey–1			Deviation Between Survey 1 and 2		
		CE	S – CE	S – BM	CE	S – CE	S – BM	CE	S – CE	S – BM
1.	Price	63	–58	–43	70	–40	–38	–7	18	–5
2.	Engineering	56	–35	–45	46	–38	–49	12	3	4
3.	Response	55	–45	–46	45	–35	–30	10	–10	–11
4.	Project Management and Timely Completion	46	+46	–3	40	–25	–30	–5	76	27
5.	Service	53	–19	–33	30	–10	–20	23	–9	–13
6.	Quality	44	–17	–44	40	–20	–38	4	3	–6
7.	Complaint Management	49	–38	–58	40	–28	–38	9	–10	–20
8.	Performance	46	–13	–35	38	–25	–38	8	25	3
9.	CSI		75.48%			36.68%			+38.80	
10.	EI or CI		61.58%			31.30%			+30.28	

- *Supplier and other Competitors* The company's strategy in improving its position on project management and timely supply has met with tremendous success and has today made the company practically the benchmark on the subject. This is also recognised by the customer and has become the company's major strength for competitive edge. The company has also made improvements at a faster pace than customer expectations in the area of service and quality but other competitors have improved at a faster rate leaving company behind. In the area of Complaint management, the company is a laggard and focused attention is required in this area. The company seems to have entirely forgotten the cost optimisation part and, today, it is in much worse condition than it was at the time of last survey.
- *CSI and EI* The Company has more than doubled its Customer Satisfaction Index and also improved its Excellence Index, a measure of competitive edge, by about 100 per cent. This indicates the overall success of its business strategy and corrective action plan put into action after the last survey but as discussed above, there are major fields where the company has fallen behind and a new strategy is required to check this decline.

* *Supplier and ... Coordination*: The company's strategy in improving its position on project management and timely supply has met with tremendous success and has today made the company practically the benchmark on the subject. This is also recognised by the customer and has become the company's major strength for competitive edge. The company has also made improvements at a faster pace than customer expectations in the area of service and quality but other competitors have improved at a faster rate leaving company behind. In the area of Complaint management, the company is a laggard and focused attention is required in this area. The company seems to have entirely forgotten the cost optimisation part and today it is in much worse condition than it was at the time of last survey.
* *CSI and ECI*: The Company has more than doubled its Customer Satisfaction Index and also improved its Excellence Index, a measure of competitive edge, by about 10 per cent. This indicates the overall success of its business strategy and corrective action plan put into action after the last survey but as discussed above there are many fields where the company has fallen behind and a new strategy is required to check this decline.

6

Market Research and Business Forecast

Why Market Research?
Role of Market Research
Market Research and Customer Relationship Management
Market Research Activities
Compilation and Analysis of Data
Extrapolation of Research Results
Report Preparation
Conclusions and Action Plan

6

WHY MARKET RESEARCH?

It is often said that 'forewarned' is 'forearmed'. In order to formulate a marketing strategy or business plan, any organisation requires information regarding market demand, business environment, customer behaviour, his decision making process and competition. Its success depends on his ability to interpret these signals. Despite the emphasis on Understanding the Customer, many companies and the whole business segment fail to understand their market. Some companies ignore important customers in favour of marginal ones. Some fail to predict or even understand when the market has peaked. Some know the market but fail to reach it, and some launch the product with an imaginary market.

Market Research is a tool that is used in professional decision making. There are three basic parameters any organisation wants to know to formulate and finalise its business plan. They are:

- Market Demand
- Customer Behaviour
- Competition

A company can do very little about the above parameters and the best approach it can adopt is to predict their behaviour in the short to medium term and keep itself in readiness to meet this predicted behaviour. The above parameters mainly depend on:

- World economic climate in general and that of the nation in particular
- The political climate
- Technology development

- Competitor's Approach and Progress
- Predicted performance in various sectors of economy
- Effect of changes and likely changes in taxation and government policies which can have a major impact on the market

The above information provide necessary basic details to the company to take well considered business decisions. The importance of this information can be compared with the two solutions—one in which a human being walks with his eyes open and the other in which he walks with his eyes closed. The outcome is well known. Market Research is like the eye to the business strategy. The business decisions taken with the second approach are more likely to make company land in a catastrophe.

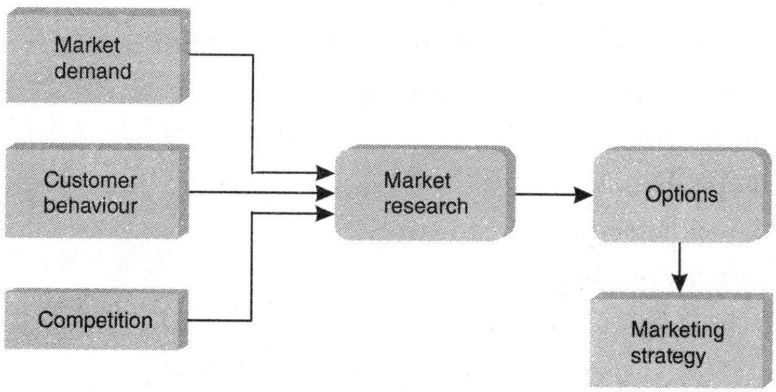

Fig. 6.1 *Market Research and Strategy*

Market Research is a tool that provides the company with the basic data to enable it to arrive at a well considered business decision. It helps an organisation in setting its business objectives, goals and business targets for itself and its executives and formulates and decides suitable business strategy to achieve them. It also allows a company to test any new idea in the market. It also gives feedback on the image and performance of the company as perceived by the market. Thus, market research provides the data for correct decision making and it also reduces the risk of such decisions. It effectively reduces the uncertainty in decision making. Even when the business plan is under execution, market research can provide necessary feedback to monitor the progress and correctness of the decision and type of mid-course correction to be applied.

ROLE OF MARKET RESEARCH

Market Research can provide a variety of information to an organisation on market expectation, market's predicted behaviour, customer behaviour and reasons thereof, type, quality and severity of competition. The type of information can include the following:

Market Demand

- Behaviour of Economy in short to medium term
- Infrastructure Sector Growth Data
- Market Size
- Market Trends
- Market Potential and Growth
- Elasticity of Market
- Technology

Customer Related Information

- Customer Perception of Economy and Growth Plan
- Customer's Opinion on various suppliers
- Customer's Thrust on Technology and Services
- Customer Decision making Process
- Customer Feedback on Supplier
- Customer Preferences
- Customer Perception
- Critical Success Factors

Competitor's Plan and Strategy

- Competitor's perception of environment and trends
- Competitor's perception of Supplier and his strength and weakness
- Competitor's growth plan and strategy
- Competitor's technology Status and plans
- Competitor's status on services
- SWOT analysis of various players in the field

MARKET RESEARCH AND CUSTOMER RELATIONSHIP MANAGEMENT

One of the biggest applications of Market Research is in the field of Customer Relationship Management. It helps a supplier to have feedback on his performance, get different customer's opinion on it and about how they rate different suppliers in the field. It also provides an opportunity to the organisation to revalidate whether strong and weak points it had attributed to itself are also shared by its customers and the kind of difference that exists and reasons for it. These issues have been discussed in more detail in Chapter 5 on 'Customer Relationship Management' and are hence not taken up here. It also helps the organisation arrive at 'Customer Satisfaction Index.' It can give feedback on the following subjects:

- Satisfaction level of customers with the company in general and more specifically with its technology, quality, service, performance and its adherence to the completion schedule and its ability to re-deploy its resources to meet emergency.
- Identify strong points for leveraging and weak points for improvements to further increase customer satisfaction
- Create data bank on the competitors and benchmark them as per customer feedback.
- To identify major areas in which the company is ahead of its peers and where it is lagging behind.
- Price Sensitivity
- Market Share and reasons for its trends

- Feedback and background information on potential customers
- Information on horizontal and vertical integration
- Reasons for poor profitability
- Reasons for typical customer preferences
- Possible business solutions to various problems
- Basic data for future growth

It may be appreciated that though in infrastructure projects, the organisation and its officials are always face to face with customers, rarely are negative feedbacks given across the table. At best negative feedbacks are passed on as suggestions for improvement. Similarly, no customer in reality gives positive feedback fully because he is afraid that this will weaken his position in negotiations. It is therefore necessary to have a professional market research agency to conduct the survey and communicate professional feedback, as many customers may not like their identities to be revealed.

Illustration

A company, which was in the business of capital intensive goods, was having a specific service department to take care of needy customers and extend them timely help. The department had a number of experts in different fields and the company used to depute them to customer's site to attend the complaints. Since it was not possible for the company to have a large number of experts, many times when complaints used to get bunched, the company could not send its experts immediately as they were busy attending other works at different sites. The company in such cases would receive distress repeat calls from these customers as their production was suffering. The company always felt that its 'Service after Sales' was the weakest department bringing it a bad name. At the same time the company felt that its manufacturing department was doing exceedingly well by maintaining time schedule as far as deliveries were concerned. It has also many times compressed deliveries by reducing the process time to accommodate the delays of its other departments.

Incidentally influenced by the modern management concept of 'Customer Perception Survey', it hired a professional agency to conduct a survey. The Market Research Company did an exhaustive work and results were highly surprising. It reveals that in spite of delay in deputation of experts even on SOS call, the customers were extremely

Contd

satisfied. This was due to the fact that whenever the experts attended; they did a through job. They were quick to identify the problem and suggest easy and permanent solutions. They were able to understand the problems of the customers and were able to mould their work to suit his requirements.

On the other hand the company found that the manufacturing department, which the company was considering their star performer, had received the least appreciation from the customers. Some of the customers even felt that the department and its work culture were the reasons for most of their site problems as in order to adhere to contractual schedules, the department had resorted to a number of short cuts affecting the quality of the work.

For the company the feedback was naturally revealing and an eye-opener.

MARKET RESEARCH ACTIVITIES

In market research the following activities are involved:

- Identification of objectives
- Planning
- Data/Information Collection
- Data Analysis
- Conclusions
- Action Plan Formulation
- Report Preparation and Recommendations

Objectives

Before a market research is undertaken, it is necessary to define the basic objectives of the work. These objectives can include parameters already discussed earlier (*refer* Role of Market Research; Market Research and Customer Relationship Management). The objective identification is necessary to give focused direction and approach to the next phase of market research, i.e. data collection. It also has a profound impact on the methodology, sample size, questionnaire and other techniques adopted for the work. While defining the objectives, it is necessary to ensure that they are focused, clear and properly sectionalised.

Planning

After fixing the objectives the next stage is to identify activities and plan for them.

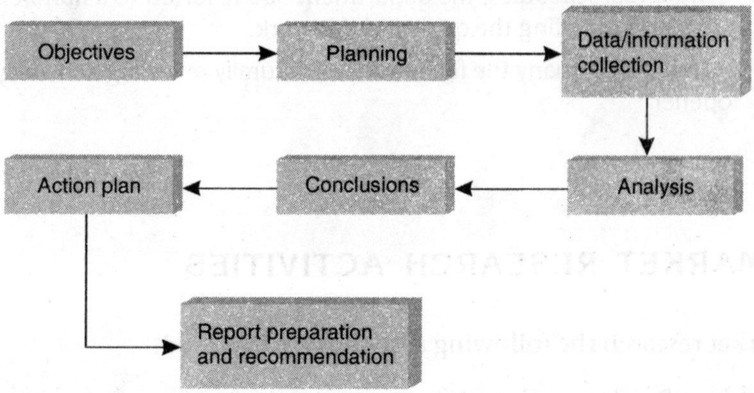

Fig. 6.2 *Flow Chart of Market Research*

Planning activities include the following:

- Identify time-horizon if research is for market trends and behaviour
- Identify information required
- Decide methodology
- Budget
- Time Schedule
- Analysis method

The kind of information required depends on the objectives. If the objective is to find feedback on the company's performance and to evaluate its performance against peers and to identify areas requiring improvements, then the type of planning activity required will be as discussed in Chapter 5, 'Customer Relationship Management'.

Illustrations

Suppose the objective is to establish market demand for use of 'variable frequency drive' (AC Motors with step less speed control), then the specific information to be collected will be:

- Total market demand for AC Motors
- Total Market demand as a percentage of motor demand necessitating variable speed application
- Range of control/speed variation required
- What would be the delivery requirement?
- Expected Prices
- Different methodology available for AC motor speed control and their critical appraisal on technical, cost and operation aspects.
- Any negative perception the market may have on this product
- The kind of service after sales and the spares requirement that the market may require.
- What kind of inclination the customer will have if he is using any other method for speed control for changing to this method? What kind of efforts needs to be made for changing the customer from other methodology to this methodology? Should the company have focused presentation to each and every prospective customer or should it have regional conferences to highlight it to invited customers?

Another example can be the market research to set up 'power project to run on municipal waste'. The type of information the researcher will be looking forward to can be:

- What kind of municipal waste is produced?
- Quantity of waste produced.
- Composition of municipal waste in bio degradable and non degradable waste
- Type of waste and its calorific value
- Method of waste collection and its transportation
- Storage facility for waste
- Unskilled labour availability and charges for removing stones, plastic and other similar material on regular basis.
- Market realisation feasible for use of bio-fertiliser which will be produced as a by-product of the process
- Readiness and charges of utilities to purchase power generated on long-term basis.

Contd

- Effect on environment and government or any other incentives, which may be available.
- Taxation and other benefits like soft loan, etc. prevailing in other countries, which can be lobbied in the host country.
- Are any other projects being run or contemplated and, if so, feedback on their performance?
- Long-term viability of such projects.
- Identification of technology and its availability.
- Expected life cycle of the project, and technology suitability for likely difference in municipal waste composition.

The above list is not exhaustive but is of indicative type to make the subject more clear. It may be possible that after conducting market research, information on many of the identified points may not be fully available or the research itself may bring out some more issues on which further information may be needed. It is also possible that one may not draw a very exhaustive list of information required thinking that unnecessary information may lead to higher expenditure, and result may not be commensurate with it, or may not allow the work to be completed in allotted time.

Data and Information Collection

There are two methods of data collection. They are:

- Desk Research
- Field Survey

Desk Research

This is the first step in any market research activity. It consists of collection of published information and a study of it. It can also mean downloading of information from the Internet. The major advantages of desk research are that it is relatively cheap, requires comparatively less time and does not require elaborate structure or manpower. Some of the research information which can easily be provided by desk research is as under:

Environment Details This is macro level information and is required in all type of business research. The movement of GDP, Index of Industrial Production, the growth rates in Basic goods, Capital goods industry and sectarian growth and their effect on the business can easily be collected through desk research. This can also extrapolate the demand behaviour in the short-term based on the expected behaviour of these parameters.

The economic data are not only available in published literature but can also be searched and downloaded from the net. Desk research can also provide specific background information that may be necessary for the work. Apart from information of general nature, specific information on micro levels are now available on Internet, Research Journals and in other published literature.

Market Trends and Size For different types of projects and specific products, market trends, size and other useful data are available in related journals and connected magazines. For example in case of electrical motors, market size demand and trends information is regularly brought out by IEEMA. Similar information on gas turbines and competitor's details are available in GAS TURBINE magazine. Fertiliser Association of India publishes regular information on Fertilisers. Similarly, National Confederation of Sugar Industry publishes information on sugar.

Information on Customers and Competitors If a supplier wants information on economic conditions, business plans and last five to ten years, performance of customers, they can be easily accessed through published documents/ business magazines/newspaper analysis or through internet. Telephones can also be used to collect information about similar industries operating in similar business segments.

Keeping track of competitors is very important. Information on their balance sheet and other economic factors, reference list, technical information and other major activities, their corporate plan can be ascertained from the web page easily.

Many newspapers and business magazines regularly publish company profile and critical analysis of their business plan. They publish sector information also. Similarly, companies bring out advertisements highlighting their achievements.

Investment reports on companies can also provide useful insight. Additionally, they also contain critical analysis and information. It is possible that much of the above information may be sponsored and not be entirely true but critical analysis of factual data, which are also available, can provide the necessary objectivity.

Market Behaviour For some of the cyclical industries like paper, cement, etc. desk research provides an ideal opportunity to predict the up and down cycle of the industry and consequently their demands and trends. Most of the companies take their investment decisions based on the projected cyclic trends and on early confirmation of their start. This gives them a lot of opportunity advantage. The projected analysis also indicates how long the good business cycle will last and informed companies stop making investment sufficiently in advance of projected downturn in the cycle.

It is also common knowledge that slow growth in GDP indicates the start of recession. Generally, in the core sector demand contraction takes about a year to set in after it has shown early signs by means of flat or negative growth in basic economic indicator.

Assistance in Fieldwork—Preparatory Another assistance that a desk research can provide is in undertaking preparatory work for Field Survey. The assistance can be rendered in following areas:

- Sample selection
- Questionnaire preparation
- Fieldwork plan

For any survey to be conducted, it is not possible to interview each and every representative of that segment as it costs both money and time. The result is not very different if a portion of that segment is only surveyed. This is referred as survey by sample. The sample size and type are chosen on the basis of desk research so that the result is fairly representative of actual conditions and error possibilities are kept as low as possible.

Every field survey requires a questionnaire which needs to be so designed as to give required information to meet research objectives. The question needs to be simple. Desk research helps in completing such type of work.

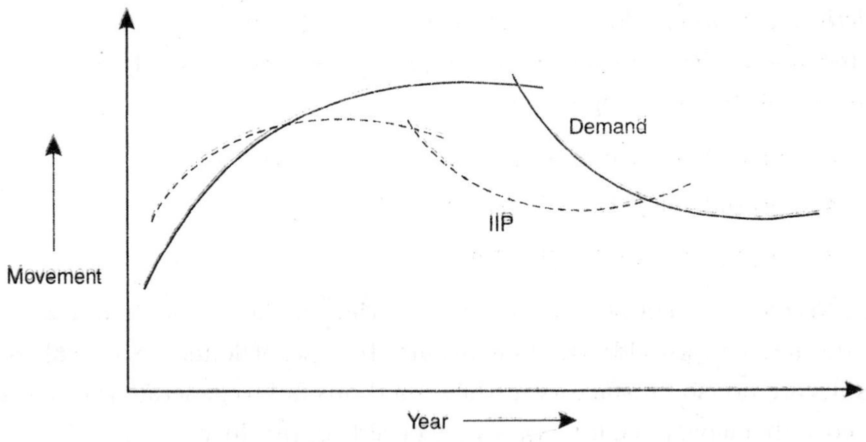

Fig. 6.3 *Demand Prediction from IIP; IIP—Index of Industrial Production*

Field Survey

Though desk research can provide a substantial amount of information, it can suffer from the big disadvantage that it does not provide any information where emotional touch and sensitivity is concerned. It is a dry piece of information without heart. Naturally desk research cannot provide complete market feedback on customer perception, attitude, behaviour, the way he thinks and other related subjects connected with Customer Relationship Management. When we talk to other party one type of communication takes place from the word spoken by each party, and the other communication is through body language, especially facial expression, which expresses the innermost feeling of an individual. They provide the reason and the intensity of the feeling of the communicator, which plays a more important role in the matter. The total message can only be understood and real picture will only emerge by analysing the messages received by both channels

The other advantage of the field survey is that it provides first hand information. It is therefore accurate and depicts the correct picture. The approach is focused. The information is complete and is objective and cannot be influenced unlike information available in articles and magazines, which can be biased and sponsored. Chances of failure or misrepresentation in field survey are negligible. In the core sector, where the number of customers is limited, field survey can provide highly useful information.

Methodology of Fieldwork Fieldwork basically consists of collecting pre-determined information from the respondents. This can be done through any one of the following means:

- Through letter/e-mail/fax
- Through telephone discussion
- Through personal interview

Needless to mention, the personal interview method, though the costliest of the lot, will provide the best results. In case of letter/fax/e-mail, the results are not so satisfactory as these methods fail to generate the type of interest that a personal interview may be able to produce.

Sample Selection In fieldwork it is not possible to conduct a survey with each and every customer. It is therefore necessary to restrict the number of parties. However it must be ensured that the selected parties represent the business segment, which is being surveyed, so that the results so obtained can be representative of this segment and can be extrapolated to reflect the total opinion within acceptable limits of error. This will ensure that both cost and time requirements are kept to the minimum without seriously jeopardising the accuracy.

Sample Size Sample size depends on the type of work and the accuracy desired. It is often seen that quality of fieldwork increases with increase in sample size till it reaches an optimum level. Any further increase in sample size will result in decrease in quality as detailed in Fig. 6.4. Another criterion for fixing the sample size is accuracy of result. It is natural that samples are randomly chosen. The higher the sample size, the higher the accuracy. However, it must be clearly understood that in an infrastructural sector, the type of customers should also be kept in mind while selecting samples. If a customer contributes a high percentage of business to the company and if he is not selected, the results will not be representative. Thus, in the core sector, random selection of sample will not be appropriate. Samples need to be taken from all business segments and it has to be ensured that high value customers are definitely chosen. Such type of sampling alone can give accuracy and quality to the work.

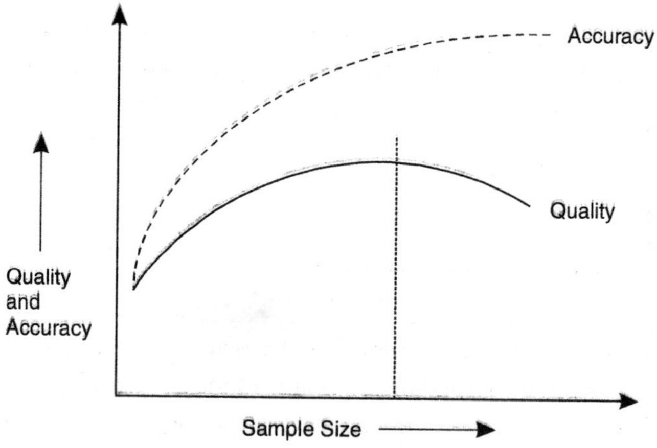

Fig. 6.4 *Quality and Sample Size*

Selection of Person to be Interviewed Having selected the samples and identified the organisations for survey, the next major issue to be addressed is who should be the person for interview. He should be one who can be reached and can contribute positively and objectively to the survey and must be connected with the work for which the survey is being conducted. For example, if the survey is to find out operating convenience and feedback on company's product, then naturally one must interview the operating personnel apart from the supervisor. One can also select the in-charge of the works where the operation is taking place to get overall picture.

One should interview such officials also who either take decisions or influence the decisions. They can be from the purchase department, operations department, engineering department or project department. Selection of right person is essential as it affects the quality and accuracy of information.

Questionnaire In order to have a structured field survey, ease in analysis and focused information collection, it is always advisable to prepare a questionnaire. Such questionnaire is useful irrespective of the mode of survey, i.e. it is required whether the survey is done by e-mail or telephone or by personal interview. It also ensures that all questions required are put up and in proper order.

A sample questionnaire is included below. Response is shown on 10 points scale. (One can chose any scale). The figure 1 indicates poor and

10 indicates the best rating. One can also use five or three point scale as may be deemed fit. The higher the length of the scale, the greater the accuracy that can be expected in the results.

Table 6.1 *Typical Interview Questionnaire*

S.No.	Questions	Mark Awarded
1.	How effective is the single window co-ordination of the company?	4
2.	How do you rate the engineering capability of the company?	7
3.	How do you rate the project management of the company?	3
4.	How do you rate the Quality Assurance System of the company?	6
5.	How do you rate the Facilities available at the company?	8
6.	How do you rate the Service Department of the company?	7
7.	Do you believe that the company normally honours its contract completion schedule?	5
8.	Do you believe that the company has resources and will to re-deploy them to meet contract completion schedule?	4
9.	Do you believe that the company gives more priority to customer needs than to its own requirements?	3
10.	Do you believe that the company has transparent and professional working system?	4
11.	How is the customer response system of the company?	6
12.	Does the company require regular follow up for doing work it should do in normal course?	5
13.	How do you rate the human resources of the company regarding capability?	8
14.	How do you rate the attitude and behaviour of human resources of the company?	4
15.	Do you find marked difference between company's personnel attitude/approach from department to department?	7
16.	Do you find people arrogant, indifferent?	2
17.	Do you think that the price charged by the company is reasonable?	8
18.	Have you ever found difficulty in contacting the desired person?	6
19.	Would you place a repeat order on the company?	8

Given above are just some of the sample questions. The questionnaire can be divided into specific sections and each section can contain five questions. It should however be ensured that the questionnaire is not very big as the respondents will start losing interest with the big list and the outcome of the exercise will be affected. It is also possible that one can use suggestions like Exceptional, Very good, Good, Fair and Poor instead of a rating scale of 1 to 10. In such a case the questionnaire is referred to as pre coded questionnaire. Normally, it is usual to provide respondents to give suggestions. This ensures that if they are feeling strongly about some thing then they find an outlet to initiate. The questionnaire should be flexible enough to enable respondent to give feedback on the situation with the force they want to put in the reply and meet the basic objective of the research. The questions should be precise, straightforward and should not be liable for misinterpretation. The question should not lead the respondent to a suggested answer like "Do you agree that company A is an outstanding company". It must also be seen that questions are not difficult to understand and should not lead to unwanted responses.

Interview Interviews are an old and time-tested methodology for collecting the information. Though such types of interviews are done very commonly in the consumer sector, they are more important in the core sector as the habits, buying behaviour, attitude, thinking, expectations and critical factors vary widely from customer to customer. The opinion of two customers may differ totally. Personal Interviews in the core sector are limited to face to face interviews only, while in the consumer sector, the interviews can be on internet, telephone or through questionnaire mailed. But in the core sector face to face meetings are highly desirable as most of the opinions an individual forms is born out of his experience with dealing with the individual of the supplier's organisation or with the equipment and it is necessary that the background information is discussed in detail along with the emotions and sentiments attached with it to appreciate the basic cause of the opinion formation and to understand the reasons behind the need of the customer.

Advantages of Interview Interviews have a lot of advantages as discussed below:

- Observation is one of the most important ways of collecting basic information. During personal interview, the researcher can collect major information on organisation, culture and practices, orientation, attitudes, value system and even about decision making process. As the interviewer enters the office premises, the treatment received at the reception, security guard and the way they conduct themselves can tell a lot. Small things do matter. If a visitor is allowed entry without even his name being recorded or pass being issued, be sure the organisation gives least priority to systems and procedures and may even be working on ad hoc work culture and decision making can also be following similar trends. If you are waiting at the reception and are suddenly extended a cup of tea, the conclusions are clear that you are dealing with a cultured organisation, and one can expect it to be a value-based company. The type of literature kept at the reception in the waiting room reflects the taste of the company. Some of the companies only employ security guards at the reception and it reflects their outlook.

At some places, the visitor is not permitted to go inside and is taken to the conference room only. This indicates that the company believes that it has something to protect and would like to maintain confidentiality. It is also an indication of secretive nature of the company.

- The second advantage is one can closely study the body language of the respondent while talking to him and can arrive at suitable conclusions. Sir Arthur Conan Doyle, in his famous creation of Sherlock Holmes had observed that the '*Face reacts faster than the Brain*'; hence, the body language and facial expressions give as much information as the spoken words. They can also tell the intensity and passion of respondent and also whether the feedback can be taken at face value or there is more to it. It provides authentic and unfiltered details.
- Personal interview can provide better feel and understanding. The way words are spoken or gestures are made indicate the depth of the respondent's commitment and desire to communicate. The higher the intensity, the more important the feedback becomes for the supplier organisation. In such conversation in addition to organisation's feeling, his personal position also gets reflected and this makes the feedback important from Customer Relationship Management point.
- There are information which can not be conveyed through written communications or in a formal way and can only be put across while

speaking. The interviewer can then record the information appropriately. Many customers do not consider it civilised to pass on negative feedback. An interview with a third party provides this opportunity to pass on the feedback without revealing the identity. Such types of feedbacks are extremely important from the vendor's point of view. The interview also provides the customer an outlet to let off steam. It is often seen that people who feel strongly become more than helpful after they have unburdened themselves.

- The information received will be accurate and comprehensive as the interview provides an opportunity to ask supplementary questions to make the point clear. One can even collect details and focused information of choice during the interview and copies of documents if so required. This provides the interviewer an opportunity to ensure that he has fully grasped the communication and is clear about the subject.
- The interview also provides him an opportunity to modify and remodel his approach or put more stress on identified areas to ensure the success of the mission. It is often seen that if the questionnaire is wrong, the respondent become bored or can become less attentive after some time and then he loses interest in the exercise. If the respondent is busy, the questionnaire will not get the attention it deserves. It can also happen that the question or the spirit behind it is not properly appreciated by the respondent and, as a result, his reply can be tangential. The interviewer, can on the other hand, ensure that the person is always kept interested in the proceedings and the questions and the reasons behind it can always be explained to him. If the respondent's personality is egoistic, then a whole lot of information can be collected by simply boosting his/her ego.
- The interview can provide better information on operating procedures, purchase practices and deciding authorities. If a respondent is really worked up on some aspect of supplier's equipment or service, then invariably while giving the feedback, the customer representative will provide simultaneously comparative information on the competitors on various facades like engineering capability, quality, attitude, service capability, frequency of breakdown or their approach to address customer complaints. This provides all the information of

competitors and helps in benchmarking the main researcher's client with his peers on various aspects and to identify the core strength and weak areas with respect to competitors, which can then be used to develop a suitable marketing strategy.

- The information so collected can help the organisation in evaluating and understanding its relative strength and weakness. It can then position itself suitably.

Disadvantages of Interview The interview system also has its share of disadvantages. These are:

- One requires an elaborate and expert organisation to conduct such an exercise. The supplier itself cannot undertake such an exercise because its area of activity is different and it may not have professional experience in conducting such work. The nature of work also demands a third party involvement to do justice to the objectives.

  In the core sector the market requirements are peculiar and at many times it requires that the third party has technically qualified interviewers and processors for the purpose. It will also take massive efforts on the part of the third party and parent organisation to ensure that proper communication and understanding exists between them because of technical nature of the work. This calls for proper training and regular interaction and reviews. This is important to ensure that the third party has understood the requirements and is proceeding in the right direction.
- The second disadvantage is a fall out of the earlier disadvantage. The cost of this methodology is very high and cannot be replicated very often. A large amount of money is needed in training and regular follow ups apart from organising the visit of interviewers to customer premises and in their lodging and boarding arrangements, which may be situated in remote and far flung areas. The amount of expenditure involved may not allow a organisation to have such an exercise more than once in five years.
- The exercise is elaborate and of non-repetitive nature because it is in core sector and may require good preparation before the actual exercise is undertaken. Normally, such work will require at least three months' time in just conducting it. Additionally, the interview will throw a

lot of unstructured but voluminous and important information, and its classification and analysis will itself take a good amount of time. It will also necessitate any analyser to go through the complete information to arrive at the main message.

Type of Interviews The interviews can be structured or unstructured. In a structured interview, the respondent will be asked questions as per the prepared questionnaire and his response will be recorded. Additionally, the interviewer may ask supplementary questions. The biggest disadvantage of this method is that the interviewer is driving the respondent. He may create such a condition where the respondent may not be left with much choice but to tick one of the options put forth before him, and he may not be able to communicate what he feels about it or his additional views. This type may also allow to monotony to set in and the communication may lose its track.

In an unstructured interview, the questioner and respondent just chat and the subject and the issues unfold in the course of discussion. In this situation, the respondent is free to mould the conversation to issues he feels are important and at the end has the satisfaction of having communicated all what he thought was necessary and the time is well spent. The issues on which they feel strongly come out clearly. The only disadvantage is that the interview may not get focused and one may not get all the details he may be looking for. The best solution may be a combination of the two styles. The respondent may be provided with a questionnaire in advance and he may be requested to fill it in before the actual conversation begins. This will help the respondent to communicate all the information the researcher may be needing. At the time of conversation, the respondent can give his side of feedback on the subjects already covered or those left out and which the respondent feels strongly about. The researcher can also utilise the meeting to ask supplementary questions or collect the details not already provided for.

Though such structured exercises in market research had their values and importance, but in core sector projects, not only the marketing but also the engineering personnel of the vendor are required to visit the customer and discuss with him or his consultant exhaustively. If the vendor has already supplied to the customer earlier, then his manufacturing and service personnel also could have extensive exposure to the customer. Such exposure and meetings can be utilised to collect all the detailed information from the client. It may be feasible that negative feedback may not be given directly due to civilities involved but there are ways of communicating and getting same during the discussion. It is often said in big corporates that one should meet the customer non agenda at least once in three/six months in a casual way to have a general friendly chat, in a relaxed manner without the tension of negotiation or settling some issues affecting the progress of the specific work. The results are mostly surprising as one gets unexpected feedback, appreciation for good work done or for helping the customer and, of course, some friendly suggestions on problems and how to solve them. Additionally, if the vendor person is maintaining good relations with the customer and is in regular touch, the outcome of such meetings will be very rewarding. The customer persons will also be able to communicate, as both the parties understand the technical terms. The major drawback is that the feedback from such meetings, particularly if they are negative, cannot be easily communicated to top management and it requires feedback from a third party for top management to give credence to it and take action.

COMPILATION AND ANALYSIS OF DATA

The first and foremost requirement is to properly compile the data so that systematic analysis can be done. Here the broad objective of market research must be kept in mind and the data must be organised in separate sections/ segments. This can be done in the following ways:

- Revisit the main objectives of the research.
- Divide the main objectives into segments.
- Establish the relationship between the segments and the business objectives.
- Classify and assign the questions of the questionnaire to each of these segments. It may be possible that one question may appear at more than one place/segment.
- Convert the replies to the question in numerical form or in such a way that it can be grouped. For example, if the question is on the capability of the organisation to provide service and the reply is on the five point scale, then one can put it as it is on the sheet. If required,

the response from 5 digits/10 digits scale can be converted to three digits scale. This may reduce the time and complexity, but accuracy may suffer. It can also be remembered that while it is possible to convert a reply from a larger scale to smaller scale, it may not be possible from a lower scale to higher scale.

- If the aim of the research is to compile similar data on competitors, then a similar compilation sheet must be filled for each and every competitor. From the sheet and data so collected, the strong attributes and weak areas can be identified for suitable action plan. If the survey was done to find out the service capability of the organisation and its comparison with other competitors, the response can be arranged and analysed as shown in Table 6.2.

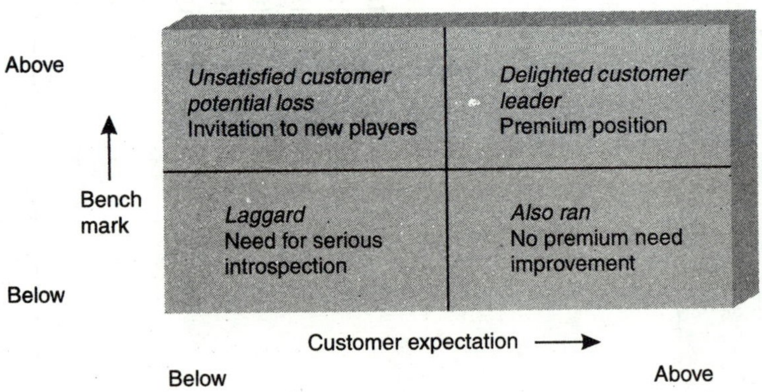

Fig. 6.5 *Strategy Formulation from Data Analysis*

It can be seen from Table 6.2 that the main objective was divided into 16 questions and the respondent's reply was recorded on a three point scale—Poor, Good, Excellent. A weighted average was calculated. Similar exercise was done for all the competitors and the best weighted average for each question was picked up from among the competitors to act as 'Benchmark'. It is but natural that the benchmark for each question need not come from the same competitor. Similar exercise was done with the customer to arrive at his benchmark. The weighted average of the company was compared with the benchmark given by the competitor and customer expectation. We can have four possibilities as discussed below:

- If the company scores more than the peers, then it is the leader. If it also scores more than the customer expectation, then we have a *delighted customer.*

Table 6.2 *Data Compilation and Analysis*

S.No.	Area	Total Respondents	Rating				Benchmark (Competitor's Best)	Priority of Customer
			Poor	Poor	Poor	Weighted Average*		
1.	Response to General call	50	20	10	20	30	20 –	10 –
2.	Response to SOS call	50	5	15	30	70	20 –	10 –
3.	Expertise Available	50	10	30	10	40	20 –	80 ¯
4.	Diagnostic Specialisation	50	20	15	15	25	15 –	50 ¯
5.	Spares Availability	50	25	20	5	5	15 ¯	70 ¯
6.	Spares Delivery	50	30	15	5	–5	20 ¯	70 ¯
7.	Price Reasonability of Spares	50	20	25	5	5	2 –	40 ¯
8.	Facilities at Works	50	10	25	15	45	30 –	50 –
9.	Facilities at Site	50	20	15	15	25	20 –	80 ¯
10.	Price Reasonability of Services	50	15	20	15	35	20 –	40 ¯
11.	Priority given for Emergency Repair	50	15	25	10	30	20 –	80 ¯
12.	Quality of Spares	50	15	25	10	30	20 –	80 ¯
13.	Quality of Services	50	5	30	15	55	30 –	80 ¯
14.	Behaviour of Service Personnel	50	5	20	25	65	40 –	50 –
15.	Importance given by Vendor	50	5	25	20	60	40 –	60 ⌞
16.	Attitude of Top Management	50	5	25	20	60	40 –	90 ¯

* Weighted Average = 2 × Excellent + Good – Poor

– Performance better than Benchmark/Customer Expectation; ¯ Performance below Benchmark/Customer Expectation

- If the company is scoring above the benchmark but below customer expectation, then we find that though the company is leader, it is having an unsatisfied customer and there is need for company to improve its capabilities. This is because an *unsatisfied customer* can easily be lured away by a new competitor by a simple promise as such a customer will definitely be looking for a substitute supplier to meet his expectations.
- If the company is scoring above customer expectations but below the benchmark, there is a need to improve as the company may get business *but not the premium as it is not the leader.*
- If the company is below both benchmark and customer expectation, it should *seriously do introspection* to find out the cause for such feedback and take corrective action.

Illustration

From the data results as tabulated some more conclusions can also be drawn as indicated below:

- The company is doing much better than its nearest competitor except in the field of spares.
- The company's weighted average in first five ranked priorities by customer is very low compared to the mark it is getting for the lower positions.

This indicates that there is a need for the company to understand the customer. Though it is not performing badly on the whole, still its performance is not driven by the market requirements but by some other factors, which should ring alarm bells for any commercial organisation. Hence, the company must redefine its objectives in terms of market requirements. The analysis also throws up critical success factors and if the bidder wants to do well, then he must concentrate on them. The result also indicates those factors in which the company is leader and by suitably leveraging it one can get a premium.

This was the simple analysis done for a case study but in actual practice the objectives and the situation may be complicated but the data and analysis can throw useful tips for strategy formulation.

EXTRAPOLATION OF RESEARCH RESULTS

Many times it becomes necessary to extrapolate trends to predict short, medium or long-term trends. This may be particularly true in case of market demand/technology trends, etc. In such an eventuality one has to use statistical methods to arrive at the results. There are four major statistical methods to have futuristic predictions. These are:

- Judgement Method
- Counting Method
- Time Series Method
- Associative Method

Each of these statistical methods are further sub-divided into other methods. We are summarising below the relative advantages and capabilities of each of the schemes under the following four parameters, namely:

- Time Range
- Response
- Resolution
- Accuracy

Judgement Method

Type	*Time Range*	*Resolution*	*Response*	*Accuracy*
Extrapolation	S/M	x	xxx	x
Scenario	M/L	x	xx	x
Delphi	M/L	x	xx	x
Historical	M/L	xx	xx	x

S—Short Term x—Fair M—Medium Term

xx—Good L—Long Term xxx—Very Good

Counting Method

Type	Time Range	Resolution	Response	Accuracy
Market Testing	M	x	xxx	xxx
Survey	M	x	xxx	xxx

Time Series Method

Type	Time Range	Resolution	Response	Accuracy
Average	S/M/L	xxx	x	xx
Exponential	S/M	xxx	x	xx
Extrapolation	S/M/L	xxx	xx	xx

Associative Method

Type	Time Range	Resolution	Response	Accuracy
Correlation	S/M/L	x	xx	x
Regression	S/M/L	x	xx	xx
Econometric	S/M/L	x	xxx	xx

REPORT PREPARATION

Market research is normally undertaken by a professional agency for an organisation, and this agency is expected to present a formal report to its hiring company. The report is generally presented to senior management officers and hence needs to be comprehensive. The report must be transparent, clear, analytical and focused. The facts must be clearly presented. It is often seen that the information furnished in tabular or graphical form create major impression and is easy to understand. It also presents facts in such a way that comparisons can be easily drawn and conclusions can be easily derived. A good report should contain the following details:

- Executive Summary of the Report
- Objectives of the Work
- Background information highlighting why this work is necessary and what advantages will result from the outcome of the work.
- Research Methodology adopted and reasons for same. Details about sample selection and the circumstances guiding it. Report should also highlight the expected sampling error.
- The report should give in detail the questionnaire and the way it has been prepared. The factors driving its segmentation should also be mentioned.
- The interview methodology adopted and salient aspects of the interview can be discussed here.
- Data and other information collected should be presented in a focused way. The main guiding parameter should be the objective of the research work. It may be possible and even necessary that the same data may have to be presented in a different form to meet the report objectives. The presentation should be prepared in such a way that it clearly establishes issues and leads to clear thinking on strategy formulation.
- If the findings need results to be extrapolated to predict future trends, then the report must extrapolate them suitably. The report must present clearly the method adopted for extrapolation and the accuracy that can be expected. It must also highlight the basic parameters or the assumption made because if these ground conditions change, then the outcome of the report will need to be suitably corrected.

CONCLUSIONS AND ACTION PLAN

The report must present the conclusions and the suggested action plan. It must highlight abnormality in findings if noted and verbatim quote certain feedback collected or given during the interview to reinforce the findings and to motivate the company to devise suitable strategy to tackle it. It is also necessary that the report may contain specific observations of the customer and his suggested action plan.

If the researcher feels that the present scope of work needs to be enlarged or further work needs to be done to do justice to the work, then he must make suggestions to that effect clearly mentioning the extra work to be undertaken to complete the assignment.

7

How to Judge Competition and Leave Others Behind

Stamina
Skill
Negotiating Strategy
Strategy
Judging the Competition and Meeting It
Pro-active Pre-marketing
Sincerity of Marketing/Approach
Time Horizon Approach

7

There are three things in particular that you (businessmen) can do; be competitive through lower cost and prices and better products and productivity; be expert minded and be calm.

John F. Kennedy
Ex-President, United States of America

Marketing is like running a marathon race with a lot of other players also competing. The winner requires stamina, skill and strategy. Thus, if an organisation has to succeed in business and stay ahead of others, it has to primarily think in terms of Three 'S' listed above. There are a number of factors which contribute to these three 'S' and play a major role in shaping them.

STAMINA

Stamina represents the tenacity of the company to remain in business as a long-term player in the identified line of business even weathering the worst storms. It also reflects the confidence and the commitment the company has in its vision and capability to achieve it. It is to be appreciated that there are large ups and downs in the core sector business and demand will vary widely depending on the economic and industrial climate. The competition will be global. There may be players, who will always try to enter and make a niche for themselves, and it is to be expected that their entry level bid will give the company much to think about on price strategy. (It is very difficult for an organisation to offer vastly improved technology, performance figures or other attractive features like low completion schedule, user friendly product for short-term until the organisation is really able to offer it on long-term basis. But price is a soft variable that can easily be changed and manipulated to achieve the company's business objective. In fact it does not require much strategic thinking to vary price in comparison to other similar factors.)

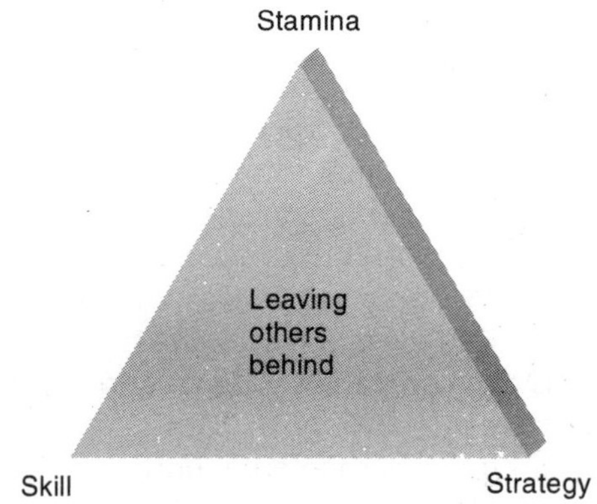

Fig. 7.1 *The Three 'S' Concept*

Many organisations believe in offering very low entry prices and then increasing it after establishing themselves in the market. Such type of strategy puts a very heavy burden on already established players as even though they are known in the market and can hope for some premium compared to new entry players, still they have to reduce their prices drastically to remain in the market. Here, the sustaining ability or stamina of the organisation comes to the forefront. An organisation that can sustain its operation in such adverse circumstances will definitely reap the benefit of its hard work. The factors which can contribute to stamina are notably the financial strength of the company, the state of technology, the service and efficiency at which it offers it and, above all, the confidence the company has in its business line.

Another notable issue the company must address is how far it is going to ensure that the commitment it has made to the customer is honoured in spite of the apparent mistake it has made during the business finalisation/ order negotiation stage. It is this sustaining ability of the company to honour its commitment, in spite of enormous heavy cost involved, which gives it the marketing image over others. It gives a clear signal to the market that it is an organisation that is not going to leave its customer high and dry and is going to fulfill its commitment in spite of enormous cost and loss to it and in future they can always count and depend on this organisation. It will be the beginning of a long-term business relationship. Let us consider some practical situations.

Illustration

In a typical tender, the customer wanted the product to not only meet stringent environmental norms but, considering that the future would see more demanding compliances on this front, prescribed very tough norms himself. Four companies submitted their bid. While company A quoted a price which was 20 per cent higher than the next bidder, it offered to comply with the stringent norms envisaged in the tender. Other companies sought various degrees of deviation but quoted a more attractive price. Most of them offered to comply with the present day environmental norms and some even went a step further to offer marginal improvement over it. The tender evaluation company had two choices—either to relax environmental conditions of the bid and accept a lower cost and reduce the overall project expenditure or choose party A at higher price though with compliance of full tender specifications. The tender evaluation committee decided that they would not relax the specifications considering the likely future laws on this capital intensive equipment, which in any case had a life span of twenty years, but would invite party A for negotiations to get better price deal as in their opinion the price difference was very high. Incidentally the price quoted by A was also their budget figure. During the negotiation, company A having come to know of the fact that it was the only party which had offered full compliance with the stringent tender specifications and under no circumstances was the customer going to relax this condition, leveraged this strength beautifully and did not offer more than a token discount. They also made it a point to tell the negotiating committee that they were technically far advanced than their peers and were thus able to comply with such stringent requirements. They also complimented the customer for his foresight in envisaging such stringent specifications keeping the future in mind. Negotiations went on for a prolonged period and company A, while offering nominal discount, extracted some additional benefits from the customer for itself. The deal was made and the customer advised that the proposal would be put to the board for formal approval and order and an advance would be released thereafter. Normally a board approval takes about a month and as the negotiation had eaten away quite a bit of time, the validity of proposal was very near the closing date. Hence, the customer requested for only 15 days validity extension which is nothing compared to the validity of 180–210 days normally

Contd

asked in such type of projects and such type of validity extension is always a formality because nobody wants to lose a settled business.

However, a new unfortunate development took place. Somebody in the Technical wing of Company A realised that they had over-committed themselves and under no circumstances would they be able to meet the stringent technical environmental requirements easily which only a few days before they were taking pride in mentioning its compliance by them. They also estimated that the cost of meeting this requirement would be very high and in any case much above the price they had settled. Thus, they would be booking heavy losses in the project.

The question was intensely debated by the higher management of Company A. Some officials felt that they ought not to book losses in this contract and in any case the validity of their bid would expire shortly and they would be within their contractual right not to extend it further. Others felt that since the validity was expiring soon, they could communicate validity extension with enhanced prices (never mind the hefty quantum jump required). These two groups concentrated on how not to take the order and, in their opinion, to come out of a messy situation, which in any case was of their own making.

They also thought that the contract envisaged free replacement if the equipment was deficient in performance and even after modification/rectification it was not able to give contractual committed performance. They felt that free replacement would put them into further financial trouble.

There was another school of thought by some managers. They felt that 15 days validity extension request was too trivial an issue and the vendor was expected to comply with it as per normal business ethics. Not honouring such a request was legally correct but could not be justified from any business practice. It would also send wrong signals to the market not only about the technical ability of the company but also make the customer sit up and take notice of the fact that company A was highly undependable, high on promise but low on delivery and could at any time leave them high and dry. They felt that the issue was not of booking an order or losses on it but of business practices, image of the company and the long-term commitment it could offer to customers. They felt that having committed to meet the performance parameters and made it their main core selling point, they were duty bound to honour their commitment. They felt that it was better to lose the battle but win the war. In their opinion loss on the contract was of very insignificant value compared to the dent it would make in the company's image and long-term business loss it would lead to.

Here, the staying capability of the company comes into the picture. It is clear that the people who want to honour the commitment are talking of correct and long-time business strategy but the company should not only be willing to bear it *but have the capacity to bear it.* It is but natural that if company is able to practise this type of approach, it will not only make a niche for itself but will earn the respect of the customer and get suitably rewarded in the business.

SKILL

This is the internal strength of the company and is a highly respected and enviable asset. This is one of the most important factors which determine the attitude of the customer towards an organisation. Skill can encompass a number of things. It can be related to knowledge, quality, engineering, developments process, system engineering, project management, financing, total project capability, etc. It may also relate to ability of an organisation to identify problems in operating equipments and solve it in the least possible time. It is one ability that is highly appreciated by the customers as it saves their down time and increases their production, boosting both top and bottom line in the balance sheet.

Table 7.1 indicates the shift in the market perception on various internal skill factors as of today compared to five years back. This also indicates the likely shift, which is going to happen five years from now. It can be seen that technology and knowledge are slowly moving up in the ladder. Five years back it was positioned at sixth place among nine parameters but five years from now, it will be the most important factor that will be much sought after. As a result, companies which are giving more weightage to upgradation of technology/engineering skills or new developments will have much better chances of success. It is however to be appreciated that development of technology is only the beginning and the vendor has to ensure and demonstrate its successful operation/utility, superiority and reliability before the market can accept it and then only he can look forward to high returns.

Table 7.1 *Changing Environment and Shifting Priorities*

S.No.	*Parameters*	*5 Years Back*	*Today*	*5 Years from Now*
1.	Knowledge/Technology	6	4	1
2.	Price	1	1	4
3.	Engineering	4	3	2
4.	Manufacturing Capability	2	8	8
5.	Delivery/Completion Schedule	3	2	3
6.	Finance	10	10	9
7.	Project Management	9	5	5
8.	Contract Management	5	9	9
9.	Human Resources	7	7	6
10.	Quality	8	6	7

During the last two decades, most of the organisations considered it economically unviable to spend resources on new developments as resources required were very high, development period long and results uncertain. The organisation was additionally required to establish the technology by conducting field trials and applying necessary corrections. Naturally, one has to do a lot of experimentation and corrections to perfect a single development. On the other hand, proven technologies were available at much cheaper price through collaboration. This arrangement also gives access in a majority of cases to the technology receiver to receive continuously news and data on upgradation and information on new developments without any additional cost or at nominal price.

It is however to be appreciated that the development of technology is only the first part of the work and it is only after successful demonstration of technology and establishment of the same that the returns will follow.

The receiving company also utilised the backup of the technology provider to strengthen his case before the customer and also to seek the collaborator's help and advice to attend to complex site problems by way of analysis and/or deputation of their experts to site to study the problem and attend to it. The receiving company also utilised technology provider's guidance and active participation on problems faced during design/engineering/manufacturing or during warranty period. Most of the customers were also happy at this as in their view they were getting the assistance and active advice from renowned companies without having to pay for it, which in the normal course would have been quite substantial.

But now with technology and knowledge assuming their well deserved premium place and with customers now ready to pay a higher price for it, it is becoming increasingly difficult, costly and unaffordable to buy the technology. Additionally, the help or guidance at various levels, which was earlier available free or at nominal cost, is becoming increasingly expensive. Knowledge-based organisations have realised the increasing importance of their assets and they are no longer willing to part with it without getting their dues. Some of them have also demanded business-sharing in hardware in addition to collaboration agreement fee and royalty as the price for parting with the information on new developments. Most of the customers are not only looking to state-of-the-art product but are also looking forward to the benefit of continuous development in the products they have bought.

The performance of the equipment is receiving added attention. The financial evaluation factors (amount by which inefficient performance of a equipment is loaded compared to better performance of similar equipment of other vendor) have increased tremendously in the last few years, giving a clear indication that customers want better performing and efficient products and systems and are willing to pay for it. Additionally, they are also now looking forward to life cycle of the product.

Illustration

My Boss never got tired of telling me one story again and again. He always felt that passion (JUNOON) and endurance can convert non-customers into willing customers and can get you the business under stiff circumstances. He often said there was an old Duchess who would often visit shops, ask silly questions and not make purchases. Naturally, she was unwelcome at stores as the owner and others felt that it was a waste of time to attend to her. One day she visited a furniture shop and was attended by one Mr John. He patiently replied to her queries and showed her the goods she wanted. As was been her habit, she came out without purchasing anything. This went on for about a week. Everyday the lady would come, spend time, see some things and go away, so much so that the owner of the shop got

Contd

angry with John and fired him. After another week the shop got a phone that the Duke wanted to place an order for 8 million Pound worth of furniture and wanted Mr John to come and collect the order. Naturally, the Owner had to search John and they then got the business. So the patience and endurance of John got the owner big business.

A similar thing happened to me. A chemical producer would regularly call us for meetings and ask all sorts of alternatives without ever taking a decision. Once he did take the decision but awarded the contract to a foreign party for reasons best known to them. After another three months, we received a call from the same customer for another requirement, which was also discussed at length at that time. Thinking that it may be another wasteful journey and waste of time, we wanted to excuse ourselves, but being in marketing, you never say No, but only put your stipulation on which you would like to have business. So we accepted the call and went for the meeting by taking an early morning flight. It was a pleasant surprise that by noon we had clinched the business. Probably one of the prerequisites of a marketing executive is also to judge when a customer is ready to take the decision.

Service and its Leveraging

Another important criterion that can give advantage to an organisation is its ability to offer fast and efficient service. Efficient service is the key dimension that influences buyer's behaviour and is a part of order winning criteria. This helps the company become a preferred supplier in the business segment in which it is operating. For this it is necessary to identify through market research the key parameters to which the customer attaches significance and to develop a suitable plan to provide him those at a reasonable charge. In the core sector industry, the buyer's decision in many ways is influenced by the opinion of its operating people.

Illustration

This is the case of a famous fertiliser company which wanted to buy capital equipments. Since this company had similar plants at two/three places and it had excellent experience with a particular company

Contd

specially for providing timely and excellent service in its hour of need. (Incidentally the vendor was notorious for delay in supply of regular spares, but had the reputation of not only rising to the occasion but also going out of the way to ensure that the equipment supplied to the customer works and he is not put to financial loss.) The fertiliser company wanted to buy the equipment from this company and, in spite of open tender, preferred to award the contract to their chosen vendor even at a premium purely for their service record.

In an infrastructure industry some of the key parameters a customer looks forward to are:

- Availability of Spares
- Service after Sales and the speed with which the organisation responds to SOS messages
- O&M Services
- R&M Services

Any capital-intensive equipment required in the core sector has a life span of minimum twenty years and they require spares at regular intervals. Non-availability of spares can lead to non-working of equipment or its operation at lower efficiencies and low availability of equipment. This can also lead to higher losses and consequent loss of revenue. Many customers therefore consider long-term availability of spares as an important factor for vendor selection. It is rather strange that though spares add more to the bottom line of the company, still many companies do not accord reasonable priority to it as this does not give them top line growth. Additionally, with amount of time and other resources required, with less top line growth, the productivity and turnover in financial terms take a beating compared to the achievement if the same resources were utilised for producing main equipments. It is therefore often seen that delay in execution of spare order is very common. But any organisation which claims to be customer focused and whose primary objective is customer satisfaction, should work out a strategy to ensure that the customer is not put to disadvantage for what essentially is the company's internal problem. The organisation should focus on assessing the customer's requirement and in meeting them specifically for spares.

During the operation of equipment in its lifetime, there are occasions when the equipment suddenly breaks down or is performing well below its capacity and the customer wants assistance of the vendor for corrective action. At this time how fast and quickly an organisation responds to SOS messages of the customer assumes added significance. Having responded to the call is only the first thing. Next comes the skill and expertise of the person deputed by the vendor. If they are able to identify the problem and quickly correct it, the services of the individuals and of the organisation are highly appreciated and remembered and may even begin a phase of mutual respect between the organisations. Sometimes, it may become necessary for the vendor/ original supplier to bring the equipment back to the manufacturing works for total repair. The amount of importance given by the supplier for early repair of the defective equipment gives an indication of the importance the supplier attaches to the customer and his work. The customer will appreciate the priority given to his work. This goodwill gives tremendous extra advantage to the vendor in getting future business.

In today's world of specialised services, now there is an increasing tendency to offload work to experts who can do it more effectively and efficiently. Hence, many times the customer may not be interested in having his own O&M staff do the work and are willing to off load it to the supplier. This is a very good situation from both the supplier's and customer's point of view. The vendor is getting additional business and the customer is getting professional and expert O&M staff and services. Further the customer does not have to employ his own people for the work and this reduces his manpower strength and associated problem apart from boosting his productivity per employee. He is also assured of constant upgradation of skills and knowledge of O&M staff as the supplier would be training them. He is also free from the worries of availability of spares.

As and when the equipment gets old, their performance suffers. Most of the customers are interested in increasing the life of the equipment by making low capital investment in retrofitting the existing equipment rather than buying new equipment. Many suppliers offer expert service in assessing the remaining life of equipment and parts and design modification required to refurbish this old equipment to give good performance for a reasonable period. This expertise also tilts the balance in their favour for order of new equipment.

Leveraging Project Management and System Engineering Capability

Many organisations have no experience or a limited presence in the supply of individual products, but they have excellent project management and system engineering ability. Bechtel USA and Larsen and Toubro, India are two such organisations, which are weak on product base, but more than compensate this by excellent project management and system integration capabilities. In the present environment where timely project completion has attained major importance, project management has assumed added significance. In earlier days, project implementation and management was done by the customer himself. This was mainly on price consideration as offloading it to the vendor increased the cost by approximately 15 per cent than if the work was done by the customer himself. But today, some of the customers feel that the additional price is affordable in the light of benefits that accrue from fast and timely completion of the project by a professional contractor and overall saving in customer's human resources which he need not divert from other work or employ specially for this work which, in any case, is of two to three years duration. Hence, many customers are looking forward to such ability in their prospective suppliers and are willing to provide reasonable premium for this extra ability.

It is to be appreciated that the project management ability is very much different from product engineering and manufacturing capability. Here a technical person is required to take a total overview of the system and generate specifications and performances required from individual products to meet the desired project performance. The person and the concerned organisation must have strong system engineering and project co-ordination capability. The task requires highly dedicated Project Management System. This is a very weak area with many vendors. While the majority of them have an excellent project monitoring system, very few understand and have a Project Management System. It is also a misconception that strong and multi layer project monitoring can ensure timely project completion. No amount of project monitoring can minimise the need for effective Project Management System. It should also be appreciated that too much of Project Monitoring can be counter-productive and may itself be the source of delay. Similarly, a strong product engineering base does not mean that the vendor has good system engineering ability.

Leveraging Quality

The quality of the product is another parameter that is getting increasing importance from the customer. Though this is not the place to discuss the internal benefits the supplier gets due to better quality like less rejection, cost optimisation, less site issues and performance problems, the external benefits to the customer are very high. Good quality equipment ensures high availability, low running cost, low maintenance and high availability. This factor plays major role in decision making as the following case example will illustrate:

Illustration

A reputed cement company 'X' was in the market to purchase capital intensive equipment for its requirement. It invited bids from a large number of national and international parties and finally decided to award the contract to a party purely on price considerations. The results were unfortunate. The vendor cuts the corners at many places as his philosophy was cost driven—one time customer. The main customer lost a lot of time and had to spend a substantial amount to rectify those equipments and even now they are having problems. The efficiency and performance have left a lot to be desired. The customer has also realised that even an excellent contract also cannot be of much help if the party has decided not to respond positively. This customer again had a similar requirement some time back and he ensured that price was not the only criteria for award of contract, but gave weightage to technology, performance, quality and above all vendor background and his customer response.

There was another textile company, which placed order for process equipment only on cost consideration. The result was that the supplier, who never believe in second time business with the same party and wanted to have all profit in one contract only, supplied the equipment to meet his business objectives and not of his client. As a result the plant had to be shut down for almost two years and customer had to spend a lot of extra money to put the plant in operation. In spite of this he continue to have off and on shutdown. This is the price one may have to pay for making COST the only deciding criterion.

NEGOTIATING STREATGY

Negotiation is the art of gaining confidence and favour of people from whom we want something. It is the use of information and knowledge to influence the behaviour to one's advantage. Negotiation is not a bad word. In our daily life we negotiate with everybody, may be at home or in the office. We negotiate with our colleagues, family members, peers, subordinates, boss and definitely with customers, when you are in marketing. However, we will restrict our discussion only to business situations. There are certain prerequisites for successful negotiation and they are summarised below:

1. One must analyse and understand the main negotiator, his style, attitude and play the cards accordingly. Two different incidents, which are reproduced below, highlight this.

Illustrations

Case 1

The president of a major company, having a turnover of about Rs 200 crore per annum, invited bids for major capital equipment and called two shortlisted parties for final discussion. He had papers before him detailing the total comparison between the parties. He informed the parties that this was the final meeting and whatever improvement they wanted in their technical and commercial proposal should be done now. One of the bidders thought that this was the normal procedure adopted by a party while negotiating and there may be at least two/three more rounds of negotiations and they accordingly decided their strategy. The second party analysed the background of the negotiator and concluded that his background and the way he communicated the message indicated that he was serious, so they decided that they would take him seriously, give their best proposal and take the risk of not offering anything in 2nd/3rd round of negotiation, should their judgment fail. They were right. The gentleman never called for another round of negotiation though his board approval took time and never allowed the first party to offer any further improvement. The reverse could have happened with the other organisation or person.

Contd

Case 2

There was another similar example in which a party, after two rounds of negotiation, invited shortlisted parties for final discussion and even mentioned it in a formal invitation letter but they awarded the contract after two more discussion without any reason. The people who took them seriously paid a heavy price for their decision.

The above two cases clearly highlight the importance of understanding the negotiator.

2. The second most important aspect is that when you encounter a stubborn negotiating personality or an unreasonable person, you cannot win even if you are right. There are instances when people negotiating are least concerned with the benefits of the organisation on whose behalf they are leading the negotiation. This happens when the organisation is headed by a part-time CEO who has no interest or commitment in the long-term business or profitability of the company.
3. The suppliers must have maximum information on the subject because the information can only help him in taking quick and logical decisions under unexpected conditions and the surprise proposals put up by the other party.
4. It is necessary to understand the negotiator—his belief, past experience, emotions, attitude and the operating style. This will help the party in formulating his strategy and having an edge over others.
5. Before starting negotiations one must ensure that the other person has the authority to negotiate and the back up of the organisation management, otherwise one will not achieve anything and unnecessarily reveal his strategy.
6. It must also be considered whether the other party believes in a one-time business deal or a long-term business relationship. In the latter case, the vendor will get an additional advantage as emotions and sentiments are involved and he will be getting additional benefit due to investment made by him in Customer Relationship.

7. Many negotiators believe in putting others under time pressure so that they give in easily. A firm stand sometimes helps or if this is expected, one should be prepared for it and should allocate a longer time period. One can also use the same tactic on him and get a better surprise advantage.

Illustration

One party always preferred to have negotiations at the other party's office and ensured that the negotiation prolonged well beyond 8 PM. Since the other party's officials were at their headquarters, half their attention was always on their families and they were willing to compromise if that helped in faster conclusion of the meeting and their going home. They realised after one or two negotiations that the other party was deliberately prolonging the meeting to put time pressure and get undue advantages. They firmly decided that either they would visit the other party's office on tour, so the shoe was on the other's foot, or they would abruptly announce that they would continue the meeting the next day as they had some emergency The pressure was now on the other party as they were caught off guard and their main strategy had failed.

Most of the executives prefer returning by the last flight so that they can use the next day completely. Many people aware of this will prolong the negotiation till the time of flight is very close and then take advantage of the pressure cooker situation. In similar circumstances, many negotiators prefer to book the next day's flight but announce that they want to return tonight and sit tight. The other party is surprised by the calmness of the person who, in their opinion, is about to miss his flight. It is now their turn to be upset and commit something they did not want to.

However there are persons who believe in the principle that *TIME IS MONEY* and would like the meeting to be crisp and brief. They get thoroughly upset if some party tries to break this rule and if they are the deciding authority, the party breaking the rule pays a heavy price for their indiscretion.

8. It is to be appreciated that in many cases, deadlines are part of the negotiation and are therefore negotiable. This should not be the reason for increasing the blood pressure or for taking a hurried decision, which one may have to repent at leisure.

9. One should not have any remorse, moral or ethical, after the negotiations.
10. The negotiator must be flexible in approach and should make the other party comfortable by his actions. He should always try to build personal rapport with the other party as such personal relationship plays an important role in arriving at the final decision and in getting better opportunities.
11. The negotiator must aim at winning the confidence and trust of the other party and getting their commitment. He should also display a positive attitude.

Illustration

The CEO of one company was very much impressed by the positive attitude and helping nature of the marketing persons of a supplier. The next time when they were discussing and finalising the second order, the vendor was surprised when the CEO sought the vendor's marketing man's advice on a subject which could have been of negative advantage to the customer, but so much was the trust of the customer in the fairness of the vendor that he not only shared with him his weakness but sought his advice in the matter.

12. The negotiator must have the ability to manage the opposition and bring it round.
13. The negotiator must have persuasive skills and should not be arrogant or lose his temper during the discussion. He must, at the same time, be able to take calculated risks.
14. A good negotiator must not over-commit him. He must know when to get up and go home.
15. The last, but most important, thing is that one should put in writing, what had been settled because the memory of other person or the language, which can lead to a different meaning, can kill the person/business.
16. Ensure that initially juniors carry out the negotiations so that the senior person gets time to understand and plan his strategy.

17. Listen more and talk less. The more the other party talks, the more they reveal. They may also blabber out their constraints and compulsions/limitations, which help in the final deal.
18. Never make it personal. It is too dangerous.
19. Stand by your commitment. You have the image and respect of your organisation and yourself at stake.

The Japanese have their own negotiation style. They will first spell out what they want and if the other party wants to deviate, they will allow him to explain why he wants a deviation and will listen carefully. Once he has completed his explanation why he cannot agree to what had been proposed, they will calmly say—*so you agree.* The other man will feel like jumping out of the window as he had just devoted his whole energy in explaining why he cannot agree.

There are persons who believe in tiring the opposition out. They consider the concessions as a sign of weakness and will use all the emotional tactics to win the battle. They will want the other party to make a concession after they have taken an extreme position. They will give very less in return and that too with considerable delay. Time deadlines will have no value for them and they will avoid reciprocity.

STRATEGY

A strategy is an action plan for optimum and effective utilisation of Resources and Assets to overcome Blockages and achieve Goal as detailed in Fig. 7.2.

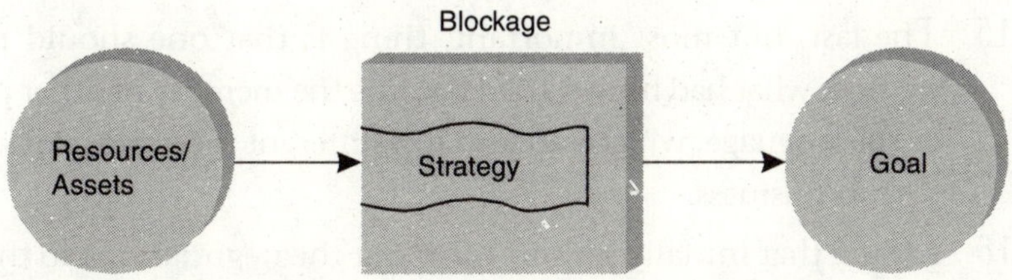

Fig. 7.2 *Strategy—Functional Approach*

The strategy is basically decided at two levels, namely:

- Corporate Level—What to do and How to do
- Functional Level—Implementation

A strategy has basically to address the following issues:

- What to Market?
- Where to Market?
- When to Market?
- Whom to Market and to Whom to Compete with?

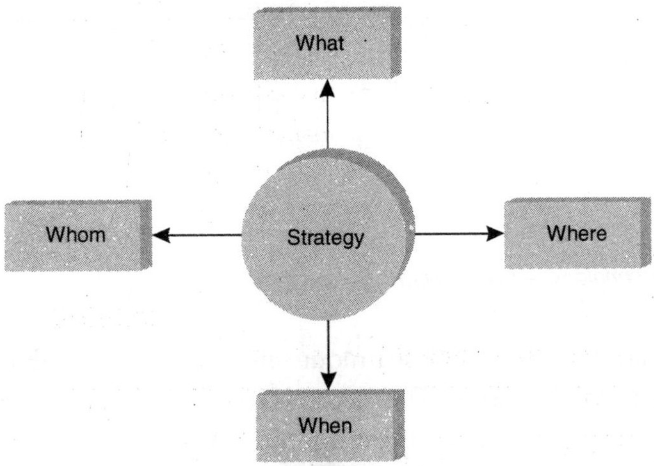

Fig. 7.3 *Strategy to Address Four W's*

What to Market?

The first part WHAT TO MARKET essentially decides the company's business profile. The company must appreciate its core strength and decide the area or the products it wants to market. The basic approach to be adopted is detailed in Fig. 7.4, which is *TECHNOLOGY—VOLUME MATRIX*. It identifies four basic segments of business based on Technology and Volume as the parameters. These segments had been identified along with their characteristics in Fig. 7.4. A company whose core competency is in engineering and new development should concentrate in high end of value chain, i.e. in

KNOWLEDGE DRIVEN QUADRANT. This quadrant is associated with low volume and hence low competition. This will result in better realisation and will provide reasonable return and enough resources to pursue future development activity as staying in this segment requires constant innovation so that by the time competition catches up, the company has already advanced further.

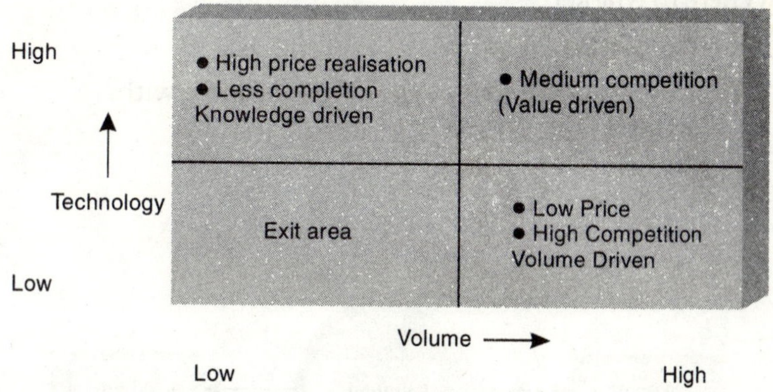

Fig. 7.4 *Technology—Volume Matrix*

There are companies whose unique selling point, i.e. USP is Price, will occupy the fourth quadrant. The customer in this segment, will compromise on technology and other specifications but would like the product/project to be at the lowest possible price. This segment is *COST DRIVEN* and is associated with low technology and high volume. The profit is mainly from the volume. The basic difference in first and fourth quarters can be compared to a general practitioner and specialist doctor. While the general practitioner will have a large number of patients, his fees will be low and he will not devote much time to the patient. On the other hand, a specialist will see very limited number of patients and will give sufficient time to them, but his fees will be much higher. The specialist is basically in knowledge driven segment while the general practitioner is in volume driven segment.

The second segment is *VALUE DRIVEN*. There are large numbers of customers who would like to have new technology but not at any price. They will buy this technology only if they get attractive returns and payback period for additional incremental cost. It is generally seen that the majority of business in infrastructure segment falls in this business segment. The tender document will itself, in a majority of cases, clearly spell out the benefit in price that a customer is willing to pass on to the supplier for better performance. The organisations, which are reasonably good in providing acceptable technology (may not be state-of-the-art), will do well in this market as can be seen from the following case.

Illustration

A CMD of a purchasing company was comparing two bids from two distinct organisations. Bid A was 20 per cent higher than the other bid from company B. Company A was having high proven reputation for supplying quality goods of high performance. It was also well known not to compromise on engineering and material quality and manufacturing/installation process to save money because they had got low price realisation on the project (Quality was not the dependent variable of price but was constant). Company B, whose bid was lower, was nowhere near in reputation to that of company A for supplying high quality performance equipment. The purchaser was also apprehensive that the quality of goods supplied by this company would be dependent on their realisation of sale price. The CMD called Company A and told them that he was conscious of the fact that once he placed an order on them he could comfortably sleep as far as performance and quality of equipment were concerned. On the other hand if he placed an order on company B, he would have to constantly monitor and inspect them at regular intervals to ensure quality of equipment but the cost of such efforts would at most be 10 per cent. Hence he offered to Company A a premium of 10 per cent over the price of Company B. He also told them that beyond this premium he would like to forget his sleep and place an order on Company B and ensure tight project monitoring. This is a typical example of *VALUE BASED BUYING.*

There is a market segment, which is marked with low technology and low volume. This is the exit area for most companies which are operating in the business. This is necessary because an organisation must come out of the loss-making segment. If one is having a non-saleable product and he doesn't kill it, then his competitor will do so. If a product is not giving reasonable return, i.e. one is not able to meet market expectations in price, technology, etc. in spite of making all efforts on technology, cost, completion schedule and other fronts, then it is better to close it down and utilise the assets and other resources in more economically viable ventures/products/projects. In the new economy, the business of Information Technology/Software Industry segment is one where human resources are very important, and it is a common rule that a person who is not '*BILLABLE* must be immediately thrown out. The same logic is applicable to other business segments also. A product that is not BILLABLE (cannot be profitably sold), must be given a decent burial. For those companies operating in the core sector this is a tough decision and normally management tends to avoid it but in the process they block the progress of the company by unnecessary attaching a drag with it which, if heavy enough, can even result in making the organisation static.

The vendor must also clearly define his market focus, viz. whether he wants to remain in Knowledge driven segment, Value driven segment or Cost driven segment and whether he has the means and capability to follow a long-term strategy based on this and survive and grow.

Where to Market?—Positioning

Positioning is a deliberate strategy formulated by a vendor based on environment, market demand, competition, price realisation and its own capability and objectives to derive benefit. It comes out of the necessity that the product may not mean the same thing to everybody. Positioning is a technique which has to be employed with a lot of understanding and planning. By taking a pro-active decision, we are committing ourselves to a particular strategy. Companies can position themselves to address business above a certain critical value. This value can be based on the quantum of business or may be based on rating of equipment or the technology requirement of the business. Positioning essentially means that you are leaving other segments for your competitors to cater to. It must be clearly appreciated that positioning can have a severe long-term effect. It may so happen that you and your competitors may be comfortable with such positioning, which essentially reduces competition and increases realisation and which you may like to continue with. It is also possible that if left unchallenged in their field of operation, they collect enough resources to pose a challenge to you in your segment after some time. It may also be possible that demand in one of the segments may dry up, creating a severe problem for the vendor operating in this range and either forcing him out or encouraging him to migrate to other segments, thus disturbing the equilibrium. Positioning is a serious proposition. A company should not hurt itself by remaining in a segment, which is not its natural strength, and must position itself to remain flexible and capable to ward off challenges from friends trying to make him uncomfortable by making forays into other segments.

There was a company which had a strong market share in a product above the rating A and was serving this segment but then it found that there was demand below this rating which was increasing. The company, in order to increase its profile and volume, decided to encash it. However, it found after two years that its profitability and productivity were declining. On analysis it was found that the demand below rating A, though large in physical numbers, was only 10 per cent in value term and wanted equal efforts as done for large rating. Naturally, the company's resources were blocked in a segment, which was contributing 10 per cent to its business. Further, this being a low rating segment, was largely price driven and there was no necessity for the company's high technology for which it was getting value in the market in the upper segment. The company soon realised that it had erred in positioning and needed to correct itself. In spite of giving good entry level price, the company realised that it would not be able to service this segment on a long-term basis as it would not have been able to recover its basic cost.

It must be understood that not all the business is there to be captured by one party. There are segments that are catered to by different vendors. It can easily be compared with food stalls and hotels. We have roadside kiosks, small restaurants, medium budget hotels and five star hotels catering to different segments. Each has positioned itself, based on the market requirement and its own capability.

Whom to Market to?

One other aspect, which the vendor sometime forgets to address, is 'whom to market to'. It is probably not acceptable in normal marketing philosophy that one chooses a customer but considering it pragmatically, helps. An organisation in the core sector must appreciate the kind of customer it wants to have and the numbers it wants to serve. Resources are limited and it is not possible to serve an infinite number of clients with that. In the core sector where business depends on close interaction, it is not possible to have a large number of clients and then provide them partial service. Some of the issues, which can decide the choice, are:

- Whether the customer has professional approach?
- Whether he has taken proper clearances on environment and in other areas that may be required?
- Whether the customer has paying capacity?
- Whether the customer is an adventurer or a serious project developer?
- Whether the customer has proper expertise in operating such projects/products or is making arrangements to develop such skills?
- Whether the customer is a first time entrepreneur and, if so, whether he has a consultant to guide him or he is sufficiently knowledgeable to promote and develop the project?
- What kind of market philosophy is the customer having? Whether he is price driven or knowledge driven or value driven and whether this philosophy is in tune with supplier's approach?

Illustration

In a particular case, a big corporate picked up a large number of orders from first time entrepreneurs. The corporation realised, in the course of contract execution, that the customers were not having much experience with such type of projects and they had gone ahead with the project implementation without proper implementation schedules and approvals. The term 'Financial Closure' was not known to them. As a result the vendor could not get timely payment and there was a huge build up of outstandings. (In a core sector project it is very difficult to stop the work after it has gathered momentum for execution. For one, the cost of remobilisation of the resources is very high and hence many contractors, in spite of payment and other problems, proceed with the work hoping that they will get sorted out soon, which is not very uncommon if the customer is professional and an experienced one.) Naturally with such build up of outstandings, the company could not provide unending service to such clients and

Contd

wanted the customer to pay before they extended help. The customer was not able to pay as he had not properly tied his finances and was unable to get revenue also because of non-operation of plant at full capacity for want of trained operation personnel and services from vendor. Forced with this situation, the customer approached the CEO of the vendor who studied the problem, analysed it and made the following observations:

- The company had picked up orders from a price driven segment which is not the segment in which the company prefers to operate.
- The order value was not sufficient for the company to recover its cost.
- The customers were typical and felt that they need not pay the full amount and were still trying to replicate their experience of not fully paying to financial institutions after drawing loans.
- The customers were used to employing all sorts of tactics like pressure, intimidation, political/administrative intervention even to the extent of misrepresentation of facts
- Due to non-payment, the company had not even recovered the low prices it had quoted and accepted initially and was definitely making losses in the deal.
- There was no possibility of getting payment for service, which the company was asked for by the customers.

The conclusions were clear. The company had picked up the wrong segment and to add to the problem, they had also picked up the wrong customers.

Many marketing experts may not agree with the suggestion that a supplier must choose his customers in today's highly globalised and competitive market environment, but it is a hard fact that when one is operating in an infrastructure sector, it is better that one also choose his customers as one must first address the basic issue why somebody is in business. Not for any charitable reason, but to make money. We worship the customer because, by serving him, we make money. If one is not getting his dues from the customer even after serving him, where is the question of worshipping him (the customer)?

One message that come out loud and clear from the above case is that one must analyse the opportunity and list the positive and negative aspects from the following perspective:

- Environment
- Customer
- Competition
- Interest of the supplier, i.e. yourself

He must then decide, on the basis of all parameters as discussed in Chapter 3, whether to enter into this business segment or the business with a particular party. Such in-depth analysis is required particularly when the company is planning horizontal and vertical integration and also undertaking diversification.

Having discussed some basic issues, let us look into how things happen really.

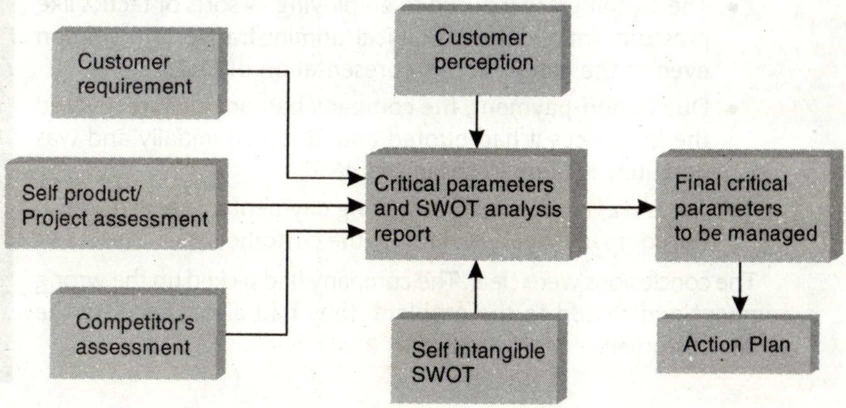

Fig. 7.5 *Meeting the Competition*

JUDGING THE COMPETITION AND MEETING IT

Business in the core sector is either through advance intimation or through formal tender. In any case, it provides reasonable time to a prospective vendor to study the situation, analyse it and develop a suitable action plan. Figure 7.5 shows an action plan chart for undertaking those activities. The first and foremost step is to identify critical parameters, which can be identified from the following base references:

- Tender specifications

- Customer's Image
- Customer's Balance Sheet
- Customer's past buying behaviour
- Feedback from similar business situations in the past

Table 7.2 *Judging the Competition and Identifying Critical Parameters*

Parameters	*Customer Perception*	*Company Status*	*Competitor –1's Status*	*Competitor –2's Status*
Qualification				
–Financial Status	3	4	5	2
–Past Experience	3	3	2	3
–Engineering Capability	4	4	3	3
–Manufacturing Capability	3	4	2	3
–Market Image	4	5	3	4
–Service Capability	5	4	5	3
–Project Management Ability	5	3	5	4
Technical				
–Performance Parameters	5	5	4	4
–Life Cycle	4	4	3	3
–Technology Status	5	5	4	2
–Quality	4	5	4	3
–Consumables Requirement	2	3	4	2
–Engineering and Human Resources	5	5	4	2
Commercial				
–Price	3	2	3	5
–Completion Schedule	5	3	5	4
–Warranty	2	5	5	5
–Commercial Condition	3	3	4	4

It is necessary that to carry out SWOT Analysis on these critical parameters. Table 7.2 shows the typical assessment procedure for these parameters. The parameters are listed on the left side of the table and customer requirement (as reflected in tender enquiry/specification), competitor's relative strength and self-organisation's strength are listed on the right side. The relative position has been shown on a scale of 1 to 5 with '1' denoting the weakest rating and '5' the highest rating. This analysis gives the relative strength and weakness of the parent organisation in comparison to the competitors with special reference to the targeted product/tender/ project.

It can be seen from the above table that critical parameters had been listed along with relative weightage given by the customer and with strength of the organisation and of its competitors. A look at the table indicates that the customer gives high weightage to engineering, technology status, service capability and completion schedule. It is clear that we are dealing with a technology/knowledge driven customer who will not mind paying a higher price for better technology, services and fast completion. It can also be seen that the company has excellent capability and is on par or better than customer expectations except in completion schedule. The company will start as a favoured supplier provided it addresses the issue of completion schedule. The company needs to convince the customer on its project management capability also. It is also clear that the critical factors for success in this business are those that are getting a rating of 4 and 5 in the customer's perception. It also indicates that competitor –2 will have a price driven strategy while competitor –1 will stress on the known weakness of the company in Project Management and Completion Schedule. The above comparison also indicates that the company can expect more close competition from Competitor –1 than Competitor –2. Based on the above analysis, the company can prepare a suitable strategic action plan for the business, taking the following parameters into consideration:

- Critical Factors
- Relative Position of Competitors (SWOT Analysis)
- Supplier's Perception of Customer (Choosing The Customer)
- Level to which an organisation is willing to go to satisfy the customer on critical parameters and price.
- Negotiation Strategy
- Strategic Action Plan

While formulating the action plan, the company may reach the conclusion that it is not possible to meet the level of customer expectancy or competition on some key parameters. It can then think whether it can change or influence the critical parameters that the customer is looking at to reduce the relative weightage of those key parameters on which the competitor is ahead of him.

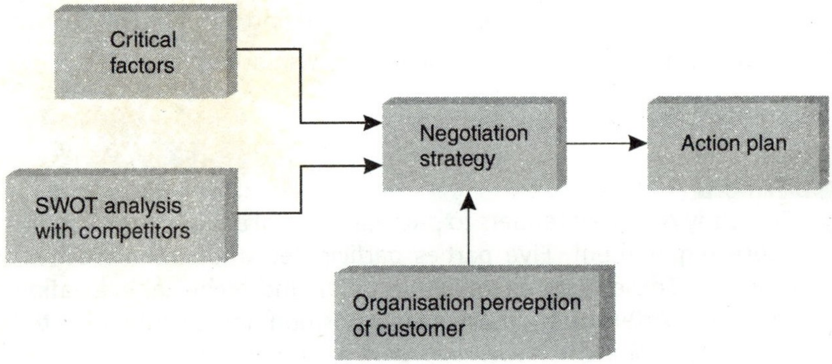

Fig. 7.6 *Business Strategy Formulation*

The reverse is also possible that the company tries to increase the weightage of those parameters on which it is strong. The company may also think whether it can change the scope or offer some other enlarged area which is its core strength and the customer may also appreciate it there by providing its competitive edge. If the bid is without financing, the company may propose financing at attractive rates. The idea is to make some revolutionary change which may force the customer to rethink in the way the company want him to think and throw its competitors off balance. The company may also suggest fundamental changes.

PRO-ACTIVE PRE-MARKETING

The other strategy is that the company follow a customer-centric focused approach. In an infrastructure sector the requirement takes a long time to get converted from concept to tender. It is necessary for a contractor to be in constant touch with the customer to understand him and his basic requirement, compare it with the company's core competence and find a common minimum requirement along with additional suggestions which should be of benefit to the customer, and at the same time, provide a competitive advantage to the company. (It must be clear that regardless of how important one may feel about certain features/scope of work for getting a competitive edge, one must not broach the subject with the customer till the supplier is fully prepared to convince the customer that it is in his interest and he is getting long-term benefits.) Such type of approach helps company to retain the customer and also create a positive impression in the customer's mind that the supplier is concerned about his welfare.

Illustration

Company A floated tenders to purchase capital equipment for its in-house requirement. Five parties participated and submitted their proposal. These were examined in detail and technical evaluation was done. After having their relative position, the customer invited them for negotiation. It was clear to all participants that the customer was a 'value driven customer'. The customer was meticulous and not only did a technical and commercial evaluation, but also worked out the premium to be paid to each bidder based on his perception and on the basis of their image in the market. Only two parameters were variable, price and completion schedule. One of the parties realised that based on his market image, the customer may prefer him provided he is able to meet the completion schedule. But he was finding it difficult to meet the expected price level. The supplier did some quick check on orders in hand and their applicability to this project and to the extent possible. He reached the decision that it was possible to meet the completion schedule by diverting material and manpower from some existing projects where progress was slow due to non-payment from the customer. However the equipment he wanted to divert were of higher capacity and rather than reducing his cost, it would result in increasing the same. But he also realised that he could make the customer see reason to accept higher capacity equipment at higher price because it would result in removing some of the bottlenecks, the customer was having in the current production schedule. This would generate additional profits for the customer and considering the long-term benefits of such recurring additional profits, their present value would really justify the additional capital cost at which supplier would also be comfortable. Encouraged with this situation, he made his proposal to the customer and explained to him the benefits. The customer realised the gain he was going to make because of these changes and awarded the contract to the supplier at a higher price. From the supplier's point of view it was an excellent situation. He got the business at his price and got rid of dead non-moving inventory lying idle due to non-payment by old customer and

Contd

to top it all, he got the appreciation and respect from the new customer for suggesting a way to increased profitability at nominal cost. *THE SUPPLIER HAD CONVERTED A PROBLEM INTO AN OPPORTUNITY AND GRABBED IT.*

There was a similar case outside India, a party who was 3rd best after evaluation walked away with the order as he offered finance to the customer (though it was not part of tender requirement) at rates and terms that were more attractive than those at which customer was arranging it.

In a third case where the strategy was similar, the supplier offered a five year Annual Maintenance Contract to the customer at extra cost. He assured the customer that this would not only ensure trouble-free operation but also high performance and availability. Additionally, he told the customer that with such an arrangement, he need not worry about the problem of spares, etc. and could also save on manpower cost of maintenance. Naturally, the party walked away with the business not only of main equipment but also of O&M. He not only got the business but also increased its quantum and return.

These cases also indicate that price reduction price is not the only option available to the vendor to get business. Reducing price hurts. As long as the price offered by the vendor is reasonable, he should try a non-price approach to increase benefits to customer to secure business.

SINCERITY OF MARKETING/APPROACH

The vendor's representative should always ensure that the promise he makes at the time of negotiation is achievable and the working is transparent. This is necessary because, in the core sector, there is every possibility that one may meet same customer or his sister company again. It is also not a good marketing practice to agree to something now and disagree later. A customer can always live with deficient performance and with non-satisfied services, but not with a vendor who makes false promises. Therefore, a supplier should always be sincere in his approach.

In a particular project there were three parties and one of them had quoted relatively high performance figures whose achievement was doubtful. On a query from the customer, the party indicated that they could further improve it. The customer was worried about their tall claims. On the other hand, the second party who had quoted relatively lower performance figures replied in the negative when requested to explore whether further improvement was feasible. They indicated that the cost of further improvement was very high and would not give the customer that much benefit compared to the extra incremental cost. The customer was impressed with their forthrightness to the extent that he awarded the contract to them even at a higher price simply because of their sincerity and logical approach.

♚ TIME HORIZON APPROACH

Sometime, some new entrants start offering unrealistic prices (as they feel that the price is the biggest determining factor) to secure business. This cannot be sustained in the medium to long run as it puts heavy pressure on the existing companies. The best approach during such a situation would be to allow this company to secure the business from some customers who want to have low prices. These companies definitely will not be able to make inroads in technology or value driven segments. Normally, a project takes two years to show results. Since these 'Fly by Night' operators would be long on promise and short on delivery, most of the customers would be able to see for themselves the folly of going with such parties and the project will become a living monument to act as a reminder to other customers not to repeat the mistakes of trusting these 'Fly by Night' operators. These will result in fading away of such parties.

8

How to Maximise Return?

Factors Affecting Profitability
Economic Value Addition
Increasing Realisation
Change the Rules

8

During the '80s, the main business focus was on business volume. Most of the corporates were more worried about the turnover of the company as it was considered to be one of the major performance evaluation criteria. The business was TOP LINE DRIVEN. But with the increasing awareness of Investors, they are demanding higher returns. It is being increasingly realised that simply winning an order is not enough. At the end of the day, one must have a reasonable return from it. Thus, the business evaluation parameter for performance is now BOTTOM LINE DRIVEN. Managements are no longer focusing their energies on volume increase in the business but more on what remains with them at the end of the transaction. At the same time it must be appreciated that growth in top line in a majority of cases leads to increase in bottom line as fixed cost is distributed over larger volume of business leading to higher growth in returns compared to business volume until and unless the volume growth is associated with decreasing realisation which is a strong possibility in a competitive market.

FACTORS AFFECTING PROFITABILITY

The concept of return is still evolving. Historically, what remains in the end in Profit and Loss Account in absolute value remains the main indicator of the profit earned by the company. As the concept of productivity gained momentum, this absolute value was converted in ratios to analytically examine its performance. These ratios are:

- Profit as percentage of Turnover
- Profit as percentage of Capital Employed

- Profit as percentage of Gross Block
- Profit as percentage of per Rupee paid

There are five major factors, which decide the level of competition and the return one can expect in the market. They are:

- Bargaining power of customer
- Bargaining power of supplier
- Competition among the existing suppliers
- Threat of substitute product/equipment
- Threat of new entrant

ECONOMIC VALUE ADDITION

During the last three years, a new concept of value creation has attracted the business world and led to new a term called ECONOMIC VALUE ADDITION, i.e. EVA. This is arrived at by deducting from net profit the cost of equity and debt. If this is positive, the business is adding economic value, otherwise it is destroying value. Simply put, this is a tool available to an investor to decide whether his investment in the industry is giving him better returns than if the same had been put in some other financial investment. During the last one year the concept has been further refined. It has been seen that many organisations, were having better profitability on the balance sheet but were having large Sundry Debtors (unrealised payment from customers) that were having the potential to become a bad debt in later years and spoil the balance sheet. Thus, the organisation's profitability today is based on positive consideration of such debts which may become bad in later years. From a business point of view the above consideration and treatment is perfectly normal, but from the investor point of view this is not advisable. Let us accept that in today's environment of performance driven compensation, a smart CEO, in spite of all the audits and checks, can deliberately declare high profits by considering on paper those amounts as realisable which may actually not be the case, or he may genuinely feel that he will make it realisable in the next two to three years, which may not happen. Such an approach is detrimental not only to investors but from organisation's point of view also and may sometimes lead to liquidation of the companies. The example of Enron is fresh in the mind of everybody. In order to protect against such happening a new term CEVA or CASH ECONOMIC VALUE ADDITION is being followed by many organisations. The simple difference between EVA and CEVA is that the profit after tax is only considered to the extent the actual cash has been realised.

Whatever may be the philosophy followed by organisations and investors in assessing profits, the fact is that there is a great deal of emphasis on increasing the returns from the business. One of the simplest ways to achieve this noble objective can be put in the following two statements:

- Increased sales realisation
- Decreased cost of operation

In real practice, the realisation of above objectives requires herculean efforts.

INCREASING REALISATION

In an infrastructure sector, the biggest advantage is that the market is willing to recognise and reward the *"DOERS"*. Thus for every right effort made, there is return.

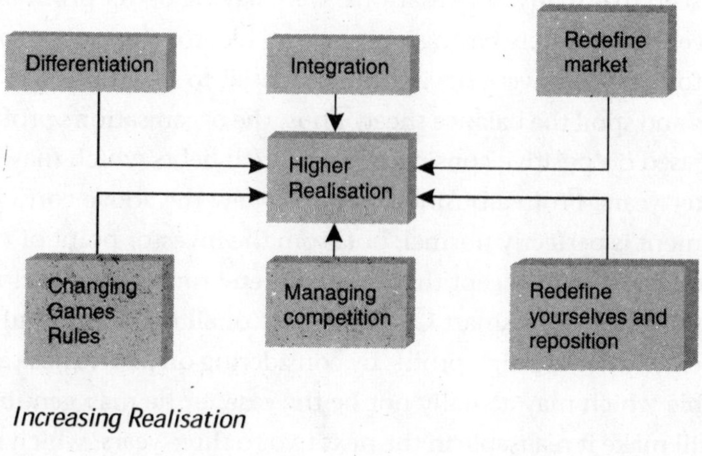

Fig. 8.1 *Increasing Realisation*

Some of the methodologies and strategies leading to higher realisation are detailed below:

- Integration
- Differentiation
- Redefining the Market
- Reposition and Redefine Yourselves
- Managing the Competition
- Change the Games Rules

Integration

Integration is the process by which the organisation starts offering more products and services to the customer through forward and backward integration, thereby not only increasing its business envelope but also reducing the competition. If the integration strategy is rightly conceived, it is welcomed by the customer as it reduces its risk and has the potential of giving him better system with high performance at competitive rates. Some of the ways of integration in business are discussed as under:

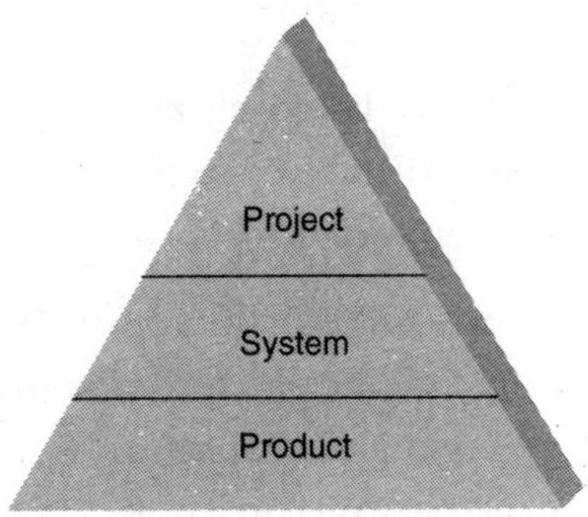

Fig. 8.2 *Stages of Business Integration*

System Integration

If an organisation is only a loose product supplier in the core sector projects, then the first logical step in business integration is to look beyond these loose products and explore the possibility of total system supply. (A system consists of a large number of small products integrated in a manner to give the desired performance.) System integration is considered to give more value addition and realisation increases much more compared to the cost incurred because it has a higher place in the value chain compared to simple product supply. The competition is also less as one moves higher in the value chain. At the same time it leads to increase in core competency of the company and probably helps in making a Brand Image for it through which it can attract some premium. System integration also creates a niche for the organisation.

Illustration

'Paharpur Cooling Tower' is one of the common examples of this. Even in large projects when the contract is awarded on the total project basis, the cooling tower part including its supply, civil works and site installation is awarded as a separate package to this company even though the main contractor might have employed a civil contractor for total work. It is common knowledge that combining all the civil works would have been cheaper but they are not willing to separate civil work of cooling tower from the overall cooling tower package. Such is the force of system integration and the niche made by Paharpur Cooling Towers in the market.

Another example is Air conditioning and Ventilation System. The realisation to the vendor will definitely be higher if he is supplying total Air conditioning system rather than individual products.

If a company is in the business of supplying loose products like transformers, switchgears, insulators, etc. for transmission projects, then it can increase its marketing edge and realisation by offering systems like complete substation. There can be similar examples in other business segments also. If a share broker or a financial agent simply offers share sale–purchase or deposit services, then he will have low realisation and competition. But if he also starts offering 'Portfolio Management Services' then he is offering total service akin to system offering and can have higher realisation due to his high value addition and consequent low competition. The incremental cost due to additional service being offered by him will be marginal. Customer loyalty will also increase, thus reducing his upfront marketing cost.

Projectisation

The next logical step in integration is to graduate from a system to a project. A project consists of a large number of small and large systems. A project executor must have the ability to break the project into systems and sub-systems and should be able to not only define their functions and inter-relations, but should have the ability to co-ordinate all these systems and sub-systems and integrate them to work suitably in a cohesive way to ensure performance and timely completion of the project. Project work involves a large amount of co-ordination, monitoring and project management work. One requires specialists and dedicated and trained resources for undertaking such type of work. The risk profile also goes high but if one has the desire and commitment the returns will more than compensate it. One can easily look forward to 10 per cent to 15 per cent higher realisation even after discounting the additional cost.

Since the returns are very attractive, there are companies which have made a special niche for themselves as Project Contractors though they may not have very high competence in the area of Systems or individual products, which constitutes the project. Such parties are basically strong in project engineering, system integration and project monitoring and management.

There is always a debate whether a company which has core competency in products or systems should logically enter a project area or not. There are companies like Siemens and GE who are leaders in individual products but do not prefer entering into projectisation. On the other hand, companies like Enron, Bechtel and Larsen and Toubro are basically project builders with nil or low base in products. We also come across companies like BHEL which have a very strong presence and competency in products and systems and feel that projectisation is the logical step in vertical integration. Thus, there are no hard and fast rules on this. It basically depends on individual companies' perception of how they can maximise their returns. Companies like GE feel that concentrating in their core area and introducing new developments can give them better returns rather than integration, while others may feel differently and so vary their business strategy.

Backward and Forward Integration

There may be occasions when the organisation would like to expand its product profile and increase its business reach and capability in order that it may lead to better realisation. Similarly, backward and forward integration can be done by project execution agencies.

BSES, which began its operations basically as a power generation company, has successfully diversified into a company that can set and operate power projects for other customers, whether they are in utilities or in more complex but small industrial field.

Similar is the case with Tata Power Company. They began their operations in Mumbai as a power generating company but have since then successfully, like BSES, established themselves as a power project construction and operation company. They have gone a step further and are now undertaking total operation and maintenance of power plants, already existing or new, and are also offering consultancy services for setting up a total power station. They are also gearing themselves up as power project developers and, if required, as minority promoters.

Reliance Industries is another example of both forward and backward integration and their business volume and profits have seen a quantum jump due to this carefully worked out plan.

Convergence in various systems/technologies can be another good reason for forward integration. Many companies have successfully increased their business envelope using this. Mahanagar Telephone Nigam Ltd (MTNL) has started offering internet services, mobile services and other value added services, in addition to normal telephone services, as a forward integration package.

Companies resort to this integration plan and diversification due to the desire to expand their business profile and to exploit new emerging opportunities. However, while undertaking such a strategy, the company must decide that it retains its basic strategic importance and core competency, which drives its marketing advantage. Diversification must add value and strength to business and not vice versa. It is often seen that backward and forward integration is the best diversification as the company can leverage its core competency, which remains relevant. It also helps in sharing skill and other expertise for ensuring greater success. This also leads to synergy among existing businesses with the new extension. Such business integrations are highly successful and help in not only increasing business volume but also by adding profit through the additional competitive advantage so built up.

Service Segment

Service is not only fast emerging as the new business area but it is also becoming an important parameter, probably at par with price and technology, for choosing a vendor. This is because all the customers have realised that their profitability lies not only in buying capital equipment at competitive rates, but in ensuring that they operate in an effective and purposeful way with high availability. Thus, if a supplier can take care of operation and maintenance of the equipment supplied by him, the customer will not mind paying a little extra to him as there is no better professionally qualified agency than the vendor himself to operate and maintain his equipment. This trend is also noticeable in the consumer household sector where the customer prefers to get the services of a supplier's authorised personnel only, even at a higher cost. Noticing this trend, there is an increasing tendency and customer preference for a supplier offering the main equipment along with accompanying service package. This not only gives the supplier a marketing edge but adds handsomely to his returns.

To begin with, companies which are only product suppliers, should start their integration process by also extending installation service. The next logical step can be to offer Annual Maintenance Contract and even operation and maintenance, i.e. O&M of the plant. Till not very long ago, O&M was always considered to be the responsibility of the customer, This resulted many times in unprofessional O&M by untrained and ill-equipped customer personnel, particularly in those cases where the customer was mainly cost driven. This resulted in problems in equipment operation which many times led the customer to think that the equipments were of not good quality and this created a misunderstanding between customer and supplier. However such situations resulted in twin actions. On the one hand, the supplier understood the value of offering an integrated supply and service package in his own interest and on the other hand, the customer realised the importance of trained O&M staff and the need for continuously upgrading their skills. The supplier is now ready to operate and maintain the equipment for a fixed number of years. Spares can either be provided by the customer or can be part of O&M package being offered by the vendor, as can be mutually agreed. In some cases even where the customer decides to have the operation under his control, he may prefer to award the maintenance contract to the supplier to derive the benefit of expert service.

Vendors are also gearing up to offer any combination of the above package of services and this results both in increasing their business volume and return. The increase in returns in many cases is reasonably higher than the increase in business volume leading to net increase in profitability ratio as a percentage of business volume.

In view of these advantages, many companies like BHEL and Wartsila have started concentrating on the service sector in a big way. This sector is a sunrise area and offers large untapped potential that can be leveraged to generate not only additional returns but, more importantly, customer satisfaction.

Banking sector is the other sector which has utilised the potential offered by service to enlarge the business envelope and profitability. Banks like ICICI have started offering internet banking and are also using the Internet to offer a variety of other services. It is possible to make investments in mutual funds and other areas through the Internet. Also facilities exist for bill payment for electricity, water, telephone and other utilities through the net at nominal charges. This approach has not only expanded the business of the bank but has given them new clients and increased returns.

In these days of economic pragmatism, many companies do not want to make fresh investment until it becomes unavoidable. They would prefer to continue with existing old equipment if it could be retrofitted and re-powered. This is highly profitable work as the customer would be willing to pay higher price if his need for fresh investment can be deffered for a reasonable period with only a part investment in existing equipment so that his work and profitability is not affected. The exercise involves assessing the life of existing equipment and identifying the work and cost involved in increasing the life and performance of the equipment, for say, another 20 per cent of life of new equipment. Many companies have created special expert groups to exploit this new business environment and opportunity. There is great potential in the service sector that is still evolving. Suppliers can formulate different innovative packages to help the customer and, in the process, boost their own profitability. The vendor can create a consultancy wing or expert group to offer technical advice and solution of operation and maintenance problems faced by the customers. This concept of *CALL CENTERS* is fast catching up and contains in itself a lot of opportunities for increasing the returns.

Knowledge and experience are invaluable and any organisation that can develop a strategy to leverage them can surely see their bottom line healthy.

Boo/Boot Approach

While infrastructure projects are capital intensive, they require a long time for completion and the return is slow. They really test the staying power of the project developer. Therefore, many times the customer either wants the contractor to take equity in the project or finance it partly or fully. The customer may also ask the vendor to set up the project with his own finances, operate and maintain it and keep the revenue. Such types of projects are called *BUILT OPERATE AND OWN*, i.e. BOO. The contractor must ensure that the project is viable and he can recover his capital cost, operating expenditure and some return. The responsibility of project viability and setting up is practically transferred to the vendor from the customer. Though the responsibility for vendor is manifold because he is now in the dual role of developer and project executor, the returns are handsome for two reasons as under:

- The customer feels free from any problem that may arise during the project execution or operation.
- The competition is negligible.

The above concept is sometimes modified in the sense that the customer may want the project to be transferred to him at a predetermined consideration after a fixed pre-agreed period. This concept is called *BUILT OPERATE OWN AND TRANSFER*, i.e. *BOOT.* Due to the reasons discussed above, the return in this case is also high but is associated with increased risk.

Such type of approach has become very common in construction sector, whether it be road, bridge or highways. The builder not only sets up the project but operates it, collects revenue in the form of toll tax and meets his capital expenditure, interest there on and operating cost. Similarly, the vendor may pick up part equity in the project. This approach provides added comfort to the main customer who will feel that there is a financial stake of the contractor on the success of the project. The vendor may also provide lease arrangement for meeting capital requirements. Naturally, the competition is limited and the return is very high.

The Differentiation

Some time back there used to be a regular advertisement of Maggi Hot Tomato sauce which was promoted with only one theme, viz., *it's different.* Differentiation is the key to life and if a product or a human being is promoted, then the only factor that is considered is how different he is from others. All goods and services are differentiable. In the world, there is differentiation everywhere. Differentiation and positive differentiation is the key to success. Everybody likes Sachin Tendulkar as a cricketer because he has skill, qualities, temperament and achievements which are different from others and in a positive way.

When there are many candidates for only one post, the only parameter to look for is positive differentiation and how it can benefit the organisation. The same principle applies in business deals.

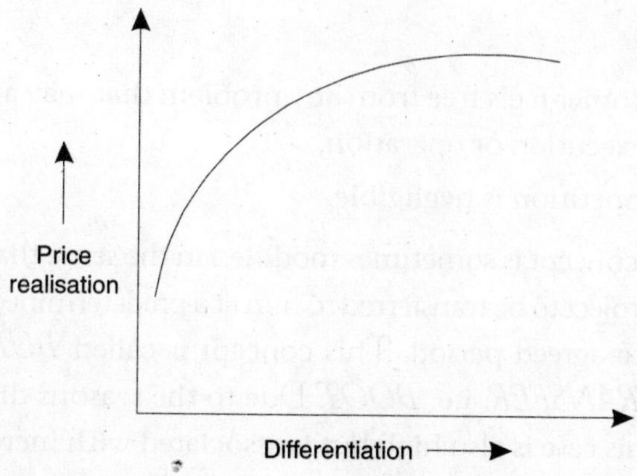

Fig. 8. 3 *Increased Price Realisation through Differentiation*

If an organisation wants to have business at premium then the main questions that he may face from the customers are:

- What is the difference?
- Is it positive from the customer's point of view?
- What additional value will it generate to the customer?
- Is the additional value generated more than the premium charged by the vendor and, if so, how much?
- The differentiation will lead to higher price realisation as can be seen from Fig.8.3.

The differentiation can be generated in the following ways with different parameters:

- Image
- Professional Approach
- Technology/Engineering Strength
- Customer Response
- Human Resources
- Past Experience
- Service
- Contract Completion Schedule
- Quality and Product/Project Life Cycle
- Vendor's Financial Position and his ability to generate Resources

Image

This is the biggest parameter that determines the inner inclination and approach of the customer. There are customers who give higher weightage to Image than any other parameter. There are many factors that shape the Image of the company. These factors include not only professional attributes like engineering/process/manufacturing and service ability but the company's culture, habits, attitude, orientation, quality consciousness and capability of its employees. The perception of customer about the vendor plays a major role in his decision making about the award of the contract and the premium to be paid.

The Image of an organisation is the combination of its culture, performance, corporate practices and commitment and is built over a long period of time. It is achieved through major investment in those areas which contribute to it. This is unique and is immediately related to the organisation and it is so important that it leads to right association.

Illustration

One organisation invited proposals for a major project and received bids from five parties. The contract was awarded to party B, which was not the lowest and the premium paid was 12 per cent over the next lowest party. The justification note for awarding the contract to party B mentioned the following points:

Positive

- The vendor is having state-of-the-art and proven technology and engineering capability
- The company is a professional company and has professional and acknowledged internal system on engineering, procurement, process, manufacturing and quality assurance apart from technology. It has high quality tools and machines.
- The company is financially sound and the present project will not face any problem on the financial front.
- The company does not compromise on engineering system practices and quality irrespective of price realisation. Thus, the customer can expect the same treatment irrespective of the price negotiated.
- The company has highly skilled and trained manpower. It has regular programmes for upgrading skills of its personnel.
- The company has high reputation for customer-focused approach and is known to help the customer in case of need.
- The company has a high reputation for providing timely quality and effective 'After sales service'.
- The company has the engineering ability to solve any design/ operational problems during the lifetime of the equipment. It also has the appreciation of its customers to avoid narrow interpretation of contractual clauses for undue enrichment.
- The company's products have a reputation for high life cycle and trouble-free operation.

Contd

- The company can provide quickly spares required by the customers,

Negative

- The company has no effective project management capability and has at best only project monitoring activity ability.
- The company lacks flexibility and suffers from inertia in re-deploying its resources to arrest the delay already set in.
- The company manpower suffers from overtime syndrome that may affect the completion schedule.

It was suggested that on the balance, the vendor is way ahead of its peers and the order with premium placed on the vendor is justified, as the customer will get higher value for the premium paid.

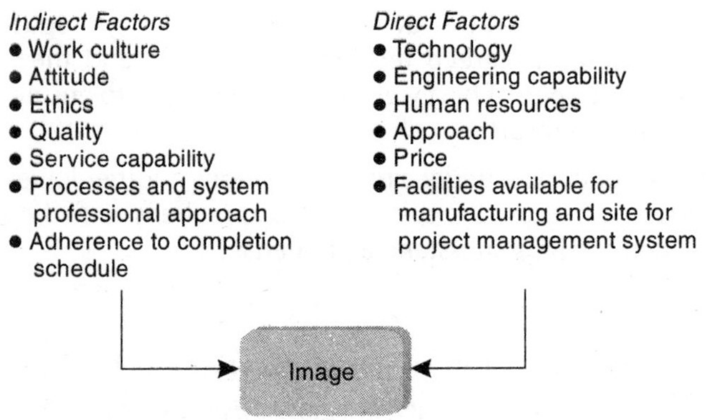

Fig. 8.4 *Factors Contributing to Organisational Image*

Many times in the case of vendors the main issue to be addressed by the customer is not whether premium is to be paid or not but how much premium has to be paid. In an infrastructure sector project, the customer is aware that he and his consultant, in spite of all the precautions they might have taken and with all the experience they might have, cannot be the substitute for capabilities and expertise of the vendor. It is the vendor, his engineering practices, his system, and his expertise that will finally decide the life, actual performance, operation and maintenance of the equipment. Hence, most of the knowledgeable customers are ready to pay a higher price to get long-term comfort and confidence.

Professional Approach and Attitude

The second major issue is the kind of approach a company adopts to the business and its attitude towards it. Many customers closely examine whether the contractor's decision on engineering, sub vendor selection, procurement, manufacturing, site work and testing are guided by professional considerations or by other reasons. The customer is also anxious about the attitude of the supplier.

Illustration

In one particular case, a well known customer placed an order on a party at a substantial price (about 20 per cent more) higher than other party as they felt that the lowest bidder was having a reputation for compromising on agreed technical parameters and they or their consultant, in spite of best vigil, would not be able to ensure that the vendor did not resort to such practices.

In a second case, under similar conditions another lowest bidder was rejected because the customer was apprehensive of the vendor's reputation for using sub-standard material.

In some cases, the customer started worrying if he found unethical practices prevailing in the supplier's organisation as he felt that this would affect the quality of equipment being supplied by the vendor to him.

In all the above cases, the major reason driving the customer's decision was the comfort and confidence he had in the vendor. He was be willing to pay a higher price if the vendor would address those requirements and give him the above two pre-requisites.

Technology

One of the biggest factors that creates differentiation is the technology, engineering capability and ability of an organisation to develop and make further refinements and improvements in the product or substitute it with better alternatives.

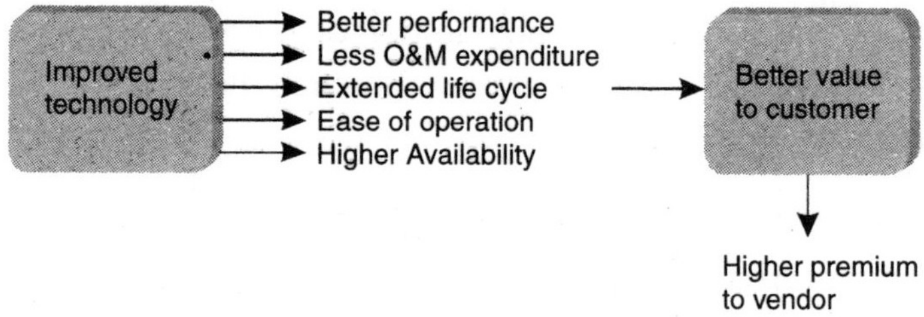

Fig. 8.5 *Premium from Technology*

Better technology can make the equipment to give better efficiency and performance not only at the time of installation but also during the life span of the equipment. This may lead to relatively higher output from the equipment for the same quantum of input and may lead to major revenue advantage for the customer who may like to work out total Net Present Value of the benefit and he will be willing to pay a fraction of it as additional price to vendor.

Another advantage that technology can give is lower operation and maintenance cost and long life span of the equipment, which will result in higher value for the money invested. The ease of maintenance may result in higher availability, lower maintenance cost and consequently higher price realisation for vendor.

In core sector projects, higher availability and lower O&M cost can give vendor higher price realisation by 5–10 per cent as lower O&M requirement may also result in lower requirement of spares and consequently saving in expenditure on account of this. It is common knowledge that any product originating from General Electric or Siemens can command about 10 per cent premium in the market due to the perceived technological superiority of the product.

Customer Response

A customer is willing to pay a higher price if he likes the vendor and he prefers the vendor if the latter had helped him during his hour of need and responded to his SOS calls. Responsiveness of an organisation to the customer is now found to be one of the biggest differentiation factors. If an organisation does not take the customer or his officials seriously, it cannot hope to get business and there is no question of any extra price. During the execution of the project a customer may approach the vendor for any of the following work:

- Improvement in the Project Completion Schedule
- Vendor's top management help in arresting delay
- Complaint on non-performance or deficient performance of equipment and urgency to ensure their rectification.
- Urgent help in case of breakdown of earlier supplied equipment by vendor or by some other party which, in the opinion of the customer, the vendor is capable of correcting.
- Spares supply

It may be possible that the vendor may not be in a position to accept or fulfill all or part of the desires/requests of the customer but, in such circumstances, if the vendor explains his position, reasons and constraints to customer, the understanding is better. Relationship and attitude is more important than actual work. The customer should be given due importance and he must feel that the vendor organisation gives him the respect and recognition that he as a customer deserves.

There had been occasions when senior officers of the vendor had refused to take telephone calls from the customer because of their preoccupation or due to other reasons. For these actions of the officers, the employer had lost business. But there had also been cases when, due to fast and positive response given by the vendor's staff, he had got business at a premium. This had been the case when the assistance had come in his hour of need and the vendor had gone out of the way to help the customer and save him from loss.

Illustration

There was one interesting case when a major corporate in India, which had imported equipment from outside, suffered a breakdown requiring service personnel from the parent company. Calling them from abroad and paying them was not an easy job but to minimise its own production loss and seeing no alternative, the company agreed. The service personnel from the vendor came and dismantled the equipment. They found the fault and advised the customer that parts

Contd

would require to be repatriated to the works for repair as nothing much could be done at the site. The customer was naturally worried about the cost and time required for airfreighting and repairs. They were aware of similar facilities available in the country with a reputed vendor whom they had not preferred because they wanted imported equipments. They approached the vendor and explained their problem and sought his help. The vendor, in spite of being earlier neglected by the purchaser, readily agreed and with his help and expert advice, they could not only repair the damaged equipment but were also able to put it in service in record time. The customer was highly impressed and when he had similar requirement later, he not only preferred the vendor who had helped him in his hour of need but gave him a reasonable premium of about 10 per cent. The customer had realised that the purchase decision is to be taken not only considering the facts and benefits available at that time but to take into account the likely maintenance problem that he is going to face in the next twenty years during the life time of the equipment and during all this period he would need the vendor more than the vendor needed him today. The premium was the value that the customer paid for past timely help and guaranteed help that he would need in future.

In a majority of cases a customer prefers to pay reasonable premium because he is conscious of the fact that the equipment he is installing would operate for the next 25 years and he would be dependent on the vendor for supply of spares and services and vendor's lack of priority would affect him more. *It is this realisation between purchaser and supplier that both need each other, which is the essence of business relationship on which the core sector business foundation rests.*

Human Resources

The supplier's personnel, their ability, capability, attitude and approach have become one of the major factors for business decision today. Ten years back the major parameter for business decision was price because the purchaser used to tell that *the price he was paying was fact. Technology, ease of maintenance and service are futuristic and are fiction.* No longer now. Ten years from now when the gap in technology will narrow down and differences between organisations in the field of expertise in engineering, manufacturing and services may not be much, it will be the quality of human resources that will be the biggest differentiating factor.

While technological and engineering gap can be bridged through collaboration, high accuracy and automated machines can be bought and installed, training programme can be arranged as desired but attitude, culture, intelligence and experience, the decision making ability are very difficult to buy. They have to be nurtured over a period of time and requires strong long-term dedication and herculean efforts to change. Employees are the biggest assets of an organisation and a company, which does not realise this, is destined to fade away into history. There is a common saying in India: *one can take a horse to a water pond, you can open his mouth and pour water in it but whether he will drink water or not is his choice.* This is also true about human beings. One can provide good environment, good compensation package, good technology, excellent machines and tools but whether the employee will work effectively, is not dependent on any of the above factors. The intention to work to excel, to honour commitment, is an intrinsic quality of a work culture to be developed over the years. When a customer enters into a contract with a supplier, he is also contracting this non-visible but important aspect that will touch his business and performance, his productivity and returns for years to come. It is often seen in some organisations that a worker or employee goes out of the way to address the concern of the customer. Many times he may not be dealing with the project but he goes out of the way to contact his concerned colleagues to address the concern of the customers. Such a positive attitude is highly appreciated by the customers and they start liking such organisations, which result in higher business and definitely higher realisations.

In the core sector, the Customer comes in very close contact with the vendor's persons. Right from the pre-tender stage to post-installation services through marketing, negotiations, engineering, manufacturing, testing installation, training, site problem solving, there are numerous occasions when the customer comes in close touch with different facades of the supplier team. During these interactions, the customer makes his opinion about the attitude, approach, expertise and capability of the supplier company, which is a culmination of the impression created by the supplier's employee. It may so happen in a big organisation that different functions may leave different footprints. Many times it is seen that while a customer prefers an organisation for a particular project, he may reject it outright, at the same time, for some other requirements

Bill Gates had said that Microsoft was an excellent organisation because it had excellent people. During the recent terrorist attack on World Trade Center, New York, the CEO of a company whose whole office records and property was destroyed in the terrorist attack, opined that nothing had been lost as all his employees were safe.

Bad approach and attitude may also lead to loss of business. A senior management level officer of a big corporate, heading an operation group, was in the habit of avoiding customer calls as he felt that these bring, with them unnecessary problems and lead to wastage of his time. Slowly, many customers became aware of his habits and, in the process, they started avoiding the officer and the company itself. This resulted in loss of business and in a few months came to the notice of the company chairman who appointed a team to find out the reasons for falling business. The team met the customers and other concerned persons and found to their surprise that the reason was the attitude of neglect of one of their senior executives, which made the customers feel unwanted.

Past Experience of Customer

It is common knowledge that the cost of retaining a customer is much smaller than adding a new customer. Thus, the business from an established customer can produce higher returns not only in marketing but also from the fact that the customer is aware of the practices, culture and other aspects of the vendor. The seller need not spend much amount or time in training him and can save expenditure. The purchaser is also well versed with the maintenance and operation procedure and this is a bonus as a well-trained customer means lesser site troubles and good operation of equipments already supplied.

One satisfied customer not only gives you further business himself but act as the vendor's business ambassador and brings further business from other clients. He acts as a verified proven reference list of the vendor. This advantage comes to the vendor at no extra cost.

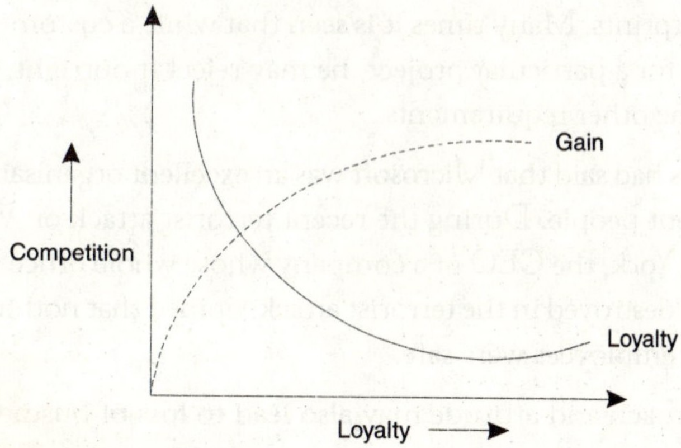

Fig. 8.6 *Competition, Loyalty and Gain*

Additionally, as new customers come to the vendor after checking the existing work of the vendor and getting appreciation from fellow customers, they are willing to even buy at a premium. If the satisfied customer is from a big corporate house, then the vendor can hope to get further business from all the companies of that corporate house. In such cases not only will the marketing cost come down, but the cost of serving the customer will also be less.

The vendor should continuously strive to retain customer loyalty as this will lead to more realisation and less cost. It is seen that loyalty is inversely proportional to competition. The converse is also true. The more the loyalty, the lesser the competition. Figure 8.6 shows the gain that can be achieved with loyalty.

The passive way of looking at the above graph will be that with the reduction in competition, the loyalty and gain will go up. A more pro-active way of increasing realisation is to ensure higher loyalty of customers which will automatically reduce competition.

In the core sector it is not uncommon that a customer specify only one vendor for many sub systems, realising fully well that he may end up paying 8–10 per cent higher price on these items. *Thus the key to higher realisation is customer loyalty that comes through higher customer satisfaction.*

Service

How do you create a perceptible difference that sets your product above the rest? The key is Service—not adequate customer service but exemplary, extraordinary attention to the customer.

At American Express, service is our 'differentiator'—outstanding, superior service quality. It is part of our contract with our customers. If something goes wrong, we view it as an opportunity to demonstrate our ability to exceed our customer's expectations. We don't want our customers to be simply satisfied, we want them to be delighted.

Terrence J Smith
Senior Vice President,
American Express Company

During the last ten years, the business environment has substantially changed and it has led to the development of new demanding customers who are also service sensitive. Many companies who have understood these changes have themselves set a higher standard of services so that the customers have not to put up with second grade services.

A survey in USA shows that 96 per cent of dissatisfied customers never complain but 90 per cent of them never return and 13 per cent of these unhappy customers will tell at least twenty others. Recent surveys have established that one factor that has influence ahead of price in the core sector is service. Thus if a vendor establishes his name for providing quality and timely service, he can get a higher price in the market.

It is often said that *customers do not buy products; they buy only benefits* and benefits only accrue through good service. It is an acknowledged fact that capital equipments in the industrial market have a high life cycle. In order to ensure that the equipment functions satisfactorily during the period, the customer needs regular service from the vendor. If the vendor can provide timely supply of spares and quality and timely service, the customer enjoys the *'benefits'* of the equipment he bought and is willing to share the pleasure with the vendor by paying him a higher price.

Contract Completion Schedule

This is one of the most well known means of increasing returns. Most of the customers are in a great hurry to complete the project early due to the following reasons:

- Normally 90 per cent of the customers get delayed in their decision making on either investment or management decisions or due to extraneous environmental factors. There can also be delay in selection of vendor. Delay can also take place due to abnormal time taken in statutory approval or in arranging finances. Having lost time at the initial stage itself, the customer wants to recover as much time as may be possible.
- Most of the core sector projects require a long time for completion and have heavy investment from financial institutions, promoters and the public. Any delay can lead not only to cost overrun but also additional financial burden in the form of interest. On the other hand reducing the project schedule is one of the surest ways of minimising the cost of project execution.
- Having made the investment decision and gone ahead with the project, the customer is interested in its completion in the shortest possible time to enjoy the benefits of the project and to start pay back by earning revenues from the operation and paying dividend to the investors.

Thus, a short completion schedule gives definite financial benefits to the customers and most of them do not mind sharing them with the vendor. Thus the concept of Bonus is prevalent in all core sector projects. It is the incremental rate of extra price the customer will contractually pay for every incremental early completion in the project. Many times during evaluation of the tender itself, the customer gives a price benefit to a vendor for offering a short completion schedule. From the vendor's point of view he not only gets higher realisation but his working capital requirement is also reduced, thereby giving another boost to his profitability. Thus it is a double benefit to a vendor. The customer, on his part goes out of the way to help the vendor complete the project early because his stakes are higher than those of the vendor.

The only catch is he should be able to offer that extra reduction in schedule and should be able to achieve it. In core sector large projects this is easier said than done but if one is able to achieve it, then there is handsome benefit. This extra benefit requires the vendor to build up a reputation for timely completion of the projects. It must be understood that as far as the bonus for early completion of the project is concerned, it is based on actual completion and if the project is really completed early, the customer will pay bonus readily. However benefit in price during tender evaluation is based on the presumption that the vendor will definitely complete the project early and it is more wishful thinking than a reality. Thus the evaluation benefit will be based on vendor's past performance of similar projects rather than the present projects and hence the necessity of image of timely completion. Penalty or Liquidated damages is poor compensation for delay in project completion.

Some of the well-known corporates do not get the benefits of upfront premium for offering short completion schedule at tender evaluation stage as they do not enjoy the reputation of keeping their word on project completion schedule.

Quality and Product/Project Life Cycle

Ten years back the word "Quality" was mostly associated with process, i.e. manufacturing, and to some extent with cost reduction by minimising or stopping the rework/rejections. However during recent years the concept of Quality has undergone total change. Today, everyone is looking for 'TOTAL QUALITY MANAGEMENT' (TQM) in total business and project execution chain. TQM covers not only the old concept of quality but incorporates new parameters like engineering, human resources, completion time, customer complaints, site problems, etc. The best part about TQM is that it also rates a company in comparison to its peers and the best in the trade. It is this feature which makes TQM a preferred tool.

This perfectly matches with the modern concept that the customer does not buy products or services; he only buys benefits. Thus quality becomes an important parameter for his decision making and for predicting his purchase behaviour. Figure 8.7 shows the importance of quality in maximising the return. If we provide quality as per the customer expectations, then we have satisfied the customer. However, taking a cue from the business philosophy of American Express Co. Vice President, if one exceeds the expectation and delight of the customer then definitely the vendor can expect suitable reward for making the customer happy. The customer has also now realised that long-term performance, service and availability of equipment depends on the quality consciousness of the parties connected with the project.

Many companies have secured ISO certification (International Accreditation) on quality and they proudly display it as a proof of recognised quality assurance system of international standards duly certified by a recognised third party. Though this creates a positive impression on the customer, the actual price preference depends mostly on the past experience of the customer and the reputation the vendor enjoys in the market. If the customer is delighted with the quality of the product and services offered by the vendor, he is prepared to give upfront price preference to the vendor.

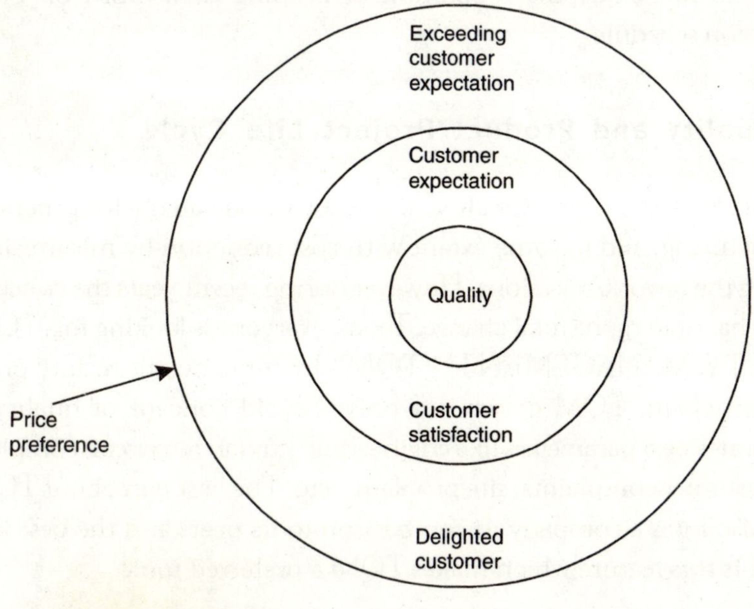

Fig. 8.7 *Quality and Price Preference*

Many companies have therefore started an internal TQM Assessment System, which not only assesses the internal system of the company but also awards marks to them relative to other competing companies. This enables the supplier organisation to not only keep in view their own improvement but also keep track of their competitors. TQM System is also designed to get actual aspects of the company from the customer, to judge his opinion of the company, to assess his expectations and his feedback on the competitors. The assessment system can cover the following major areas:

- Customer perception and feedback
- Engineering practices and improvement
- Manufacturing Technology/Process
- Installation Feedback
- Service
- Cost leadership
- Project Performance

TQM Assessment can cover a wide area like Price realisation, productivity, profitability, after sales service, rejection rate, performance of the equipment and can make relative assessment of the customer's expectation and supplier's readiness. Such assessment helps the supplier in constantly working towards exceeding customer expectation and delighting him to get that extra gain. It should always be appreciated that the 'customer delight' is a journey whose destination is mobile and changes with environment.

Vendor's Financial Position and Ability to Generate Resources

We have discussed in earlier sections that completion schedule is very essential from the customer angle to ensure that he is getting better results. The customer is also aware that no vendor can meet his contractual commitment, much less exceed it until he has sound financial position and adequate resources. Further, if the project is getting delayed, then the delay can be minimised or eliminated if the company is capable of increasing its resources, which in a majority of cases would be higher than what would have been required in the normal course. For example, if the assembly of major equipment is getting delayed due to non-availability or delay of some small parts, then the vendor who is resourceful may even think of air freighting them at his own cost rather than transporting it by train or ship. Similarly he can pay for more shifts/overtime or invest more resources to arrest the delay or expedite, project if he had the financial ability. Many vendors may not be able to get timely loan from financial institutions and, ultimately, this may delay their project for which the customer may have to suffer. Therefore, many knowledgeable customers are willing to pay a premium to a financially sound party having proven capability to add/re-deploy his resources to ensure timely completion of the project.

Redefine the Market

If the supplier is not able to meet the competition or want to increase the realisation then he has to change the market perception, i.e. he must ensure that the customer requirement is re-worked in such a way as to increase the benefits to the customer and, at the same time, it provides advantage to the vendor. The three possible ways to redefine the market are:

- Integration
- Substitution
- Moving up the Value Chain

We have already discussed in detail the Integration in business where we are expanding the envelope of business based on our strength to add value and benefits to the customer and its advantage in maximising the gain to the supplier.

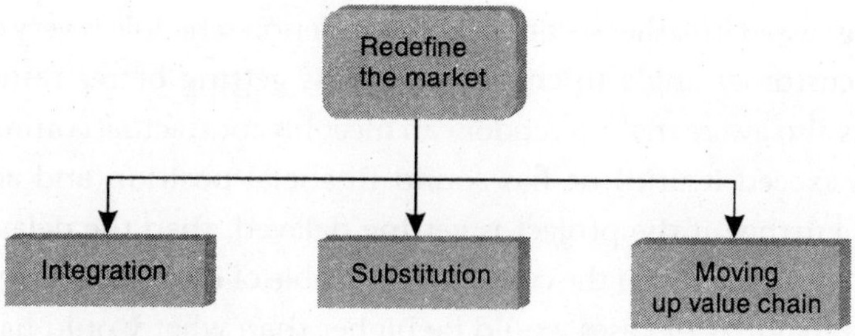

Fig. 8.8 *Redefining the Market*

Substitution

The second most profitable strategy is *substitution.* Here a vendor introduces an entirely new concept/product/philosophy to give additional benefit to the customer at a small incremental price. The whole package is made in such a way that the customer gets more return than before and is therefore attracted to the new concept. Though there are numerous examples in the core sector on this concept but in order to have more clarity, let us pick up some examples from the consumer sector.

Illustration

OTG (Oven–Toaster–Grill) is a very common product. Some companies who were finding it difficult to survive or wanted to increase their return, substituted the same with 'Micro oven' and brought it to a level where it give OTG stiff competition. As a result many customers who wanted to purchase OTG shifted to Micro oven gladly paying the extra cost for the additional benefits they got.

Every household has MIXI (Grinder and Mixer). Some companies, in order to get higher realisation, introduced, Juicer also with this. Some others went a step ahead and discovered the 'Food Processor' which gave tremendous benefit to the customer and good money to supplier and, in the process, destroyed the near monopoly of a well known vendor. This is probably the best example of what a substitution can do. In a single strategy three objectives were achieved, namely the established vendor's market share was badly hit; the customer was provided substantial additional benefits and naturally the new vendor made the money.

A well-known colliery wanted to set up a captive power plant using coal. Naturally many parties were interested. One of the companies, along with customer help, found that washery rejects from the collieries could be used as fuel. The customer was delighted as he was getting value from a resource which, for all practical purposes, was of zero value to him.

Moving up the Value Chain

The other way of redefining the market is to ensure that we encourage the customer to move up the value chain. Such movement will ensure that we are not allowing the market to remain static. By forcing the change, one is creating a challenge to the existing major players and allowing the market to re-adjust it. The customer gets more value and the entrepreneur and persisting vendor gets more return. The example of microwave oven was just an example of moving up the value chain to maximise the return.

Redefine Yourselves and Reposition

The supplier should make a careful assessment of profitability and volume of the equipment he is offering. He may find out that in some products, in spite of all the efforts he is making, he is not getting the return he was expecting. It is then time for serious introspection. He should decide whether he should continue to market this product further. Every product/equipment/theory has its life span and it should be allowed to gracefully fade away from the scene as soon as its period has expired. This will help the organisation to concentrate on the equipments and the projects in which it is strong and consequently increase its realisation for same amount of efforts. The vendor can also redefine his marketing strategy. He should consider whether his basic approach as a value supplier, knowledge or cost based supplier needs to be changed in the light of changed market conditions. He may also decide whether he would like to remain a product supplier or wants to graduate into a system and project supplier. The main idea is that every supplier discovers his core strength and uses it to increase his return as much as feasible.

It can also happen that the supplier finds that he is competitive only in a certain range or above a certain capacity. Then the supplier should re-position himself. Positioning is the outcome of a well thought out strategy based on the market conditions, the competition to sell the product in a certain bandwidth with respect to capacity or industry segment, etc. to derive maximum benefits. Positioning is to be decided with a lot of thinking and planning as we are committing that product to the certain decision and restriction to augment its appeal and monetary value

Managing the Competition

One of the major reasons for less return from the supplier's point of view is the ever increasing competition. Thus if a supplier is able to manage the competition, then he is on the right path to increasing gains.

Overcoming the competitor or acquiring a sufficient foothold in its decision making is the most common tool presently employed by the parties to manage the competition. Gujarat Ambuja acquired shares of ACC to acquire a 'say' in managing ACC, reduce competition and leverage their combined strength to maximise return. Similar philosophy was followed by Birla Group in acquiring shares of L&T which was in the process of divesting its cement division to concentrate in its core area of projects. Grasim group, the Flagship Company of Aditya Birla Group in cement, readily concluded that L&T with its large capacity could be the deciding factor for the competition in the field. If it fell into wrong hands, i.e. say with their competitors like La–Farge, it would not only create stiff competition but a strong base for La–Farge to expand cement business in India and offer them intense competition. This would have resulted in serious erosion in their profitability. So they decided to block the move by acquiring a stake in L&T from Reliance at a price higher than the market price thus effectively blocking L&T's move to come out of the cement business. Grasim, by its pro-active approach, has not allowed competition to build up.

Another example of managing the competition is to submit joint bids for a project and share the business. Such an arrangement reduces competition and thereby increases return. In some places where there is excess capacity, this is standard practice. OPEC control on production of crude oil is the most visible example of business sharing by managing the competition for maximising the gains.

Business sharing, wherever successful, can result in increased realisation of around 10 per cent in normal cases. It also helps the vendor organisation reduce its cost.

CHANGE THE RULES

The supplier can possibly attempt to change the scope and condition of the project to derive the advantage. In one particular case in an international tender, a supplier who was not the lowest evaluated bidder arranged financing to win the business at higher price. One can change the scope, specification and even evaluation criteria by submitting proposals that give higher values to the customer and definitely higher price to himself.

to manage the competition. Gujarat Ambuja acquired shares of ACC to acquire a say in managing ACC, reduce competition and leverage their combined strength to maximise return. Similar philosophy was followed by Birla Group in acquiring shares of L&T which was in the process of divesting its cement division to concentrate in its core area of projects. Grasim group, the flagship company of Aditya Birla Group in cement, broadly concluded that L&T with its large capacity could be the deciding factor for the competition in the field. If it fell into wrong hands, i.e. say with their competitors like La-farge, it would not only create stiff competition but a strong base for La-farge to expand cement business in India and offer them intense competition. This would have resulted in serious erosion to their profitability. So they decided to block the move by acquiring a stake in L&T from Reliance at a price higher than the market price thus effectively blocking L&T's move to come out of the cement business. Grasim, by its pro-active approach, has not allowed competition to build up.

Another example of managing the competition is to submit joint bids of tender and share the business in such a way that it reduces competition and thereby increases return. In some places where there is excess capacity, this is standard practice. OPEC control on production of crude oil is the most visible example of business sharing by managing the competition for maximising the sales.

Business sharing, wherever successful, can result in increased realisation of around 10 per cent in normal cases. It also helps the vendor organisation reduce its cost.

CHANGE THE RULES

The supplier can possibly attempt to change the scope and condition of the project to derive the advantage. In one particular case of an international tender, a supplier who was not the lowest evaluated bidder arranged financing to win the business at higher price. One can change the scope, specification and even evaluation criteria by submitting proposals that give higher values to the customer and ultimately higher price to himself.

9

Market Share and 100 per cent Market Share Syndrome

Market Share and its Importance
Market Share Trend
Low Market Share
High Market Share
Optimum Market Share
Negative effect of increasing Market Share beyond Optimum Level
Advantages of Competition
What should be the Optimum Market Level?

9

MARKET SHARE AND ITS IMPORTANCE

Market Share is one of the parameters to measure the performance of the company and that of its competitors in the market. It is a measure of the percentage of the business a supplier is enjoying for a particular product or system or in the particular business segment. This also determines the presence of the company in that particular segment. The market share can be defined for a product or project. If the company is in the business of selling 'cranes' then the share of business it can pick up in this segment should become its market share. However, in the core sector, rarely does one company operate to cover the entire range of the product. It generally operates in a segment of the capacity range. In the case of the crane itself, the company may decide that it will operate in the range from 5 MT to 120 MT. Most of the companies, in order to assess their presence in the market, start defining the market share as the percentage of the business they have secured in this range. There are others who, in addition to getting information on market share in their interested range, also try to simultaneously collect information about the market share in the total product range to assess how much business they are attempting. The business growth can then come from expanding the company's range of operation to unserviced portion. The basic purpose of market share is:

- To access the quantum of business secured by the company in a particular product/business segment in total and in a particular range.
- To access the quantum of business secured by other competitors in same product/business segment in total and in a particular range.
- To identify future growth areas

- To identify competitors and their market presence
- To act as a parameter to measure relative change in business secured by various suppliers over a time period and to ascertain whether the supplier is on the right track or needs course correction.

Many business experts do not consider the market share alone as a parameter to measure business success. They also consider the capacity of the company along with the market share to judge the success of the organisation's business strategy. One company may have 40 per cent market share but may have only 20 per cent installed capacity utilisation. On the other hand another company may have 30 per cent market share but 80 per cent capacity utilisation. Definitely, in spite of lower market share, the second company's business strategy seems to be better.

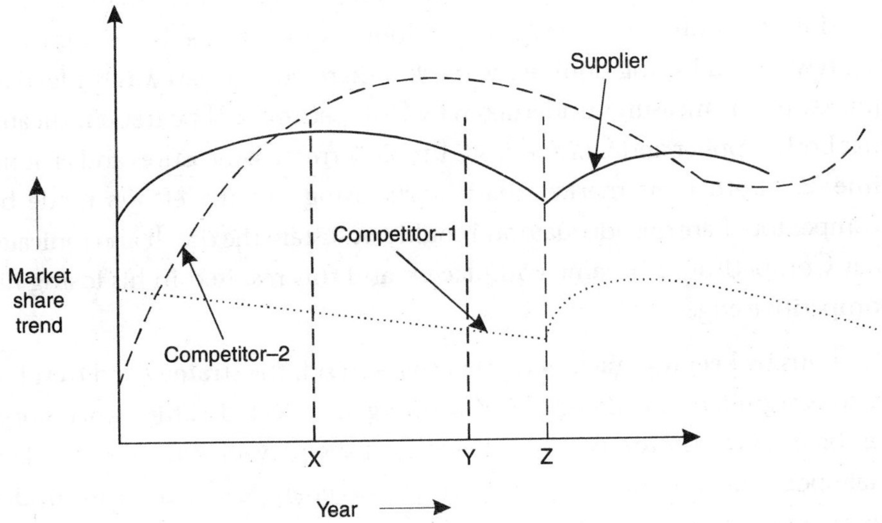

Fig. 9.1 *Market Share Trend*

MARKET SHARE TREND

The trend in market share of the supplier and of the competitor also gives an indication of the outcome of the strategy followed by the supplier and the competitor. Figure 9.1 shows the trend in market share of the main supplier company conducting the study along with two other competitors.

The market share of the supplier was increasing slowly but continuously and reached a maximum at the instance 'X' and then started decreasing thereafter. The market share of Competitor–1 is continuously on a downward path, which indicates his indifference to the business or lack of proper core competencies. But Competitor–2 takes the business seriously. Its market share picks up at a rapid pace and surpasses that of supplier whose business share is also increasing at a slow pace. But Competitor–2 soon starts eating into the business of supplier and Competitor–1. Long-term positive market share trend indicates that this competitor had done major work in building competitive edge. This may have been in the form of new technology, price or by way of enhancing value to the customer or due to other strategic measures taken by him which resulted in increased business to him. The measure was serious and productive as the sharp and sustained upswing indicates. They were strong enough to propel him to market leader position from number–3 laggards in double quick time. The supplier to begin with was having double the market share but the gap was bridged in quickly by the measures undertaken by Competitor–2. The trend indicates that both supplier and Competitor–1 took corrective measures and around time 'Z', both their market share starts rising but the efforts made by Competitor–1 are not adequate and could not sustain the rise. It also indicates that Competitor–2 became complacent and this resulted in his losing his competitive edge.

Thus by keeping track of market share trend, the strategy and trend of various suppliers and the speed of action gets reflected. This information can be used to summarise the behaviour of the players and to extrapolate their possible reaction in the future to the changes. In the case under discussion, Competitor–2 seems to be seriously interested in the business and tried everything to become business leader. He challenged the supplier who was probably taking his position for granted due to low market share of Competitor–2 and lack of challenge from Competitor–1. It appears from the above case study that anybody who is the market leader takes his position for granted and stops adding value to the customer until challenged. This brings out another positive aspect of a competition, i.e. that it brings out the best in a vendor and competition is a must for improvement.

LOW MARKET SHARE

The last important function referred to in the earlier section is very important because it acts as a dynamic parameter to measure the success of the company's product and marketing strategy. It is possible that a company's business may be increasing in absolute terms, but its market share may be decreasing. This situation arises when market demand is increasing at a rate faster than that of the increase in company's business. Thus while the company may celebrate due to its business growth, in reality there is cause for worry because the growth is not what it should have been and the company is losing its competitive edge. It indicates that the company is not able to make full use of business opportunity and is lagging behind due to either improper marketing strategy or due to uncompetitiveness. It calls for a re-visit and re-evaluation of company's business strategy. On the other hand there may be situations where the business, in absolute terms, may be decreasing due to a rapid fall in demand, but the market share may be increasing. This indicates that the company has a healthy and competitive product along with a matching business strategy, which will result in business growth as soon as demand picks up, but the demand behaviour needs to be ascertained.

Market share acts as a major parameter in deciding the company's business strategy. Low market share indicates that the company is not able to utilise the business opportunity available before it. It gives direction to the company that it should re-examine both the product and the critical success factors and identify those factors, which need immediate attention and take corrective measures. Falling market share is a sure sign of the company losing its competitive edge. Low market share also indicates that the company is only a marginal player and is not in a position to influence the market.

The definition of low market share needs some discussion. If there are only three competitors in a business segment, then 40 per cent market share appears to be low. On the other hand, if a business segment had ten competitors, then 20 per cent market share will be reasonable.

HIGH MARKET SHARE

If a company is enjoying a high market share, it indicates that the company is a market leader in the particular business segment. It is able to understand the market and customer needs and the customer is relatively happy with the performance of the company. It also suggests that the products and services of the company are having a competitive edge. This suggests that the company is a dominant player in the segment. A supplier having high market share or dominant position has its own advantages. Most of the customers, who do not have consultants or do not know the art of selecting the supplier, prefer well-known supplier and invariably land with a dominant player not by matter of choice but as a matter of convenience. Even those customers, who are knowledgeable, find it difficult to neglect suppliers with a high market share. They are generally considered market movers for the business segment and changes introduced by them find easy acceptance compared to those introduced by marginal players. They are considered as path setters and their movements are watched both by customers and competitors. They have tremendous influence on the market and can be considered as trendsetters. They generally make a 'niche' for themselves and there is some 'uniqueness' associated with them and their products. They get high price realisation/premium in the market. Technology changes introduced by them are readily accepted.

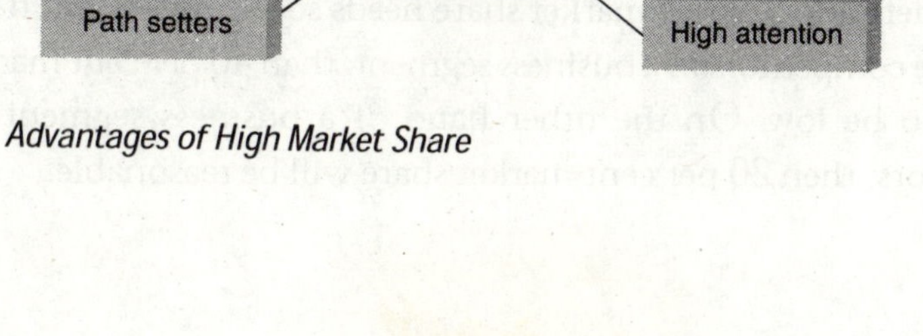

Fig. 9.2 *Advantages of High Market Share*

OPTIMUM MARKET SHARE

In any business, while deciding strategy, one of the major questions addressed is: What should be the optimum market share? It is often said that "*success increases ambition*". Human beings and organisations also follow this universal truth. If one is currently having a market share of 60 per cent, the natural tendency is to increase it further. The term market share is being used in a more generic sense and may also be considered as "Success Rate". However some individual may be so carried away or may be so obsessive in thinking that they may be aiming at the ultimate, i.e. 100 per cent success rate. They do not want to lose anything. Such a tendency is called "*100 per cent market share syndrome*".

The 100 per cent success comes at a price and one should be willing to pay that price. Let us first discuss both the positive and negative effects of such an approach. The 100 per cent market share aim acts as a great motivator for an individual achiever and as a challenging target for an organisation. With this as a driving force, the company marches ahead on the path of growth by constantly improving on its performance. It introspects factors inhibiting its forward movement and develops strategies to overcome them. In a globally competitive market it motivates an organisation to remain ahead of others by trying to offer better value to customer for its money. This can be in the form of better performance, technological innovation, cost optimisation or better service.

In order to ensure that even a small amount of business is not lost, the company stretches itself to meet diverse and varying needs of the customer. This makes the organisation flexible and customer-responsive. It also adds to the business profile of the company and may lead to entry into new business segments but too much of flexibility may lead to loss of business focus and resources getting distributed over a large chunk without providing effective return. This also leads to killing of competition which every supplier prefers, is counter-productive in the long run. Some of the disadvantages of lack of competition are described as under.

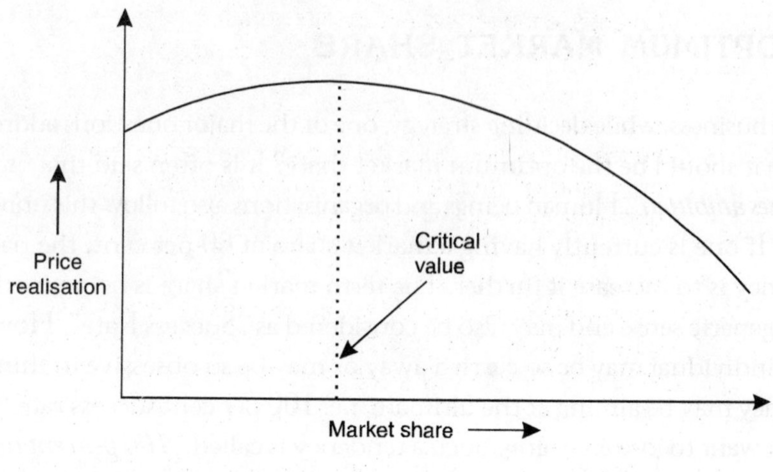

Fig. 9.3 *Price Realisation and Market Share*

NEGATIVE EFFECT OF INCREASING MARKET SHARE BEYOND OPTIMUM LEVEL

Falling Price Realisation

However there is a negative effect of this syndrome. In economics we often refer to the 'Law of Marginal Returns'. This is applicable here also. The success rate and price realisation generally follow an inverse relationship, i.e. higher the success rate, lower is the price realisation indirectly indicating that the growth in top line of the company will come at the cost of bottom line. Some economists may not agree with this concept as it may be argued that higher capacity utilisation may lead to fixed overheads getting distributed over a larger cake leading to lower cost or what may be called as achieving economics of scale but this effect works up to a point. In actual practice these two are having different bases. While one is connected to the internal capacity of an organisation, on the other hand 100 per cent success is connected more to the actual pie available in the market, which apart from supplier others are equally keen to gobble up. This phenomena leads to reduction in price realisation after the company decides to go above critical market share as shown in Fig. 9.3. The competitors, in order to maintain their business, try to work out a different strategy that revolves around providing more benefits and value to the customer for his money. To meet this competition, the supplier has also to do better than one being tried by other competitors, which increases the cost and reduces the profitability of the business. Reduction in price is the first strategy, which is tried by every one because it can be put into action quickly. As the attempt to increase market share continues, the price realisation falls drastically.

The relationship is rather complex in a globally competitive market. Each point improvement in the company's market share puts its competitor that much out of business and they try all means available at their disposal to halt the other's progress. The results can be disastrous. Companies, in order to survive, can come out with suicidal strategies like quoting below variable cost, subsidising, offering financing for a product which may be a small part of the project and the financier may not have much control on project dynamics. In order to reduce cost, some companies may start compromising on basic design and quality or offering products having lesser life span normally expected from them. The companies doing this generally ensure that the product life lasts for the period they are contractually bound but deteriorates rapidly thereafter. Some even go to the extent of compromising designers margin, which are generally provided to take care of aging. This life period of product can be referred to as "Warranty Period Life". Some customers are equally guilty as they often use this designer's margin, kept for taking care of aging and ensuring long-term trouble-free life, for operating the plant beyond its rated capacity to earn better short term profit but putting themselves and their shareholders at a disadvantage in the long-term. Any company which is operating in the infrastructure sector must realise that the sector by its very nature, is a long-term market and any strategy for marketing has to be a long-term one, if it has to succeed.

It is therefore necessary that one must carefully evaluate the incremental cost one has to pay to achieve incremental improvement in market share and arrive at an optimal level. 100 per cent market share may be very good for publicity but is a sure recipe for "Winding Up" in a competitive market.

The concept of cartelisation has its birth in above truth. About competitors and long-term survival it is often said that you should not have hungry wolves around you. Either you should 'kill' them or ensure that they are fed also.

Lack of Competition

No supplier wants competition. Everyone enjoys monopoly as it generates high profits. If a supplier is working in such an environment then he becomes accustomed to getting business without trying and loses focus and competitive edge. As the profit from monopoly operation increases, it attracts competition. If a company, which has lost its competitive edge and ability to face competition, is suddenly required to face intense competition, it gets shock treatment and may not in many cases be able to face it. Survival in the business segment itself may become a problem. It may also happen that by the time the organisation gears itself to face the competition it may be too late. HMT is barely surviving today but BHEL is prospering. The reason is simple enough. BHEL had always faced competition with global companies; so when the Indian market opened up, it adjusted to new order just like a duck taking to water. It was also able to prove that in spite of being a PSU, it is surviving on its own strength because it had always strived to maintain its competitive edge and not due to protected policies. This was only feasible due to the competition it was facing even earlier.

ADVANTAGES OF COMPETITION

Brings Best out of an Organisation

Competition acts as a motivator for the organisation and its human assets. It provides them the challenge. The urge to come out at the top is the biggest motivator and acts as a catalyst for improvement. The company gets a purpose for improvement rather than setting its target on customary "Improve your Performance". It sets for itself a quantitative target. It makes employees at all levels to understand the challenge faced by the company and it requires very little prompting from management to make people work. Slowly, this type of working provides company with a very healthy work culture as a long-term gain.

Cost Reduction

The first and foremost benefit of the competition is in cost reduction. In order to provide better value to the customer at lower cost, the suppliers works to optimise design and reduce material content. They also work out ways and means to reduce wastages. The process is also improved to reduce labour charges. Other cost optimisation methods are reduction in power, fuel charges and reduction in overheads. In the absence of competition, the approach of the supplier is "Cost Plus" but the competition puts a restriction on 'price'. Thus the supplier, in order to look for profit and survival, starts thinking and implementing the action plan to reduce cost.

Technology Upgradation

I recall my meeting twenty years ago with a Managing Director of a reputed private company which were supplying us with a component for our drive system. The component was using outdated technology and was not having certain vital technical features, which we as system designers thought were very essential for good and safe operation of our equipments. The other alternative was to use imported components from GE and other companies. It was thought by us that with little technological inputs from us, the product from a Pune Company could incorporate the same features as their imported counterparts. We as a customer wanted to develop not only indigenous vendors but also competition in the field. With this objective, we went to Pune to offer this company our technical expertise for technological improvement along with a proposal for a guaranteed minimum order quantity for the next five years. The vendor was required to invest capital for upgradation of his machinery and training of some of his engineers. The payback period of this investment was three years. After detailed discussion with operating personnel and design engineers, we met the Managing Director of the company. I was shocked to hear from him that with the existing product, he was getting comfortable profit and good business so why should he bother about improvement. He informed us that he did not believe that he would go out of business due to technology. His argument was simple;

technology is irrelevant in a controlled economy. We returned disappointed but this is what happens when there is no competition.

Performance Improvement

Like cost reduction, competition encourages performance improvement for providing more value to the customer. This results in incorporation of user-friendly features, reduced operation and maintenance and higher efficiency. The supplier strives to build features to create differentiation about the product in the market. He tries to give more benefits to the customer. One of the best ways of passing these benefits is to make it result in positive differentiation of the product to the customer in the market resulting in higher price realisation to him.

Customer Satisfaction

Many customers, who are highly demanding, always feel that the supplier is not doing enough and that they are in trouble because of lack of proper co-operation from the supplier. These types of customers are such that the more a supplier tries to satisfy them, the more unsatisfied they feel. Lack of competition antagonises them further as they do not have options. On the other hand, the supplier feels that the customer is highly demanding and unreasonable, and thus starts losing interest in the customer. It is always better with these types of customers to let them try alternatives and the presence of competitors always helps as they provide ready alternative options to the customer. In case the competitor provides better service, it removes misunderstanding at the supplier's end and he will strive to improve upon and provide better service to the customer. On the other hand, if the competitor is not able to provide the same kind of service as the supplier was providing, the customer will stand corrected and will be more satisfied with the supplier. The true worth of a product or service is known only if there is competition.

WHAT SHOULD BE THE OPTIMUM MARKET LEVEL?

In view of the foregoing, the company should aim for the optimum market share. What should it be? It is the level at which the company derives maximum possible price from the market and remains a dominant player who can also influence the market but at the same time allows the market not to feel restrained or constrained due to its dominant position. This allows the product to find its optimum price level and provide enough incentives for improvement and innovation.

The 100 per cent market share can sometimes be used for reducing competition in the long run. If one has strong financial muscle and can sustain loss for a reasonably long time then one can aim for 100 per cent market share so that some of the competitors who may be having less sustaining ability, down their shutters. This strategy is very useful on another front also as companies, which have less sustaining ability, generally quote lower prices and have a naturally lower quality. On the one hand they cut into the quality supplier's margins and on the other hand, they want him to lower quality standards to survive in the market and thus want to strike at carefully cultivated image of a quality and reliable supplier. Such strategy is also not in the best interests of the customer and should be discouraged.

10

Marketing Executive–What You Must Possess

The Importance
Total Marketing Approach
Essential requirement for Marketing Executives

10

THE IMPORTANCE

In earlier chapters, we have discussed the increasing importance of Human Resources in securing business and maximising returns. In time to come, when due to fast improving communication system, the world will become smaller and technology gaps will become narrower, human resources will become the main differentiating factor.

In an Infrastructure sector, a business settlement requires many rounds of formal and informal discussions, which may be face to face or over the telephone before a decision is finally arrived at. The customer comes into contact with different personalities in various functional areas of an organisation and in the process learns about the organisation and its human resources. The kind of response he gets, the attitude and the approach the officials and the workers exhibit, the innovativeness and resourcefulness they show, the importance and the attention the customer gets, leave a lasting impression on him and plays an important role in shaping the *IMAGE* of the organisation in his mind which later plays a decisive role in the business relationship. It is often seen that the customer builds up like or dislike for certain type of personalities and feels comfortable in dealing with them. He will contact them whenever he is in need and the relationship fast develops into friendship. Such persons slowly become his friend, philosopher and guide and this relationship plays a very important role in influencing his decision in spite of other overriding factors.

Marketing executives are the front end of an organisation and they are the persons who first come into contact with the customer. They are the first to make an impact/impression on the customers. It is often said that the first impression is the last impression. It is often seen that if the first impression that the marketing executive leaves on the customer is positive, then the customer, in spite of not getting not a positive response from other organisation personnel, remains loyal to the organisation as he believes that the organisation has other people also who can always address his problem and on whom he can depend in case of emergency or urgency or who can always act as his ambassador in the supplier's organisation. He thus tends to neglect the negative attitude or experience with the other personnel. But if the front end, i.e. marketing executive on whom he depends, is non-responsive then he gets the wrong message at the beginning. He cannot but have the impression that the organisation itself may be non-responsive. He has no other experience to compare with. There is no way the customer will come. Thus it is not the beginning of the end but *the end of the beginning.*

It is often seen that in big corporates, the other functional persons in contract, engineering, project management are introvert looking. They are more concerned with themselves than with the customers. By virtue of their functional area and long working in that function they can neither appreciate nor understand, in the same way as a marketing executive, the issues bothering the customer. Their approach is anything but customer-centric. In such circumstances it is highly essential that a marketing executive presents himself as a well-wisher and friend of customer and as a customer's representative in the supplier's organisation and provide necessary comforts to him. His role becomes of paramount importance not only to customer but also to his own organisation as he can also leverage his relationship with the customer to resolve issues that are blocking the progress of the project/ work. He can always create an impression on the customer that his interest is safe in his hands and with such a relationship the customer also finds it difficult to ignore his request which may be in the form of early release of pending payment or settlement of some disputed clause. The issues can always be settled in the spirit of give and take.

Another most important aspect that the customer wants to understand is the role the marketing department is going to play during the total contract execution period. Most of the marketing executives still see themselves as the order booking executives rather than total business executives. Most of them pass on the order *and in the process, the customer to* the contract/ project management department as soon as the order is received. This is not the correct approach and shows a very narrow outlook of the marketing personnel. While passing the order for execution to the contract department is okay, they should 'retain' the customer with them. A customer passed is difficult to be reclaimed in most of the cases. For this the marketing executive must keep himself appraised of the project progress and should pro-actively try to resolve the problems which may during the progress of the project. The customer only approaches marketing executives during the execution of the project if and only if he has problems with the executing people and they are not able to address it. As a last resort he approaches the marketing executive thinking that he will understand his problem better and will resolve it. But if the marketing executive also becomes indifferent then the customer feels that he has hit a roadblock and his decision to place an order on the company was wrong.

It will not be inappropriate to compare this situation with the marriage in an Indian family. When a new bride comes to her in-laws family, it takes time to adjust. Even if we neglect the dowry issue, the culture and background difference between the two families itself creates problems for the new bride to adjust to. On top of it there are long and unending expectations from the bride. If these conditions are not fulfilled, then the tension starts building up along with the problems. At this stage one man she expects to stand by her is her husband. If his support and encouragement is there, she is able to withstand all the problems in the in-laws' house. On the other hand if she finds that her husband's support is missing or he is not on her side or his attitude and approach is not balanced, she becomes disappointed and broke n-hearted and the marriage relationship receives a setback. A marketing executive's role is not very different. The customer expects him to understand his genuine problem and fight for it in the supplier's organisation so that the contract proceeds on the agreed lines and the commitments are fulfilled. In order to meet the customer's expectation, there is need to re-define the role of marketing executives in the organisation. In the quality management a term called Total Quality Management is very common. In line with this we have to adopt the concept of 'Total Marketing' as shown in Fig. 10.1

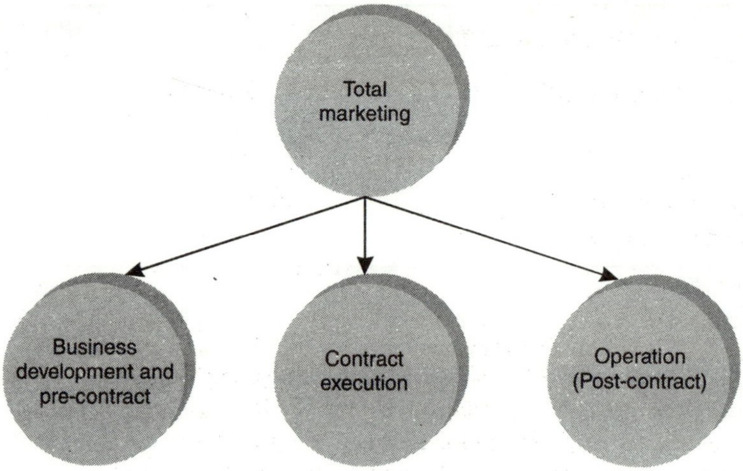

Fig. 10.1 *Total Marketing Concept*

TOTAL MARKETING APPROACH

Table 10.1 shows the blueprint of the Total Marketing Philosophy. There are three phases of marketing namely:

- Pre-Contract Stage
- Contract Execution Stage
- Operation or Post Contract Stage

Table 10.1 *Customer Expectation from Marketing Executive at Different Stages*

Pre-contract	*Contract Execution*	*Operation (Post-contract)*
EXPECTATIONS • Business Developer • Understanding the requirements • Meeting it or Offering better alternatives • Helping in improving specification/ performance	• Help in monitoring the progress and in taking appropriate corrective action to ensure timely completion • To act as a honest broker to settle disputes	• To help in ensuring spares supply • To assist in ensuring timely overhaul • Help at SOS calls and in emergency • To help in attending service calls

Contd

Pre-contract	*Contract Execution*	*Operation (Post-contract)*
• Advisor offering constructive suggestions for betterment • Flexible, Pragmatic • Decisive • Aggressive Player	• To act as customer's representative and watchdog	• To offer advice for retrofit/repair/re-power
REQUIREMENTS • Innovator • Flexible • Decisive • Calculated Risk Taker • Strategist • Creative Thinker	• Watchdog • Helper • Progress Chaser • Monitor • Problem Solver • Elder Stateman/Arbitrator	• Helper • Pusher in the supplier organisation • Guide and Friend

The table highlights the expectation of the customer from the marketing executive at each stage.

Pre-Contract or Business Development Stage

This stage is business development/tendering or negotiation stage. At this time the customer only comes into contact with the marketing executive. He gets the first impression of the supplier's company from the way the marketing executive functions. He expects the persons to understand his (Customer's) needs, not what have been specified in the tender documents but what is required by him based on his ultimate requirements. If the supplier's representative is able to understand his requirements then only will he be able to offer suggestions for improvement and cost effectiveness. The relationship between vendor's representative and purchaser is often misunderstood. It is often considered only as a relationship between purchaser and seller. They are always considered as two poles separated at 180° sitting on the other side of the table.

Though it is a fact that they are purchaser and seller but in the core sector their relationship is more complex. The purchaser and his consultant appreciate the fact that the seller is an expert in his area and there cannot be a more knowledgeable advisor in the field than the seller himself to suggest optimum solutions. The tender specifications are drawn to achieve the best solutions to the needs of the customer. However in the core sector, the purchaser always looks forward to suggestions from the suppliers to improve upon his specification and to get the best possible solution to his requirements. In fact many times the tender specifications undergo many changes after discussion with the supplier and some of them may be major in nature. It is therefore to be appreciated that both supplier and customer are partners in this venture and sitting on the same side of the table and their purpose is the same, i.e. to meet the needs of the customer in the most efficient and cost-effective way. The customer expects the bidder to help him in identifying the critical factors, which may have a bearing on the long-term performance and life of the equipment.

It is here that a good marketing executive can help both his organisation and customer. He can act as an advisor to the customer by suggesting changes that can give additional benefits to the customer and at the same time also explain to the customer how his company is capable of offering him these features. It is the first opportunity that a marketing man gets to leave his impressions on the customer. By making transparent and pragmatic suggestions, he is not only helping the customer but his own organisation also. This is the way that the relationship of mutual faith and confidence begins. Such type of assistance is highly appreciated by the customers and they start having respect and regard for the marketing man.

Illustration

There is a major capital goods manufacturing company which was operating 18 MW captive power plant to meet its in-house production power requirement. The power plant was about 20 years old and was operating at 44 Kg/cm^2 pressure which, though the commonly chosen system pressure, was not economical nowadays, when the pressure of steam is to be higher to derive the maximum efficiency. The boiler was more than thirty years old. The customer was interested in replacing the boiler only as the STG (Steam Turbine Generator) was only twenty years old and was in a position to give further service for another fifteen years. The customer therefore floated tenders for a new boiler and wanted this new boiler to be the exact replica of the existing boiler. Five parties showed their interest by purchasing the tender documents. One of the participants indicated to the customer that he could suggest a better solution and wanted an appointment

Contd

with him for explaining his proposal. During the meeting, he suggested to the customer that the 44 Kg/cm^2 pressure system was highly uneconomical and outdated and that the customer should replace it by a high pressure 84 Kg/cm^2 pressure boiler. However, he comforted the customer by suggesting that the existing STG set which the customer wanted to retain could still be used. His plan envisaged that the new boiler would feed steam at 84 Kg/cm^2 to the new STG set (Topping Turbine) and steam could be exhausted from this turbine at 44 Kg/cm^2, which can then be fed to the existing turbine. The new turbine would give additional power of 8 MW. The proposal had a number of merits which appealed to the customer and are summarised below:

- The existing 18 MW turbine was productively utilised.
- The customer was getting extra power of 8 MW and thereby increasing the total power availability to 26 MW.
- The overall efficiency of the system greatly improved due to high pressure use.
- The incremental cost of high pressure boiler and topping turbine compared to earlier envisaged replacement was getting paid back in three years' time making it a highly economical investment.
- In future when the existing 18 MW STG set would need replacement and the boiler would be relatively new, the customer need not go for inefficient 44 Kg/cm^2 STG again as the boiler was now capable of delivering steam at high pressure. The customer could go in for identical replacement or do away with topping turbine and go in for single efficient high pressure turbine.

The customer liked the idea and accepted it after some more detailed interaction. He was happy with the marketing executive for saving him from making investment in an outdated product and for suggesting him a better product and giving him more value for the money. The vendor organisation also got benefited. In the end it was the innovative, analytical and pro-activeness of the marketing executive which had given benefits to the customer and his own employer.

There was a similar case in a 'Flyover' Construction at a road junction. The requirement was made known to the vendors and many of them visited the site for on the spot inspection before submitting the tender. It occurred to one of them that the way the flyover was being planned would further complicate the traffic. He felt that the present planning of the flyover would simply shift the traffic congestion from the present crossing to the next crossing. Normally, flyovers are planned on the busiest traffic roads and their construction should

Contd

ensure that the bulk of traffic was through the passage. In the present case the design was not on these lines. The person did some traffic density calculation present at various road crossings which were going to be affected by the flyover in the present planned position of the flyover and also for the position he had in mind. He prepared the anticipated visuals of traffic flow in both the cases and then gave a presentation to the customer. The customer, after seeing the presentation, realised that the way that they planned the flyover would only add to the problems rather than solving them. He accepted the vendor's suggestion and thanked him for saving him from falling into a mess. The vendor naturally benefited from this. Normally such foresight has little to do with organisation but more to do with the individual's capacity and personality.

A marketing executive can play another role. We have discussed in an earlier chapter on marketing that it means not only utilising the opportunity but creating it. The marketing executive can play an important role in conceiving the project for the customer and thereby creating the demand where it did not exist. The customer has to be made aware of the opportunities coming on his way or the assets he is having which can be put to profitable use. Some of the cases will clarify this.

Illustrations

In India the disposal of household waste or municipal waste is becoming a major issue. Its high volume itself is creating a major headache. The municipality does not know what to do with it and it is proving to be a major health and environment hazard. Some of the municipalities are trying to make fertiliser out of it. However nothing of note has occurred. The problem remains. This liability can be easily converted into an asset. In many countries this waste is converted into gas through bio-methanisation process. The methane gas, produced has high calorific value and can be burned in gas engines to produce electricity, which can be sold to Electricity Utilities to generate regular revenue. The other remains of bio-methanisation process can be used as bio fertiliser and sold in the market. The payback period is very attractive. Thus the municipality can convert this problem into a means of revenue generation to supplement their income.

The other example is of House Builders. In big cities, with the paucity of land, the builders are finding it very difficult to get land at

Contd

a prime location and in sufficient quantity. They therefore approach existing plot owners or even the occupants of the old bungalows, who apparently do not have sufficient financial resources, to repair or construct new ones with the offer that they can give their land for construction of multi-storied houses. The builder gives one or two apartments free of cost to the owner of the plot and sells the balance to the public. The owner is thus getting a new apartment free and the builder is getting his business. The concept has picked up very fast.

We have another example from the enterprising service sector. The people today are very busy particularly in cosmopolitan cities. They have everything except time. Many people have made it a business to do work like electricity/water/telephone bill payment at a small charge. Some people have gone even further. They come on alternate days in the evening to collect orders for vegetables and deliver it fresh from the Mandis at their doorsteps at a price cheaper than the person selling in the colony and definitely of better quality. All this comes due to the pro-active approach of the individual. They are sensing the opportunity and creating the market.

During the pre-order stage, the customer expects the marketing executive to understand the requirement and adopt a flexible and pragmatic approach. They also want him to be pro-active and decisive in nature and he should be sufficiently informed or having the ability to collect the information and decide during the meeting and not postpone the problem to the next day or for other person or if he so desires to reply within the stipulated time period without reminder.

Since in a core sector both the customer and the supplier are knowledgeable and there is always a consultant, the customer expects the marketing executive to be frank and straightforward and to be a value adder. They want him to be sure of what he is offering and what he cannot offer, i.e. what he can accept and what he cannot. There is no use of committing to something which is not feasible or which cannot be achieved.

Contract Execution Stage

This is the post award stage. Most of the marketing executives feel that their work ends with securing the business. This is not correct. They must appreciate that they are the people who have the closest contact with the customer in their organisation and the customer is placing the order partly because of the confidence and comfort generated by them and they cannot leave him just high and dry, though it is also a fact that the baton, with the receipt of the order, passes to the contract and project management division. The foremost responsibility of the marketing executive is to formally introduce the customer to his counterpart in the contract execution and project management department and to inform his colleagues in the presence of the customer of the salient features of the project, the expectations of the customer and a written and verbal commitment given to the customer at the time of business finalisation and the circumstances prevailing at the time of deal. The marketing executive must also understand that he is handing over only the project for the execution and not the customer who remains solely his responsibility. This is also the stage where the customer also changes his perception of marketing executive *from vendor's representative to his representative in vendor's organisation.* He expects the marketing person to ensure timely completion of the project and to solve the problem that may crop up during the execution period. These problems can be over the interpretation of the contract agreement or over the technical issues. It can also be due to some new issue which may crop up because of changed circumstances from the one envisaged at the time of order finalisation. The customer expects the marketing executive to resolve the issue so that the contract can proceed without hindrance.

It is often seen that in core sector projects in spite of all the care taken by both the parties, there can be chances of dispute on scope particularly at terminal points or due to different interpretations by the supplier or the customer or his consultants. These issues are of a serious nature and can lead to major reasons for delay and cost over-run apart from spoiling the relationship between the two parties. It is often seen that the contract executing personnel from both sides take a very narrow view of the problem and a long-term view of customer-supplier relationship is farthest in their mind. Both parties need each other and the disputes can be resolved amicably if they want. It is here that a marketing background and approach, taking a long-term business view of the situation, can help.

Many times the customer may need changes to suit his new requirement. The contract department is generally allergic to changes as it jeopardizes their plan but all reasonable changes of customer should be accepted if required with implications. The marketing executive has to safeguard the interest of both his employer and customer like a daughter-in-law has to safeguard the interest of her father's and father-in-law's house. He is expected to resolve the issue so that the work and relationship does not suffer. He is expected to play the role of the Helper or Facilitator. Sometimes, he has also to act as an arbitrator between his own organisation's contract/operation division and the customer. This time he is expected to act as an independent jury to resolve the dispute between his own operation wing and that of the customer.

Post-Contract Stage

During the long operation of the product/project, there are several occasions when the customer may face problems on various counts. They may be due to:

- Sudden deterioration in the performance parameters
- Damage due to accidents
- Renovations
- Upgradations required due to new developments in the technology
- Changes required due to changed environment/new policies
- Repairs/Overhauls
- Difficulties in sourcing of spare parts

The customer generally always contacts the marketing person and expects him to provide the information/assistance he is looking forward to or arrange to provide the same from the relevant persons in the supplier's company. He also looks forward to the advice that the marketing man may give to address his concern. The customer in the above case puts total faith in the marketing executive and proceeds ahead on the path suggested by him. It is also to be understood that during the operation period whenever the problem occurs, the customer gets panicky as in a majority of cases his production/ revenue suffers and he appreciates anybody helping him to overcome the problem. This also provides an opportunity to the marketing executive to build a relationship, which can prove to be rewarding in the days to come.

Illustration

In this case a chemical factory situated on the west coast of India purchased major capital equipment in 1992. While drafting specifications the factory and its consultants never took into account the highly corrosive nature of the climate and never specified extra protection to retard corrosion. As a result the equipments were ill suited to withstand the climate prevailing over there. Within five years of operation, heavy rusting was noticed in the equipments. The customer, having exhausted all avenues, turned his attention to a marketing friend in his vendor company (a different vendor from the one who had originally supplied the equipments but in the same trade) enquiring whether he knew of any expert in his organisation who could be of help to him. He was expecting his marketing friend to act as his advisor and guide. A question that may arise is why he did not ask the marketing department of the original supplier? This was because in the customer's eyes this marketing person was more suitable. For the customer he was more important than the original supplier. The customer was having more faith in him and he was more comfortable with him.

Let us now debate what are those factors which make a customer more comfortable with the marketing executive and provide him confidence.

ESSENTIAL REQUIREMENTS FOR MARKETING EXECUTIVES

There are five major requirements for a marketing executive. They are:

- Personality
- Skill
- Knowledge
- Communication
- Hard Work

If we consider the relative importance of these parameters in the requirement chart of a marketing executive, then Skill will occupy the highest slot with 30 per cent followed by Personality and Knowledge. Communication and Hard Work will follow other factors. Skill has been given more weightage because while the personality and knowledge decide the potential, skill decides the actual action.

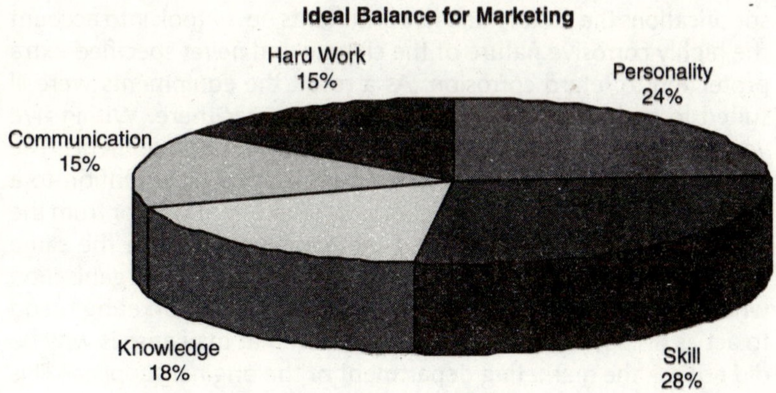

Fig. 10.2 *Ideal Balance for Marketing*

These are detailed in Table 10.2. We will discuss them in detail.

Table 10.2 *Marketing Executive—Requirements at a Glance*

Personality	*Skill*	*Communication*	*Hard Work*
• Attitude • Orientation • Temperament • Approach • Initiative • Charisma • Creativity and Risk Taking • Passion, Transparency, Determination	• Personality Understanding • Negotiating skill • Strategy • Diplomacy • Pressure Cooker Survival • Solution Finder • Decision Making and Response	• Understanding others • Conveying his views • Empathy • Good speaker	• Perseverance • Sincerity • Tenacity

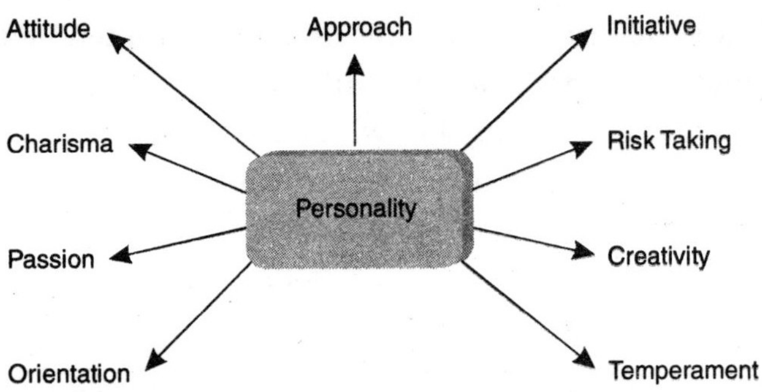

Fig. 10.3 *Personality—Many Faces of It*

Personality

It is the foremost requirement that the marketing executive has the right type of personality. Needless to say, he should be of pleasant disposition with a positive outlook. But that alone does not make a person suitable for marketing. There are a whole lot of essentials that he must have and they are discussed in subsequent sections To begin with, the marketing executive must be conscious of the fact that he is representing an organisation and the way he speaks, listens, acts, behaves or conducts himself will not only reflect on him but more importantly on the organisation he is representing. He is present there not in his individual capacity, but as a part of his organisation. The way he conducts himself may leave a lasting impression on the customer and may decide his like or dislike for him. To begin with, the marketing executive must develop the right chemistry with the people who matter in the customer organisation. For this he should have the right mix of attributes that shape his personality. The factors that shape a person's personality are shown in Fig. 10.3 and will be critically examined here.

Attitude

This is the foremost parameter of an individual which has a major bearing on the result. It is often said in marketing requirement that for a executive to be successful 98 per cent knowledge and 96 per cent hard work will suffice but 100 per cent positive attitude is required. There is no use of having knowledge, excellent skills, etc. until they are intended to be used. It is like going into the battlefield with all the sophisticated arms and ammunition and skilled army but with no intention to fire a single shot. The result is defeat. You cannot win until you intend to win. There is a problem and there are possible solutions but until one intends to solve the problem, there is no use of having solutions.

In management games, one of the exercises assigns mark 1 to A, 2 to B and so on to Z with 26. If we now break the words as under, the result is interesting.

Hard work = 8+1+18+4+23+15+18+11=98

Knowledge = 11+14+15+23+12+5+4+7+5=96

Attitude = 1+20+20+9+20+21+4+5=100

The above exercise indicates that Knowledge can give a person 96 per cent, Hard work 98 per cent but attitude only can give 100 per cent success.

Most of the HRD Managers are engrossed with what they call the 'Attitude Problem'. They are having bright, energetic and dynamic executives, but they are not of much use as they do not want to deliver because they do not intend to. In daily life there are many cases which separate success from failure because of lack of attitude.

Illustration

In a company a senior management official was having a reasonably bright officer but the top man was surprised that he was not being given responsibility by his immediate seniors and, as a result, his career was also showing pedestrian progress. The top man had tested the man in question and found him to be of reasonable IQ. He was wondering why his superiors were neglecting this officer. He started calling this man also along with his boss for discussion and, at the same time, gave him direct responsibility and also guided him how to proceed though that instruction was not necessary. He gave him double the time but when he rechecked, he was surprised that the officer had not visited the customer from whom he requested him to collect details about customer requirement in the new project in which the company was interested. The worst part of the case was that he not only had no details about the person who was handling the project in

Contd

the customer's organisation, but he had also made no attempt to collect other details. When the officer was questioned about the reasons why he had not collected the details, the officer told him that he could not get the time. The super boss was shocked that a marketing man, whose most important assignment given to him was to collect the details about the future upcoming requirement of a customer, could not even find time in a week to collect the name and telephone number of the officer dealing with the project at the customer end, what to talk of the customer plan, financing arrangement, consultant's name, etc. The reason was lack of a positive attitude. To have such people in marketing will mean doing great injustice to the marketing function and to the organisation.

In core sector projects, during technical and commercial discussion, a lot of problems crop up and different solutions are thrown up. If the marketing executive exhibits a positive attitude and takes these problems and solutions on merit and contributes positively in decision making process, then he will find the other party also reciprocating. But if he starts avoiding the decision under the pretext that he cannot decide or is not authorised to decide or that he is not an expert in the field, then he is definitely not fit to be in marketing. Everybody knows that a marketing man is not an all-rounder who knows each and everything but they also understand that his job is to co-ordinate, to facilitate and to collect information required from the concerned people and pass on the information to the customer. Many executives have the habit of putting the decision either on their subordinate's head or on their boss's head. They will tell their boss, "Sir, it would be better if you talk. You know he always want to talk to the you." Yes, the customer wants to talk to the boss because his problem gets addressed by him but this makes the other man redundant in the marketing department. Not only the customer, but also his own colleagues in other functions get fed up with him and start avoiding him resulting in a break in communication and as a result business suffers. On the other hand if the marketing executive takes the position that unfortunately he can't reply immediately but will contact the concerned person in the organisation and collect the details required, the customer extends him the communication facility like telephone/fax/e-mail to enable the vendor to complete the work.

Illustration

A fertiliser company wanted to adhere to its schedule of tender opening in spite of some changes made in the specification. They gave all the vendors two hours to inform the changes particularly in performance parameters, which were essential for tender acceptance. It was a rainy day and one of the vendors, in spite of all the efforts made by him and the assistance provided by the customer, could not contact his design department and was worried that he would miss the deadline and his bid may not be accepted. As a last resort he contacted the customer and informed his problem that he did not know the calculation procedure and was unable to contact his office. The customer offered the assistance of his technical person to do the required calculation so that the bidder could complete the work and submit the bid.

Thus, attitude is the most important part of an individual's personality.

Orientation

If attitude decides the basic willingness of the person to contribute, then orientation decides the direction of the move. Basically, orientation of a person decides the end result on which he is concentrating or is trying to deliver. This also describes the process and methodology of his working. There are four basic orientations and an individual has all of them in different strengths. The most predominant and the next predominant decides his work orientation. The four basic orientations are:

- Goal Oriented
- Task Oriented
- Process Oriented
- Query Oriented

The personalities, who are goal oriented will work relentlessly for achieving the end results. If they have set their target on securing a particular business, then they will work relentlessly to achieve it. If there are constraints in their path, such type of personalities will always work out a way to overcome constraints. The biggest advantage with such type of orientation is their 'never accepting defeat attitude'. They are assets to any marketing department. I know of one of my colleagues who caught a flight to submit the proposal. The completed tender was filled in six volumes and was required to be submitted in ten copies. The gentlemen checked nine copies as checked-in-baggage and carried the original with him. On reaching the destination he found that the baggage had not arrived thanks to the goof up by the airlines staff. This gentleman had exactly four hours to meet the deadline of tender submission. Each tender copy was 600 pages long. So it amounted to photocopying 600 pages in 10 sets and sign, seal and submit it. So determined was this person that he engaged five photo copiers to do the job and they took exactly 1.5 hours. He took the same time to sign and pack the tender and was able to submit the proposal well in time. It was his goal orientation and determination which drove him to plan his work under heavy odds and achieve the target.

Normally such goal-oriented persons do not bother much about the system, and will not become slaves of rules and regulations. They are more likely to find a way to overcome these blockages and will not allow the process/system to keep them chained. They are decisive and risk-oriented personalities and will be impatient if the work is not moving at the pace they have desired. They are more likely to push others also to match their pace.

The second type of personality is *task oriented.* They are similar to goal-oriented personalities but they divide the goal into a number of tasks and start concentrating on achieving these tasks. Many times this results in their concentrating more on smaller issues rather than in totality and, in the process, the overall project may suffer. Another disadvantage with this type of personality is that if there is an enquiry and a tender is to be submitted in a short time then they will concentrate in achieving the deadline and sometimes due to this focus the quality of tender work will suffer. In their eagerness to submit the tender before the due date, they will forget that their main job is not tender submission only but to submit it in a such a way that it results in business to the company. They should rather ensure that the proposal is not only submitted but is competitive and gives the desired information to the customer; also, it is not just submitted to meet the deadline of submission but is comprehensive enough to enable the customer to take a decision. Like goal-oriented personalities, they are resourceful in overcoming resistance, blockage and are not deterred by rules and regulations coming in their way of achievement but unlike goal oriented personalities, they are not visionaries. Though they have high potential, they will never set their targets high. However, such personalities are very good at work and can produce excellent results under a goal oriented leader.

The third type of personalities is *process oriented.* They have great respect for rules, regulations and system. Whatever work they do, they will do it methodically and systematically. Thus if we consider the same case of tender submission as was considered for a task oriented personality, this type of executive will ensure that the quality of proposal is given due consideration. They will also believe in going to every person through the proper channel and will not drive or strive to go beyond the system to achieve the objective. Hence they will find it difficult to achieve the desired time objective for tender submission. Not only will they find the pressure of meeting the time dead line but also the team working with them will also be constantly under pressure and at the last minute will not know what to do. They are more likely to take the help of others to meet this deadline or, in the process, may lose control to a task/goal oriented personality. In their eagerness to be systematic and methodical they are natural accumulators of backlog and work progress will be slow. Such type of personalities is not suitable for front line and specially for marketing where speed of response is as much essential as the accuracy of work. They are more likely to irritate a customer as during meeting or negotiation they are not capable of giving a reply or commitment across the table. They will wait for communication/ information from their colleagues or approval from their bosses. They are not the ones to take calculated risks and naturally are not business oriented. They will do well in engineering, quality or other similar departments but are certainly not suitable for marketing functions.

The fourth type of personality is the one who will question or challenge everything. They will find queries everywhere. Though they themselves may be incapable of working and completing a task, if somebody else can do it, this type of personality will be able to find a large number of faults in it. If they are in marketing then rather than spending their time in understanding the customer, project requirement, identifying critical success factors, they are more likely to question the project requirement or technical specifications or the work done by their own colleagues rather than themselves doing some constructive work. They are most suited to examine investment proposals, for project monitoring or for critical appraisal of a report. They will do an excellent job in such positions but they are not the ones who can do business development or marketing. Strategy formulation and long-term approach is not their cup of tea. They are not the ones who believe in building a relationship. You can depend on them to antagonise the customer. While they can do project monitoring, they cannot do project management. They do not have professional friends and find it difficult to get assistance from their friends and colleagues. They are certainly not team men. Their colleagues and friends are more likely to avoid them rather than seek their help. They have tremendous nuisance value in an organisation. Assigning them to a marketing function is a sure way of losing both the customer and the business.

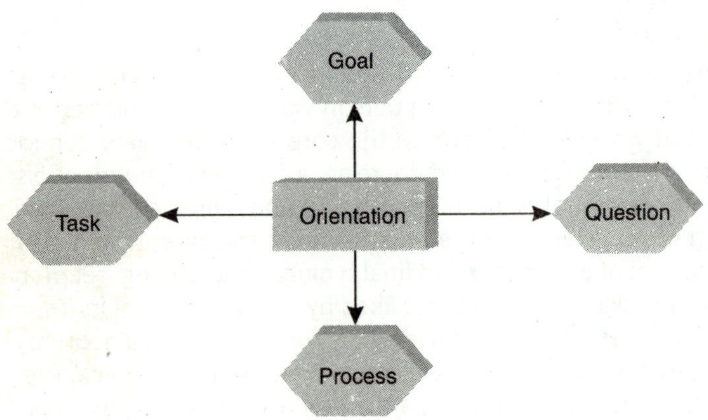

Fig. 10.4 *Personality Orientation*

In all human beings we get all the four types of orientations, which is natural and essential for a balanced personality, but one or two types always dominate and are referred to as primary orientations and ultimately decides the personality's style. For a successful marketing executive, the ideal mix of relative orientation in percentage should be:

- Goal Orientation 40%
- Task Orientation 20%
- Process Orientation 25%
- Question Orientation 15%

Approach

The next important attribute required of a marketing executive is his approach and the way he conducts himself. One of the most preferred ways is that the marketing executive becomes a part of the customer team. For this he should adopt a more pro-active approach. He can start discussions with them in an informal way and should start getting their confidence. As the small wall distancing them slowly collapses, more closer interactions will follow and slowly the marketing executive will become part of the customer project team and even influence his decisions. The individual can have even greater acceptability with the customer with his suggestions. From the vendor he transforms himself into an advisor for the customer.

Illustration

We reproduce here two different instances where the approach adopted by the marketing person was different and hence the end result was also different. In the core sector it is very common that prior to submission of bid, there are a number of rounds of discussion and record notes are prepared and annexures and appendices are attached. Preparing the minutes and attachments and getting the consent of everybody and final typing/photocoping, set preparation is a thankless job and is not liked by many in spite of its importance. In the present case the marketing guy has made it a habit to do such type of work himself. The customer and supplier's colleagues used to only modify the minutes and the balance work was done by the marketing person. In the process he not only became a part of them but also started taking a lead role. It became easier for him to develop a mutually co-operative relationship with the customer and was successful in resolving many contagious issues in a spirit of give and take. He always gave the impression that he would go out of his way to ensure that all pending issues were resolved and even if he had to compromise something he would do so in the overall interest of the project and not take sides. The customer seeing his positive and impartial approach also contributed his side of help to ensure that compromises were made from both sides so that the project progress would not be affected. The marketing person could not only show better results but also retained the goodwill and confidence of the customer.

Contd

On the other hand the second marketing man believed in a laid back style of working. While he would take part in discussions, he would not assume a leadership role. He waited for others to sort out issues for him. He adopted a role more suitable to a passive leader. He would never take the lead in 'minutes' preparation and restricted himself to correcting the 'minutes' and waited for others to complete the work. The customer and his own colleagues saw in him a person who was more interested in finding faults rather than making a constructive contribution. Naturally the customer and his own colleagues started losing interest in him and he could not get the support of the team from both sides. It was not feasible for him to push through a change and get acceptance of others or get concessions from the customer, which a person in the earlier case was easily able to do. The relationship between him and the customer was formal and most of the issues use to travel to and fro between supplier and customer without getting settled without the help of third person. As a result the project progress was affected and, in the end, both customer and supplier were unhappy.

These two examples just indicate the importance that the approach of an individual can make in business.

Initiative

There is a small saying displayed at the table of a Chairman and Managing Director of the company. It reads *"THE BUCK STOPS HERE"*. Similar is the position of a marketing executive. He represent the company before the customer and he cannot take recourse to statements like 'I do not know, I am not dealing with it'. His job as a marketing executive is to understand the customer requirement and contact the appropriate persons in his organisation or outside and inform back the status to the customer. One of the major roles of the marketing person is to act as catalyst for promoting business. He has to identify the 'Needs' of the customer and find the ways to convince him about the capabilities of his organisation to meet them. For this purpose he has to meet the customer often at various levels. He must make a presentation at different layers to the customer to prove that the idea he is proposing is workable and will give benefit to the customer. During the presentation the marketing executive must keep the customer in focus and then present his capabilities in such a way so as to indicate to the customer that they can effectively meet his requirements. The presentation can be purely technical or techno economical as the case may be. The basic purpose of initiative is to create an opportunity and then demand. If on the other hand demand exists, then it should be utilised for business growth. Initiative is always based on identifying the customer's 'Needs' and then developing a product or service to meet the 'need'.

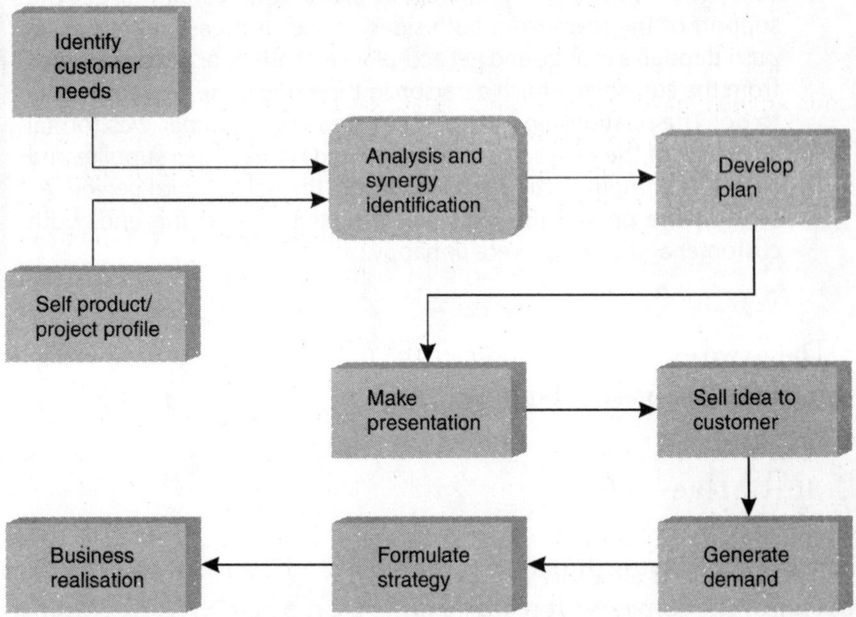

Fig. 10.5 *Business through Initiative*

Charisma and Positiveness

A marketing executive needs to have a magnetic personality which attracts the individual. He must have the image of helper and should be able to establish beyond doubt that he is a problem solver rather than a problem creator. He should be a good coordinator and should have the ability to understand the other personality. He should 'OWN' the project. Sincerity only comes from ownership; otherwise it is a routine practice of taking a position that if customer wants it, then somebody will do it.

The customer must get the message that the person with whom it is dealing is serious and that its interest is safe in his hands. He must present the image of a confident and calm personality who is at peace with himself and is in command. He must not only show commitment and be a personality with clear thinking, but he should be consistent in his stand.

In core sector projects during pre tendering and contract execution stage, the customer may require information on subjects which may be connected or not connected with the projects, but it is expected of a good marketing person that he will either himself provide the correct information or will ensure that somebody else provides the same. He is not going to deflect the customer to another person. Many officials have the habit of directing the customer to other persons in order to save themselves from uncomfortable situations. This is not liked by the customer in a majority of cases. A more acceptable way is to inform the customer that you are not the concerned person but will ensure that the related person provides the customer with the desired information. If the customer himself desires that he, of his own accord, will contact the concerned person, then it will be appropriate to provide him with the details. Otherwise, the marketing person should ensure that *'the customer gets the call rather than he making it.'*

Creativity and Risk Taking

These are two very important aspects of a personality. Though they are two different attributes, it has been found that in order to predict the thinking, approach and style of an individual they must be considered together. Every person have these two attributes in varying proportions and different combinations of them throw up different type of personalities some of whom may be better suited for marketing function.

To win a business it is necessary that a marketing man is able to out think others, including the customer and competitors. He must find out different ways to attempt the business and provide comfort and confidence to the customer. The more radical the working idea a marketing man has, the greater his chances of success. He must be able to think, from different angles and different perspectives, the same issue in order to find the optimum way to address it.

Risk taking is another attribute required in a marketing person. Many times while discussing the issue or negotiating the contract a situation may arise when the marketing executive has to take decisions for which he may not have the authority. One simple way is for him to communicate to the customer that he does not have the authority and that he will ask the customer's boss or his boss to take the decision and communicate it to the customer. This approach can only be used in case of serious issues on which the customer may also appreciate the marketing executive's difficulty but using it frequently will make the customer wonder about the status and power enjoyed by the executive who has come for negotiation. This will also raise the question of the individual marketing executive's ability and capability to occupy the post. The customer may also like to talk to persons who have the authority or who can take decisions. The customer will also develop the allergy to talk to or deal with such type of marketing executive and will always like to bypass him. He will also have a bad impression about the vendor organisation for neglecting him and sending a junior level person who has no authority or is incapable of deciding. In either case both the marketing man and his organisation have gone down in the eyes of the customer. This is a case where all the three namely the customer, supplier and the marketing man suffer.

In negotiation or discussion, nobody can envisage all the possible situations and one has to respond mostly based on the information available. So if one wants to be a successful marketing executive he has to think and take risk. However, one should not take blind risk. It should be a calculated risk. Before taking a decision, the marketing executive must be sure that he will be able to muster support for the decision from his own organisation. For every decision one has to pay the price and he should be willing to pay the same. Telling 'YES' to the customer will definitely result in business to the company, but the price and other terms at which he is accepting the same must be workable for his own organisation. Otherwise, it is will be the start of problems for both the parties and spoiling of relationship. Similarly saying 'NO' may mean loss of business, which the company may not be willing to lose. It must be remembered that it is very easy to lose a business or customer but extremely difficult to get the business or new customer. It is therefore essential that risk and its level be decided from a pragmatic point of view and not from an emotional and sentimental angle.

Many management experts have found strong correlation between creativity and risk taking ability of an individual and based on these parameters, eight different types of personalities are found as detailed in Table 10.3, which segregates them on the basis of creativity and risk taking and also mentions their brief characteristics and suitability for marketing functions. It is to be appreciated that not all types of personalities are suitable for all types of work.

Table 10.3 *Characteristics of Different Personalities and their Suitability to Marketing*

Type	*Risk Taking Ability*	*Creativity*	*Characteristics*
Reproducer	Low	Low	• Does repetitive job • Resists Change • Does not have new ideas • Not suitable for marketing
Modifier	Medium	Medium	• Good at incremental changes • Incapable of giving brilliant new ideas • Excellent for Number–2 role in marketing but cannot be the leader of marketing team
Challenger	High	Low	• Unhappy with everything • Has no new ideas • Can agree to anything and everything customer wants without blinking eyes • Will blame others for their loss making and irrational decisions • It is suicidal to keep him in marketing in any role but can be ideal for Project Monitoring, though they will be a failure in Project Management
Planner	Medium	Low	• Very good coordinator • Process oriented • Likes new ideas but lacks ability to implement • Misfit for marketing but most suitable for project management

Contd

Type	*Risk Taking Ability*	*Creativity*	*Characteristics*
Practicaliser	High	Medium	• Likes new ideas and has the persuasive skill to convince others to accept it. • Can take people along • Has clarity of purpose about what can be done and what cannot be done. • Pragmatic Decision Maker • Takes calculated risk • Will settle for what is possible • Ideally suited for marketing
Dreamer	Low	High	• Full of unusual ideas but has no implementation ability • Impractical • Always dissatisfied • Unsuitable for marketing functions
Synthesiser	Medium	High	• Goal oriented • Can create fresh ideas • Can take people along • Suitable for marketing function
Innovator	High	High	• Full of new ideas • Can create many options • Radical Thinker • Blames others and system for impractical ideas failure • Loner • Disastrous for Marketing

As the above table indicates, any organisation must keep a 'Practicaliser' as the main marketing man. In his absence a 'synthesiser' can also fit in but no other type should be at the top of the marketing team. A 'Modifier' can be a very good asset as a supporting officer but should not be made the leader. Unfortunately in practically all the organisations nobody gives serious thought to the type of personality required to do a particular job. They feel that everyone can do every thing. This concept does not allow the organisation to use its human resources productively in an optimum way. Sometimes, in extreme cases, such type of approach can be suicidal as can be seen from the following two illustrations.

Illustration

In a major project from a well-known corporate house, five bidders participated. The tender conditions were quite stringent and naturally all the bidders took different degrees of deviation. During the discussion, the customer wanted all the deviations withdrawn. He also used threat of summary rejection to put pressure on bidders and to coerce them to accept 'No deviation' clause. Most of the bidders fearing adverse commercial loading on them withdrew major portions of deviation except for the unavoidable bare minimum, which was required in their opinion at any cost if they were to execute the contract. However, one of the very reputed corporate's marketing executive withdrew all the deviations as he thought that otherwise they would lose the business. He was afraid that if such a major order was lost, it would reflect badly on him. He also did not explicitly inform the others. It so happened that after long negotiation, this man's organisation got the business. As the contract execution started, the mystery also started unfolding. The marketing man had accepted some unacceptable and unachievable conditions. The organisation and his colleagues were willing to honour all the commitments made by their marketing man but did not know what to do with some clauses and conditions, which were not feasible. One of the clauses stipulated destructive testing of some major capital equipment worth 15 per cent of the contract value. The marketing man had made no provision for that in his cost estimates or in the completion schedule for such an expenditure and work. The management was angry with the executive for picking up a net loss contract but the fact remained that the fault really lay with the management themselves because they had put a 'Challenger' in the marketing department and nothing better than this could have been expected of him. Naturally, the marketing executive himself was also unhappy. In his opinion he had done a great job by picking this order and he felt that his own colleagues were making an unnecessary hue and cry rather than thanking him.

In another instance a "Reproducer" was representing the organisation in the absence of his boss who was a practicaliser. The order was bid and negotiated by the team of these two persons and the reproducer was very happy in faithfully following the instructions of his boss. However, during detailed contract finalisation, the Practicaliser had to go out on some urgent work and the 'Reproducer' had to face the customer alone along with some other junior member of the team. During discussion, this gentleman was not even prepared to agree to reasonable and justified demands of the customer because, in his eyes, they constituted deviations from the terms proposed by

Contd

> him and accepted at the time of ordering. Though he was convinced that what the customer was requesting was just, he lacked the courage and boldness to agree to it. This resulted in a deadlock and even after three meetings, each lasting a full day, no agreement could be arrived at. This made the customer unhappy and irritated and he complained to higher management of vendor about intransigent approach of the official. The management had to send his boss, the Practicaliser, for another meeting along with the Reproducer and they reached the agreement in two hours to the fullest satisfaction of both sides. What could not be settled in 24 hours was settled in two hours.

The above two case studies indicate the power of personalities which affects the course of business, and it is therefore essential that one should have the right man for the right job.

Determination/Tenacity

Many persons give marketing a black and white treatment. They meet the customer, make opinions and if they do not find the customer's attitude favourable to them in getting business, they lose interest in the customer. During negotiation they always take a position regarding the price at which they want to quit, and if the customer is demanding a lower price than this, then they quit. Though they have clarity, they do not appreciate that there is nothing like "black and white" in marketing. A marketing man gets chances for securing the business not only till the order has been received by the other party but till the advance has been released to successful bidder, and if he pursues it, then he has a chance. In the core sector about 20 per cent of the deals fall through during the issue of 'Letter of Intent' and release of advance. The reasons are many but if a marketing man keeps track of these, he can latch on to chances provided by such development. Also, there are no terms such as 'Final Price' or 'Final Decision' till the advance is paid. The vendor can offer better than the best price and term and the customer can also improve upon the so called final offer/counter offer he has given. Thus, determination and tenacity are two most essential qualities that a marketing executive in the core sector should have. It can give extra business to his employer and can always help in retaining customers who want to jump out.

Skill

The second most important prerequisite of a marketing executive is skill. As shown in Fig. 10.1, it is the most important parameter that determines the effectiveness of a marketing person. While Personality indicates the 'Potential' which may result in a benefit or not, 'Skill' is the reality which gets delivered. Some of the major attributes are detailed as under.

Personality Understanding

This is the most important requirement of a marketing executive. While he holds discussions with the customer and consultant, there may arise situations where he may have to furnish information to the customer as a supplier. It may also happen that he may himself volunteer certain information, which may prove useful both to the customer and vendor or may give competitive advantage to vendor. It is therefore necessary for the concerned person to first assess to whom and in what manner the information can be passed on. Judging a personality is very important. Normally, there can be three possibilities.

(a) The person is interested in you and your organisation.
(b) The person is interested in one of the competitors.
(c) The person is neutral.

It is clear that there is no use of giving confidential information to personality (b) as it can be counter-productive and will amount to cutting the branch of the tree on which the person is seated. If the person is of type (c), then one can pass on neutral type of information to him provided he is receptive and will not mind having it. The information to be passed on to him should be neutral, and the objective should give the appearance of having been communicated to protect the best interest of the customer and to get from the customer best performance and long time service. Of course, it is natural that no vendor gives such information until he is looking forward to some competitive advantage.

If the customer person falls in category (a), then definitely the marketing person can talk to him freely and provide him more detail and focused and direct information which can be used for the benefit of the person providing it.

The second advantage of knowing the personality can be used while talking to the higher officials in the customer's organisation. During discussion/negotiation, there are occasions when the CMD or other officials of the customer may ask for certain impossible prices or completion schedule, which may not be possible. Normally, it is common practice not to say NO during negotiation but if the other person will not mind a frank reply then many times after judging the personality, it is better that we gave him factual status after explaining the position. For this it is better to find out what kind of personality one is going to meet during the meeting. Further if the CEO himself is going to conduct the discussion, then he may adopt any of the following positions:

(a) CEO may prefer to talk himself and may not allow any other colleague to talk.
(b) CEO may take the lead role but may allow others to talk and participate.
(c) CEO is of (b) type but is well informed and may prefer to talk himself.

Not much can be done with Category (a) types. One can only prepare well but sometimes these personalities do not even allow others to reply to their queries and want only a 'yes' or 'no'. When dealing with such type of persons, one must be prepared with a final reply as these persons are short tempered and can get easily tripped.. They are also the 'I know all' type. Nobody can handle them in a meeting as they are the player and umpire and hence the best way to handle them is prior to the formal meeting. Fortunately such type of personalities is rarely endowed with desire for in-depth study or preparing for them well before the meeting. They basically depend on the preparation and briefing of their juniors and act accordingly. Hence, the best way to negotiate with them is to identify their advisors and settle with them the details that can be formalised in the later scheduled meeting.

In the case of (b), one should identify a senior and influential colleague of the CEO who is logical and can explain to him the position. He can then help in bringing up the desired subject during the proposed meeting which may provide the opening for further discussion on the subject.

Discussion and negotiation with type (c) can be very interesting, They will prepare themselves well and will employ all charm with pre-planned strategy to disarm the supplier. They do not get influenced by anybody and will do what they think is right. They will also provide sufficient opportunity to the other party to put forward his case and will prefer to deal at the level of equal footing. In fact they are the toughest negotiators that one may face.

Illustrations

I had the personal experience to talk and negotiate with one such personality, who is an IAS officer and CMD of an undertaking. He is an engineer by profession. We had a scheduled final meeting with him as it was told that the final negotiation would be conducted by him personally. Before this meeting I collected the information on the person who was to conduct the final negotiation and prepared a psychological profile of him and got the feedback that this gentleman preferred free and frank discussion and was a transparent person. He was not very particular about protocol and was an egoless personality. I also got the feedback that while he listened to all and sought advice from all his colleagues, he kept his own counsel and decisions were taken by him. With this feedback, we prepared ourselves and went for the final negotiation meeting at 3 PM. The gentleman wanted to know about our technological standing, strong points of our bids and completion schedule. After this preliminary the main discussion started and he enquired about our shop floor loading (to ascertain that we were in a position to complete the supply in stipulated time) and then settled down with the technical issues on which he allowed his colleagues to discuss and finalise. When the turn came for negotiation on prices and completion schedule, the gentleman was in his elements. He took the negotiation in his hands and quoted statistical figures on our past performance and price levels and also furnished similar information on our competitors to make a strong case for further betterment. He had really done solid homework on the subject. We explained to him the reasons with detailed explanation why we were not in a position to accept completely what he was looking forward to. He gave us a patient hearing and seemed to grasp well the technical details as some of his supplementary queries indicated. He had sensible counter queries to most of our replies. When the deal was finally reached at 9 PM, it was a business secured after tough negotiation

Contd

and we came out with a lot of appreciation for the personality who, despite being CMD, pent a full six hours to finalise the business without any hint of irritation or dominance.

In a similar other negotiation where again an IAS officer was involved as he was the CEO of the company, the meeting lasted only ten minutes. The CEO was late for the meeting and kept us waiting for more than 30 minutes as he was getting briefed during the period. The effect of lack of preparation was reflected during the negotiation as he neither displayed any intention to reach to the bottom of the problem, nor was he consistent in what he was looking forward to for his company. He had no idea of the technical details and his own colleagues were not willing to talk as all the talking was done by the CEO. The party called for negotiation was L–1 and he was willing to give a token discount also, considering the importance of the occasion. The CEO did not ask for the discount but changed the basic scope of work. When the party wanted to explain that this was not feasible and if they wanted to change the basic scope then they must go for re tendering, the CEO last his cool and fired the party. Naturally, the deal fell through and the requirements were re-tendered with the loss of another one year with the price going up by about 5 per cent. The customer, vendor and everybody were losers.

Negotiating Skill and Strategy

Negotiating skills and strategy formulation are equally important. They have been dealt with in detail in Chapter 7.

Diplomacy

A marketing executive must have diplomacy particularly when he has to say 'No'. Many persons do not say No and leave the problem open for some one else to solve on their behalf. This is not correct because it unnecessarily leads to wastage of time for themselves and others. It is therefore necessary that the final answer should be given and if it is a No, then this must be conveyed without offending or antagonising the customer. During negotiation or discussion, we come across situations where one has to resort to diplomatic means to achieve the ultimate aim. Most such moves should also focus on removal of blockages and hindrances.

Illustration

In one of the projects, a vendor found that one influential member, GM (Technical) of the customer was passing on his and other vendors' technical performance and price details to one particular vendor. This information was utilised by this particular vendor in modifying his proposal to get a competitive advantage. This vendor, who found this unethical state of affairs, was naturally very upset and wanted the GM (Technical) to be removed from the negotiation committee, which had called all the vendors for discussion and negotiation. The vendor did not wanted to cast aspersions on one of the senior officials of the customer and so he found a way out. He suggested to the negotiation committee some useful technical tips to reduce cost and optimise performance. He also suggested that other vendors also could similarly offer constructive suggestions of benefit to the customer, and it would be appropriate for the customer to form a separate technical committee to solicit and examine such suggestions and the cost reduction connected with it. The suggestion was highly appreciated and a separate committee was formed, and there was no better person to head the committee than GM (Technical). While GM was happy that he was given an important task and was heading an important committee and the customer was happy that he was getting suggestions for cost reduction and enhanced benefits, the vendor was happy as he had removed the person from the main negotiating committee who was giving undue advantage to the other vendor. GM (Technical) was applying his expertise on 2 per cent of the contract value, while he was totally cut off on what was happening on the balance 98 per cent of the contract value. The vendor who was getting undue benefit could see through the game but could do little.

Pressure Cooker Survival

A marketing man will always find himself in a *'pressure cooker'* situation. On one side he will be under pressure to bring business and, on the other side, his management will desire him to bring higher realisation, more business and definitely with lesser resources. The customer will always give him half the time to respond though he himself may take any time. It has been generally observed that decision taking time in any infrastructure project is higher than the completion period. Added to that will be different pressure from engineering groups for not agreeing to certain specific requirements of the customer because it amounts to deviation from the otherwise clear specification. The marketing man should always consider himself as the engine of a train where he has to provide the higher initial torque to overcome the inertia and once the train picke up speed, then he has only to exert maintenance torque.

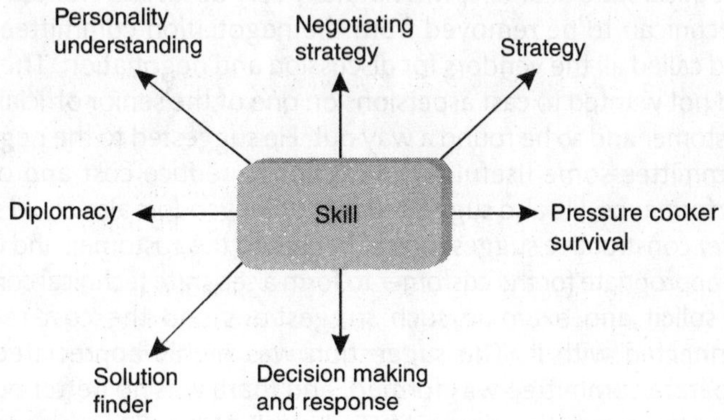

Fig. 10.6 *Different Skills*

Many times the customer will tell the marketing man that if he does not agree to a particular technical feature, price or completion schedule, then he will be losing business. This may be the reality or it may be only a tactic to get further concession. Many people give in without assessing the situation and suffer loss. The more appropriate approach would be as follows:

- Judge from other information whether the customer is telling the truth or trying to bargain.
- Whether the customer's counter offer suits him or he has reached his limit and will not be able to compromise further. In the latter case he should sit tight.
- If he is comfortable with customer's counter offer then it must be seen whether "yes" should be communicated immediately and if he accepts this proposal, whether this will become a new milestone or position for the customer to demand more or whether other competitors can out bid and set still more demanding levels and lower price levels.
- Timing and the manner of communication are also equally important.

Solution Finder

The job of the marketing man is not to create problems but to find solutions to existing problems and to ensure that new problems do not crop up. He has to look for convergence and find and enlarge areas of agreement. He must ensure that complex differences are narrowed down and the gap between customer expectation and his organisation's ability to meet them is eliminated.

He has to work with different divergent groups in the engineering, finance, legal, taxation and commercial departments to find common acceptable ground. With so many functional men present on all sides, there is no shortage of problems and divergence, and the marketing man must channel his positive strength to find a solution. He must have the art of carrying the people of different opinion along with him, and he should have patience, calmness and persuasive skills to achieve the objective.

Decision Making and Response

These are two essential prerequisites for the marketing man. It is necessary that he must respond fast as delayed response means no response. The customer gets disheartened and disillusioned with delayed response and will start looking elsewhere.

Decision making is another attribute required in marketing person. He has to make up his mind fast by ensuring that he has all the information required for it, and that alone will help him in responding quickly. He therefore needs to be logical and methodical and should have good analytical ability to work out the action plan from various angles to evaluate different options and finally choose one. He must believe in the principle that there is only one way to work and that is to 'SOLVE' the issue, and he cannot 'SHELVE' or 'SHIRK' it. The decision making ability requires generation of various options/alternatives and taking a calculated risk in choosing an option. This has already been discussed in detail in Chapter 8.

Knowledge

No marketing man can take a decision until he has examined the pros and cons of it. In order to take a well considered decision he is expected to have at least knowledge of the subject and information connected with it. Today, information and knowledge are the biggest tools in the hands of a marketing executive to have a competitive edge. With computers and PCs easily available, everyone—the customer and the competitors—are full of details and analysis. In order to meet this challenge it is essential that the marketing person is having equal information on all the aspects connected with the business. He is expected to keep track of technical development and comparison, reply to the queries generated by customer based on doubt created by the competitor, taxation laws and other economic parameters. He must be aware of his other competitors in the past and problems faced because of the equipments and is expected to give a reasonable reply.

The marketing person has to be an extrovert but while facing the customer and meeting the challenge of the competition he is a loner. If he is a successful there will be a large number of persons to share this luck, but if he is unsuccessful then he alone has to bear the responsibility of failure. It is therefore essential that he must develop sound knowledge of the product/ project, which will add to the quality of his decision making. He must have sharp memory and must be able to recall minute details of the past with ease. He must have a sound technical base as more often he is expected to double up as an engineering person. His technical knowledge can provide him a marketing edge over others.

Communication

Communication is the most important skili a marketing executive must possess. He has to understand the customer and his consultant's requirement and at the same time he has to ensure that others understand him. Many times business opportunities are lost because of misunderstanding and lack of communication. The basic purpose of communication is to ensure that the supplier understands the customer and his needs and the customer understands what the supplier is offering and is capable of offering. This helps in clarity and good understanding and avoids problems during contract execution.

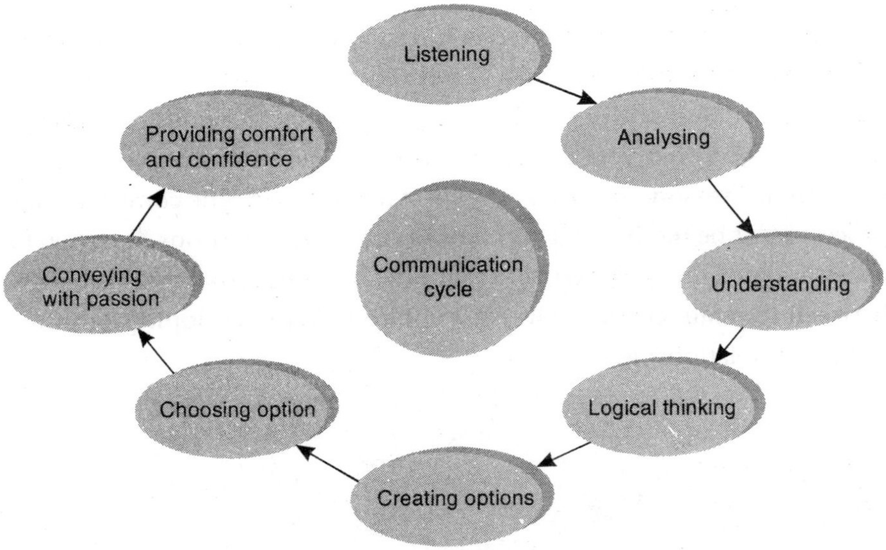

Fig. 10.7 *Communication Cycle*

Figure 10.7 indicates the communication cycle. A marketing man must be a patient listener as it is from this point the communication process begins. He must first listen and understand the requirement of the customer and must analyse and understand it. He must then create various options depending upon his organisation's ability to meet them and the requirement of the customer. Finally, he must choose the option best suitable under the circumstances and convey this to the customer. It must carry the conviction of the conveyer and should be communicated with passion so that it creates comfort and confidence in the customer. For this the marketing man has to be a good speaker and his voice should be well modulated. He must also convey facts and figures with frankness and without attachment and sentiment. It must give the impression that the views being conveyed are the outcome of deep analysis and thinking by the supplier based on the customer's requirements. He should address the issues completely and comprehensively with clarity and details. Sidestepping the issues or ducking them will not help. The more uncomfortable the problem the more the need to address it thoroughly to explain to the customer the position. It is better that the marketing man himself address the uncomfortable issues rather than leaving it for the competitor to do it. The sincerity must get reflected as well as demonstrated.

Most of the customers prefer a frank reply as it brings clarity to them. The manner of speaking should clearly reflect that you are transparent and narrating fact and nothing else and suppressing nothing. It must also give the impression that you are 'firm' but not 'rigid' and flexible enough to consider any reasonable views or request from others. The communication process must be methodical and should not be monotonous. It is therefore necessary for a good marketing person to ensure light-hearted exchange in between to retain customer interest and to help in developing a mutually acceptable relationship.

11

e-Business and e-Marketing

Difference Between e-Commerce and e-Business
e-Marketplace
Market Exchange
Advantages of e-Marketing
Disadvantages of e-Marketing
Prerequisites of e-Marketplace
Types of Marketplaces
Content Management System (CMS)

Customer Response

11

The Marketplace is constantly evolving due to changes introduced by environment, globalisation, technology, customer assertiveness and government policies. The INTERNET has changed the way people the world over think about communication, buying, selling and their expectations. What took Radio 38 years and Television 13 years to reach the same level of popularity, has been achieved by the Internet in just 4 years.

The business done through Internet is called e-Business. During the last four years it has received tremendous momentum to the extent that it has now become necessary for any business to use this medium for not only faster growth and profitability but to remain competitive. e-Business is changing the way the business is done. It is expected to bring rapid economic growth and provide new business opportunities. e-Business will help in development of new business models. Its impact will cover all areas of business. It will increase depth of reach of the supplier by creating new markets. It will increase response by faster transmission of quality information and reduction in operation cost.

DIFFERENCE BETWEEN e-COMMERCE AND e-BUSINESS

The term e-Commerce is generally associated with buying, selling and related transactions of the business like invoicing, payment authorisation and confirmation and other monetary transactions. On the other hand, e-Business covers the total activities along the business chain like business development, marketing, purchase of raw material and component, production, total project management, system integration, sales transaction, invoicing, payment, financing and leasing, services, insurance, etc. As shown in Fig. 11.1, e-Business encompasses both CRM (Customer Relationship Management) and ERP (Enterprise Resource Planning). e-Marketing is a part of CRM package and we will restrict our discussion in this chapter to e-Marketing.

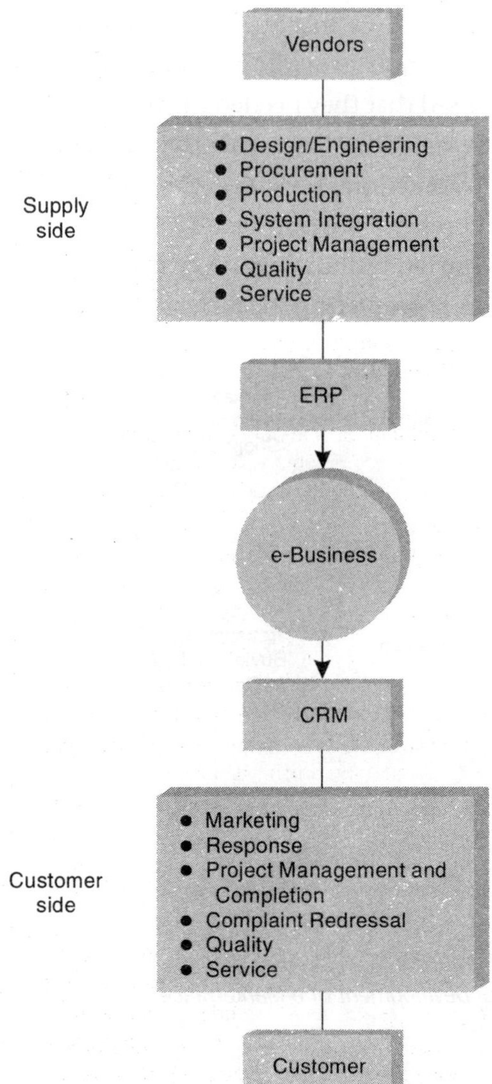

Fig. 11.1 *e-Business*

e-MARKETPLACE

e-Marketplace are the venues where the buyer, seller and other connected agencies meet and explore various options, evaluate, negotiate and effect transactions and payment. These are the places where buyers can advertise their needs and shop. They also help suppliers to display their product range, capabilities and market them. Business through the Internet and Marketplace has evolved gradually as shown in Fig. 11.2. Initially it began as a pure window shopping place simply providing catalogues and literature. Slowly these marketplaces realised that they needed a revenue stream to survive and thus began online buying and selling with the marketplace charging the commission for the transactions provided through it. They also started providing auction and reverse auction facility. Slowly as the competition among marketplaces started building up, they started providing complete value added services and completing the e-Business chain.

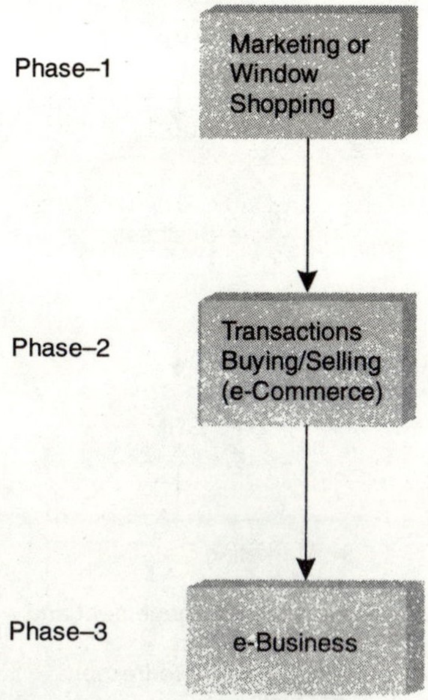

Fig. 11.2 *Chronological Development of e-Marketplace*

MARKET EXCHANGE

e-Marketplace is also at times referred to as 'Market Exchange' as a large number of customers and suppliers visit it for different purposes, different products and different services. The transaction can take place on real time basis with price and other parameters getting decided based on market needs. Such exchanges allow trading in various commodities and brokers can also participate. In days to come, such exchanges can also start operating in the core sector. The electric power distribution agencies can have access to different generation companies and can negotiate on real time basis, fixed quantity of power at 'Power Exchange' from different generation companies depending upon the benefit that can accrue to the purchaser.

ADVANTAGES OF e-MARKETING

e-Marketing provides a number of advantages to both the customer and the supplier. Some of them are:

To Customers

- Can pre-qualify prospective suppliers by readily assessing their financial and technical status, production facilities, past references and through other literature.
- Can create competition by bringing in a large number of suppliers.
- Can upgrade specifications of his requirements by downloading information from other related sites of other customers and suppliers.
- Speed of Response.
- Can get best price, optimum efficiency, delivery and other terms by reverse auction.
- Easy spot purchases for emergency situations.
- Single point facility for Buying, Financing, Leasing, Tax consultations and other services like Insurance, etc.
- Reduction in Inventory.
- Transparency in total buying process.

To Suppliers

- Increased Market Depth.
- Reduced cost of Marketing and Market Promotions.
- Fast Response.
- Authentic information on critical parameters for business success through reverse auction.
- Can verify financial status of Customer and his paying capacity or can arrange direct payment through other financial agencies through marketplace.
- Transparent process.
- Better CRM.

DISADVANTAGES OF e-MARKETING

e-Marketing lacks one-to-one contact. Emotional benefits and contacts are as much essential as functional parameters.

PREREQUISITES OF e-MARKETPLACE

A good e-marketplace or market exchange should have the following features which are also shown in Fig. 11.3.

Security

Both suppliers and customers want security of transactions. Additionally, the market place should ensure that the information hosted by customers and suppliers should not be used for the purpose other than what is intended. Those marketplaces that are connected to CRM system of supplier and ERP system of customer should have additional security protection. The marketplace should limit access to enrolled users only and should support digital certificates and encryption technology. But the system must allow work across the public network without sacrificing the security.

Reliability and Scalability

The marketplace should ensure reliability and extension as the need may arise. It should also allow simultaneous operation of multi users at high speed with reliability on the same file or at different files. The marketplace should allow addition of customised or stand alone applications. The market platform should enable such modules to be easily plugged in.

Fig. 11.3 *Essential Ingredients of e-Marketplace*

Search Engines

In order to afford the 'Visitor' easy access, the marketplace must have its own powerful search engines, which should be able to help the visitor to search products, service, catalogues or details about a company or any other information and produce shortlisted results. These search engines should be able to provide linkage to other connected networks or linkage to ERP or CRM system, if permitted by the host party.

Cross -Communication Compatibility

Any marketplace/exchange must be compatible and capable of connectivity with fax, e-mail and other digital data interchange formats. It should be accessible with standard software tools.

Reporting

The marketplace should have the facility to enable users to generate reports on total business done and check on total outstanding. It should also be possible for users to generate requisite details about the business or visits to their place.

Registration

The marketplace must allow users self-registration with password and enrolment. It should be able to screen members before providing facility for transactions to genuine and serious visitors.

Flexibility

In each marketplace the host should be able to establish and effectively enforce rules transparently to all users. But this rule must not restrict the flexibility of the marketplace and should allow both customers and suppliers to establish and use their own procurement and marketing system.

Confidentiality

Marketplaces and Exchanges dealing with products at the high end of the value chain need certain special features to suit their clients. Suppliers would like the marketplace owner to protect their relationship with customers and confidentiality of the price and other commercial and technical terms settled. Similarly customers would also only patronise marketplace if it protects confidentiality of information.

TYPES OF MARKETPLACES

Marketplaces can be classified in different ways as shown in Fig. 11.4. These can be based on the following parameters:

- Based on Business Type
- Based on Business Application
- Based on Facility

Classification Based on Business Type

As shown in Fig. 11.4, the marketplace can be classified under the following three types. They are:

- Business to Business Marketplace, B2B
- Business to Consumer Marketplace, B2C
- Consumer to Consumer Marketplace, C2C

In B2B marketplace, the business takes place between business houses, corporates and industries. Such business transactions are for raw materials like steel, copper or components. Even finished products can also be transacted through the marketplace. It must be appreciated that in a majority of cases the transaction takes place on B2B marketplace after parties have initially discussed the proposals in detail and marketplace is only used to re-discover the price and get best efficiency and other important parameters through Reverse Auction. B2B deals are high value deals and visitors to B2B marketplace would require personalised attention from the marketplace, including value added services like Project Management, Payment Status and Progress Reports. Such visitors would also like integration of marketplace with their own CRM and ERP system and will require customised services at the marketplace. Such visitors always have repeat requirements and hence retention of their loyalty is important. Unsatisfied visitors can cause serious problems as they are more likely to share their dissatisfaction than non-marketplace customers.

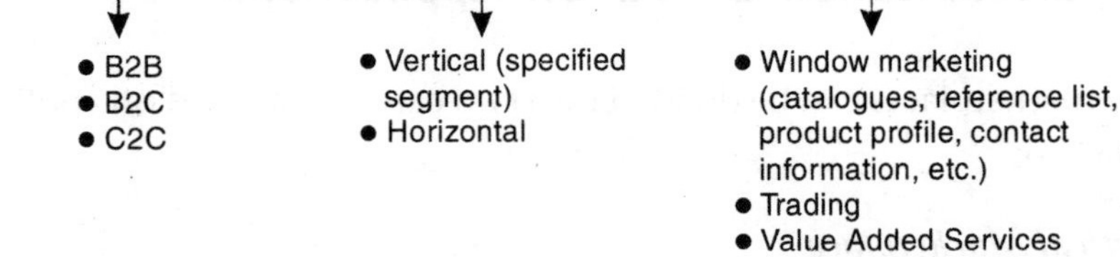

Fig. 11.4 *Classification of e-Marketplace*

B2C transactions are between Business to Consumer as illustrated in Fig. 11.5. The third type of marketplace is one where transactions take place between Consumer to Consumer and is referred as C2C type. The visitors in both these types of marketplaces require fast speed of response. They do not require customised service but they do appreciate and require fast service. Some marketplaces provide software that welcomes them by name and they appreciate that. They do not require many value added services like visitors on B2B marketplace but the Supplier and Buyer are unknown to each other and they do business only as a result of trust of marketplace.

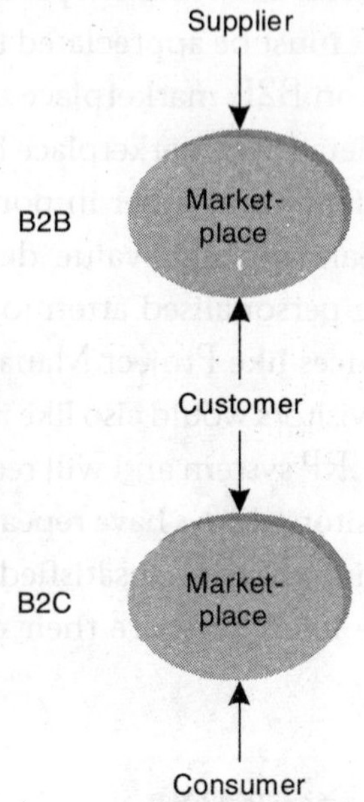

Fig. 11.5 *B2B and B2C Marketplace*

Classification Based On Applications

The marketplaces can be divided into two categories based on applications. They are:

Vertical Marketplace

These are marketplaces that are devoted to specific business segments. Products and services traded here suit to both customers and suppliers as their requirements are common. This commonality in requirements helps in content specialisation and standardised e-commerce network for specific industry or business segments. Such vertical marketplaces are likely to grow at a fast pace in days to come.

Some of the large companies are setting up their own marketplaces, which are primarily for their own requirements, but they have plans to extend it to other parties who are operating in the same business segment.

In some cases, industries operating in a common business segment have joined together to have a common vertical marketplace. Some of the examples are marketplaces of steel, chemicals and automobile manufacturers. Such marketplaces have high chances of success compared to independent marketplaces due to high volume of captive business the promoters will bring with them. Additionally, the marketplace can easily build up value added services specially required by this segment.

Horizontal Marketplaces

These marketplaces deal in multi products and multi services with several buyers and sellers. They are not designed to cater to any specific business segment or product. Thus standardisation or business specific facilities are not possible at these marketplaces. They largely depend on the revenue generated through operation through them and value added services provided. How many of such marketplaces survive in the future is open to question. Some specific segment orientation may become necessary for most of them to stay afloat.

Classification Based on Facilities

A marketplace can only contain window-shopping material or can provide a total range of operations from marketing and trading to total service required for business. They can be classified under the following categories:

Window-Shopping

Such marketplaces provide information to prospective buyers and sellers and are mostly for marketing purposes. They are important for the core sector as they act as the first marketing point for the company and help in making customer aware of its range and capabilities. Most of the core sector business is done in a conventional way and a small fraction of it only comes for final settlement to the marketplace to negotiate price and other vital parameters through reverse auction. the following information can be hosted on the marketplace:

From Supplier

- General profile of the company, including business segments served by it.

- Financial and performance reports for last three years
- Product/Project/Service Profile of the company
- Detailed catalogues and brochures.
- Technical literature highlighting company's specific expertise and achievements.
- Reference List
- Enquiry Proforma
- Contact Information and addresses
- Any other information that a supplier feels may be needed by a customer or can create differentiation for him.

The marketplace can also include 'Call centers' to provide specific advice or reply on queries. The marketplace should have feedback facility.

From Customer

Following details can be hosted from the Customer's side:

- Customer's Profile
- Customer's Financial reports
- Customer's Purchase Requirement along with specification, terms and conditions, delivery requirement.
- Payment conditions, term and mode.
- Service requirements

Marketplaces of this type are static and are not suitable for trading on real time basis. They are intensively used for advertisement. They must have self-guided search engine facility to locate Suppliers/Customers or their catalogues to enable the visitor to quickly access information of interest. Their main purpose is to act as single window information centres to interested visitors. The marketplace mainly plays the role of making the customer and supplier aware of each other and after their introduction they can decide the future course of action.

Trading Marketplace

These marketplaces are designed for actual trading. They have facility for spot purchase and auction on real time basis. Spot purchases are normally done for standard products that are mostly available on 'ready to deliver basis' and do not require intensive discussion between supplier and customer about specifications or other technical features. The customer can mostly choose from catalogues of different suppliers and can place an order and effect payment through either credit cards or payment gateway provided by the marketplace. Such purchases are generally resorted to for emergency purchases of standard equipments and products in the core sector or for purchase of operation and maintenance spares and are based on catalogue prices. In the consumer sector, a majority of purchases on B2C and C2C marketplaces are spot purchases.

However in the normal course in the core sector, the customer will prepare his purchase specifications and terms and conditions and will shortlist parties from the marketplace depending upon shortlisting criteria that he may devise. Most of the marketplaces concentrating on value added services and core sector business have inbuilt filter facility to help the customer prepare a list of suppliers listed on the place and meeting criteria designed by the purchaser. The customer can then e-mail his enquiry to these parties and request for bids. Most of the proposals from the suppliers will have to be evaluated and discussed by the customer for clarity or modification in the proposal or even in customer's purchase requisition. Only when the discussion reaches a decisive stage of negotiation, can the customer either resort to conventional negotiation methods or take help of the marketplace for negotiation through Reverse Auction.

The negotiation on Trading marketplace takes place in two different ways, either through Auctions or through Reverse Auctions.

Auctions

Auctions, as the name suggests, are resorted by the Supplier/Seller. There are not many cases of auction in the core sector. This is resorted to dispose off excess inventory or to sell finished product for some other customer who has since cancelled the order. This is also done in the case of liquidation of a company or when it is effecting a major change in its business profile. Auction can either be of open type or closed type. In open auction sellers, after preparation of specification, terms and conditions, advertise the date, time and duration of auction and the marketplace of auction. The open auction, as the name suggests, is open to all but the supplier can put certain restrictions by allowing only those parties who satisfy certain minimum criteria. This can eliminate non-serious participants. The seller can also incorporate in the software, reserve price and minimum conditions to be satisfied by the bidder so that bids not fulfilling these conditions can be immediately rejected.

In case of close auction, Supplier shortlists the parties himself based on his requirements and sends them an invitation to the auction along with the detail specification, terms and conditions and informing him the name of the marketplace, date, time and duration of auction. The auction is normally of one hour duration, but may need an extension if the last quote is received 60 seconds or any other time fixed prior to the closure of auction. Many parties deliberately try to extend this process by timing their bid in such a way that extension of duration may become mandatory; hence the Auctioneer may like to build some safeguards if considered necessary. The auction process brings dynamic and real time changes in pricing and other parameters offered for negotiation. The supplier can highlight the parameters open for negotiation and incorporate suitable software that can display on real time basis the evaluated figures based on the pre-informed evaluation criteria. Even bids on different parameters can be displayed on real time basis if the supplier decides to have total transparency in the process. The names of bidders are generally not displayed on real time basis.

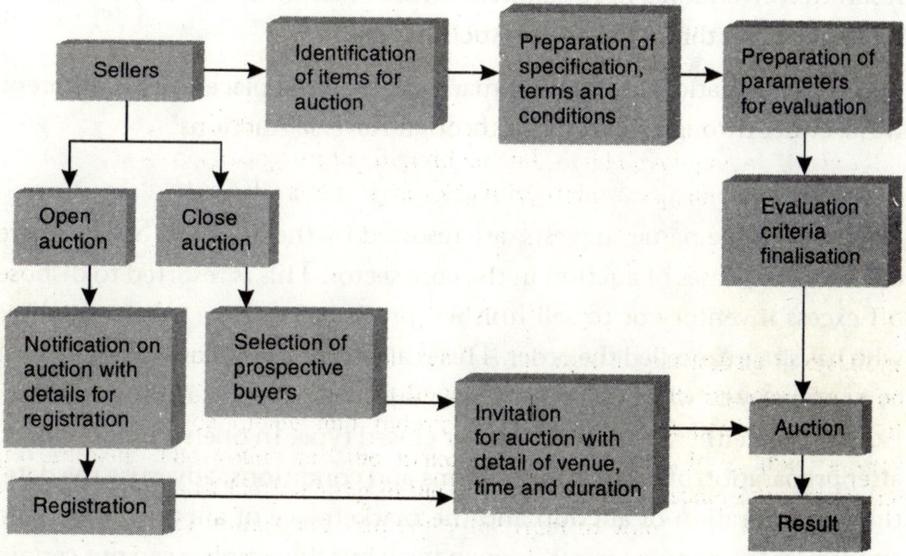

Fig. 11.6 *Flow Chart of Auction Process*

It is seen that auctions result in 15–20 per cent higher realisation to the Supplier. Such auctions are very common in B2C and C2C transactions. Fig. 11.6 describes the flowchart of the auction process.

Reverse Auction

Auctions done by Customers are called Reverse Auction. The Customer can prepare a specification and generate an enquiry for purchase. This enquiry can either be posted on the Internet or can be sent to selected suppliers who meet the prequalification criteria of the customer, who can then request them to join for reverse auction. In the case of complicated projects, the customer may like to seek clarification from the selected parties before short-listing them for auction. The customer can identify important parameters on which he would like to negotiate and declare the evaluation criteria to all the shortlisted parties. These factors can be price, delivery, efficiency and other performance parameters. The reverse auction process has been illustrated in Fig. 11.7 and is the same as the main Auction process described earlier. Reverse auction is the most transparent way of negotiation and allows the Customer to discover the real price and other important factor levels in the market. It helps him get the best efficiency, quality and delivery period at an attractive price. The customer can also determine how much information he wants to share with the participants in reverse auction.

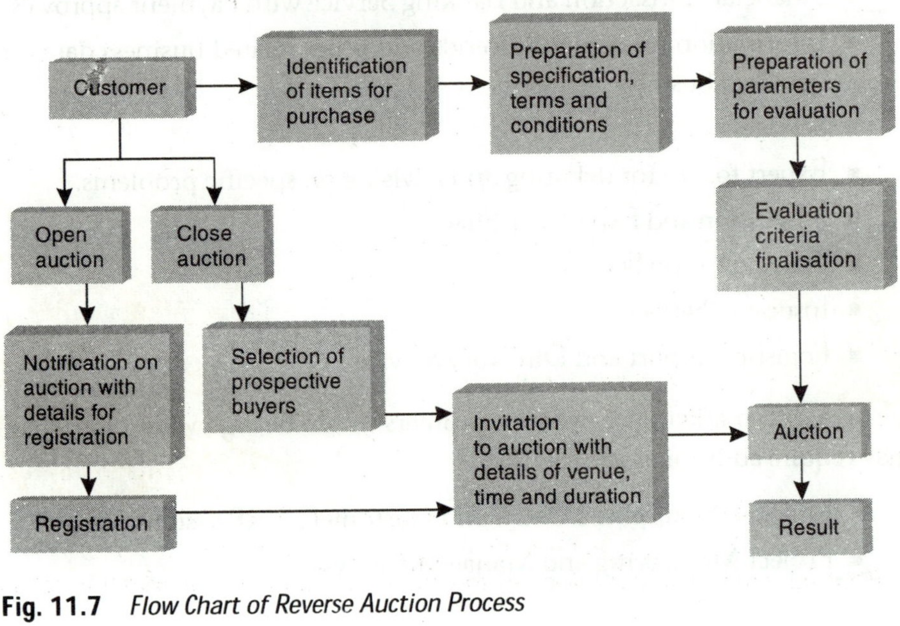

Fig. 11.7 *Flow Chart of Reverse Auction Process*

A marketplace which allows determination of price and other parameters through online negotiation is called a 'Dynamic Marketplace'. These marketplaces adopt different types of flexible business models to suit the requirement of their clients and charge a percentage of transacted business as the fee for effecting business.

Value Added Marketplace

Simple trading cannot provide enough revenue and differentiation for a marketplace to survive and grow. Similarly, advertisement cannot adequately help the marketplace to survive on its own in a competitive environment. It has thus become essential for a marketplace to act like a "Super Market" and provides at one place all the information, facilities and services that a business deal or visitors undertaking business through the marketplace may require. Such services may include the following:

- Feasibility study guidance.
- Information on rules, statutory approvals, taxation, statutory clearances. The marketplace can provide a 'Call center' or 'Help line' for this purpose.
- Consultancy Services
- Project Financing/Leasing
- Financial Transaction and Banking Service with Payment approvals.
- Information on demand, trends and other related business data on specified business segments
- Services
- Expert forum for debating and advising on specific problems.
- Discussion and Experience Sharing
- Transportation Service
- Insurance Service
- Logistic Support and Directory Service

In a B2B marketplace, where customers would be high value ones, they may require additional services like:

- Linkage to Supplier's CRM and Customer's ERP system.
- Project Monitoring and Management System.

- Status on raw material procurement and production.
- Status on Invoices and Payment.
- Complaint Management System
- Call center/Help line.

The higher the value services, the higher would be the preference of the visitor to do business on the site. Some of the marketplaces also provide advisory services to both buyers and sellers.

CONTENT MANAGEMENT SYSTEM (CMS)

Content is the most important part of e-Business. Accurate, complete and informative content improves the quality and speed of the transaction. On the one hand it helps the buyer to search multiple vendors and shortlist those who meet his business requirement; on the other hand it helps the supplier to communicate to the customer his ability and capability to meet the customer's need. Content helps the supplier to communicate to the Customer his ability to serve him. It helps the supplier to impress upon the customer how different he, his products and services are from others. Content is the relationship medium between customer and supplier. It is essential for success and a good marketplace must have excellent content management system. The following features are essential in a Content Management System (CMS):

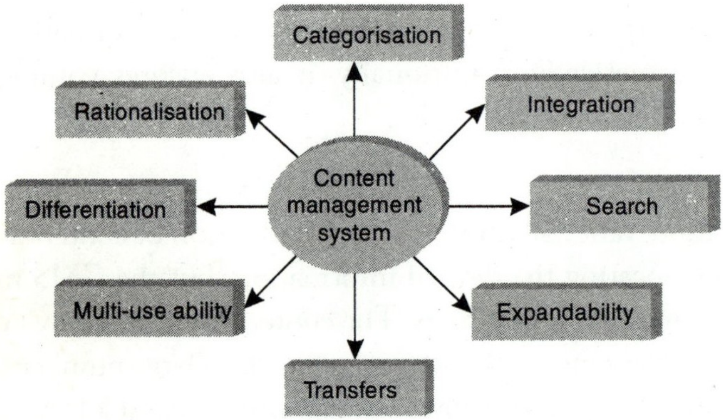

Fig. 11. 8 *Content Management System*

Rationalisation And Standardisation

Standardisation and rationalisation of information is essential as they help the customer to immediately compare different suppliers and arrive at the considered conclusion. It helps a supplier to create differentiation. However, it is not very easy to realise this objective. Customers/Buyers would like information to be available on the marketplace in a way they prefer and which addresses their needs. Suppliers would prefer information to be placed in a way that it highlights their ability and suppresses their weaknesses and thus creates a positive image about them. The core sector business may not allow rationalisation and standardisation until it is a vertical marketplace.

However, the marketplace host can handle such diverse situation with his experience. He can standardise the data and information format based on the basic information required for the business. CMS must be capable of not only providing this data and also automatically updating it from the Supplier's CRM and Customer's ERP.

Such rationalisation helps in arranging scattered and unstructured information through proper categorisation, which enables the customer to search/access them easily in a structured way. This enables the customer to have complete information on his needs and provides him with alternative options for consideration and use. Easy location and downloading of information is very essential for the success of B2C and C2C marketplace.

Integration

The CMS must have integration with ERP and CRM system. This ensures that the marketplace is always providing the latest information as it gets updated automatically. Additionally, it also ensures completeness of information.

Search

Categorisation, rationalisation and standardisation of content help in the visitor easily locating the desired information, but the CMS must allow total search and easy accessibility. The content must be easily available to external search engines so that it can be used by a large number of visitors. CMS must allow search and downloading with standard software packages. A well-integrated and dynamic CMS should automatically direct visitors to supplier's CRM and customer's ERP for additional details.

Differentiation

Though one of the main objectives of CMS is rationalisation and standardisation, it must allow both the buyer and the supplier sufficient leverage to exhibit their uniqueness in their content to create differentiation. CMS should be able to support and promote 'Diversity in Unification'.

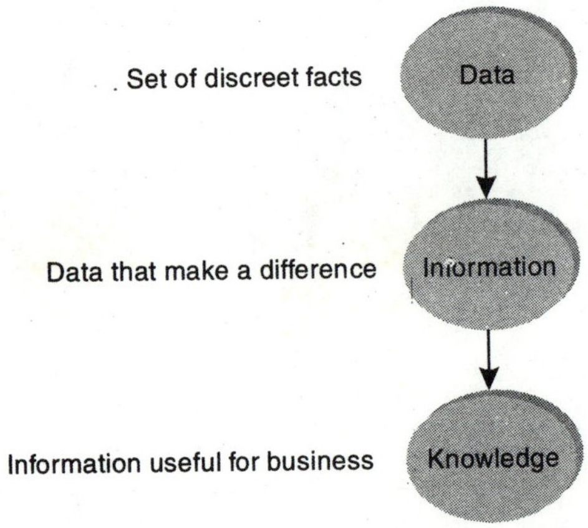

Fig. 11.9 *Usefulness of Details*

Knowledge

The CMS must provide details in the form of knowledge. As indicated in Fig. 11.9, there are three different forms of furnishing details. Data refer to a set of discreet facts which are of little use as they do not communicate anything. Information is again a set of data which are able to discriminate and differentiate between them to provide certain analytical information. But a CMS should aim at providing 'Knowledge' which is the information that can be leveraged for business decision making, both by the supplier and the customer.

Expandability

CMS should allow easy addition of information by interested parties. It should be easily scalable and expandable.

References

1. All India Management Association — Managing Enterprises—In the Era of Uncertainty
2. Cunningham, Cunningham and Swift — Marketing—A Managerial Approach
3. Gary Hamel and C K Prahalad — Competing For The Future
4. Herb Cohen — You Can Negotiate Anything
5. P N Hague and Jackson Peter — Do Your Own Market Research
6. A K Jain — Critical Success Factors
7. Margaret Crimp — The Marketing Research Process
8. Martin Christopher — The Customer Service Planner
9. Michael E Porter — Competitive Strategy
10. N K Singh and Omita Paul — Corporate Soul
11. Peter F Drucker — Management
12. Peter Gloor — Making the e-Business Transformation
13. Philip Kotler and Keith K Cox — Marketing Management and Strategy: A Reader
14. V S Ramaswamy and S Namakumari — Strategic Planning for Corporate Success
15. Warren D Raisch — The e Marketplace—Strategies for Success

Index